ESCALATION IN DECISION-MAKING

ESCALATION IN DECISION-MAKING

The Tragedy of Taurus

HELGA DRUMMOND

OXFORD UNIVERSITY PRESS
1996

Oxford University Press, Great Clarendon Street, Oxford OX2 6DP

Oxford New York
Athens Auckland Bangkok Bogota Bombay
Buenos Aires Calcutta Cape Town Dar es Salaam
Delhi Florence Hong Kong Istanbul Karachi
Kuala Lumpur Madras Madrid Melbourne
Mexico City Nairobi Paris Singapore
Taipei Tokyo Toronto
and associated companies in
Berlin Ibadan

Oxford is a trade mark of Oxford University Press

Published in the United States
by Oxford University Press Inc., New York

British Library Cataloguing in Publication Data
Data available

Library of Congress Cataloging in Publication Data
Drummond, Helga.
Escalation in decision-making: the case of Taurus/Helga Drummond.
Includes bibliographical references (p. 212).
1. Taurus (Project). 2. International Stock Exchange—Data
processing. 3. Stock exchanges—Data processing—Case studies.
4. Decision-making—Case studies. I. Title.
HG4577.D74 1996   332.64'2421'0285—dc20   96–21020
ISBN 0–19–828953–7

1 3 5 7 9 10 8 6 4 2

Typeset by Hope Services (Abingdon) Ltd.
Printed in Great Britain
on acid-free paper by
Bookcraft Ltd., Midsomer Norton, Somerset

For Janet

It is not given to human beings, happily for them, otherwise life would be intolerable, to foresee or predict to any large extent the unfolding of events. In one phase men seem to have been right, in another they seem to have been wrong. Then again, a few years later, when the perspective of time has lengthened, all stands in a different setting. There is a new proportion. There is another scale of values. History with its flickering lamp stumbles along the trail of the past, trying to reconstruct its scenes, to revive its echoes.

(Winston Churchill, in Robert 1974: vi. 307)

PREFACE

In the summer of 1991, Peter Rawlins, the chief executive of the London Stock Exchange, was uneasy. Taurus, the long-awaited IT project intended to replace London's antiquated system for processing share transfers, was substantially over budget and seriously behind schedule. Rawlins had been unhappy about the whole venture from the start but had been unable to stop it:

Intellectually I said, 'We should not be doing this.' If we are going to have the system changed, for Christ's sake let's do it properly so we build one central register. I said, 'Why don't we do this properly?'. The great advantage was that nothing had been built at the time I was there. 'No, sorry Peter, we have had all those arguments. Great idea but no, we have been arguing about it for twelve years, forget it.'[1]

Taurus was originally due to be implemented in October 1991. Earlier that year the deadline had been postponed until summer 1992. Now it was becoming clear the earliest possible date for implementation was April 1993 and then only assuming that there were no more delays—a perilous hope given the history of the project. The board of directors were not pleased and the chief executive wondered whether he should cancel the whole thing:

They [the board] rounded on me as chief executive, was I satisfied about these budgets, budgets to time as well as money. They were worried about how much more time because it was seen as an embarrassment.

I said, 'Fellers we can stop this.' In my view the issue was not . . . is this the right cost or the right time, as to which there had to be respectively doubt, the question I said we should be asking is whether we should be doing this at all . . . is this the right project?[2]

The project was allowed to continue but the doubts lingered. 'I just didn't like the smell of it,' said Rawlins.[3]

In January 1993 Richard Waters, a journalist for the *Financial Times*, was conversing with Andrew Hugh-Smith, chairman of the Stock Exchange. Hugh-Smith said that he was worried about Taurus. Waters thought little of it. The Stock Exchange had a long history of 'muddling through' on projects; 'No one thought so much money would just go down the drain,' he said.[4]

There was indeed a great deal of money at stake. The Stock Exchange had already spent over £80 million on developing Taurus, whilst various organizations in the City of London were reported to have invested £400 million in preparing their own systems. In January 1993 it seemed as if the market would soon see a return on its investment. Although there were still many problems to be resolved, an air of stability had descended over the project at last. More tangibly, the testing programme which would make Taurus a reality would shortly commence. Taurus, in popular parlance, was 'just round the corner'.[5]

Then the unthinkable happened. On Wednesday 10 March 1993, a member of the Stock Exchange technical team returned from lunch with a copy of the *Evening Standard*. The newspaper claimed that Taurus was about to be cancelled. The Stock Exchange staff and contractors working on the project were sceptical. One said, 'We were all lulled into a false sense of security by the fact that this [Taurus] may be a bit of a dog's breakfast coming up, but they've spent so much money on it, surely it would be ludicrous to jack it in now.'[6]

The next day, however, on Thursday 11 March, an announcement was made over the Stock Exchange Tannoy system. All Taurus staff were instructed to report to an 'off-site' building away from the Stock Exchange. 'Aye, aye', said a programmer, 'something's up.'[7]

An hour later he left the meeting clutching an envelope. The envelope contained a letter advising him that he was now redundant. The letter instructed him to telephone the Stock Exchange next week to arrange to collect his personal belongings from his desk. Almost all of the 360 or so staff working on the project were likewise jobless. As the programmer left the building he embraced his manager. Both of them had been working eighty-hour weeks for nearly three years in a desperate effort to deliver Taurus. 'Thanks,' said the programmer to his manager, 'you couldn't have done any more.'[8]

In the days that followed, and as City houses counted their losses, hard questions were asked. Taurus was intended to do for stocks and shares what cash dispensers and other forms of electronic transfer had done for banking. It had the support of the securities market and the Bank of England. It was staffed by a powerful team of analysts, programmers, and strategy experts, led by a highly respected project director, watched over by boards and committees. How could such a superbly resourced project fail? And why, less than one week after Taurus had been scrapped, could no one suggest any good reason why it should ever have been built?

Escalation in Decision-Making

The case of Taurus contains important implications for decision-making in organizations. The focus of the present study is a phenomenon known as escalation. Escalation is concerned with how and why organizations become involved in fiascos such as Taurus, and why they seem to persist with failing ventures long after any sensible person would surely have given up.

Although there are many books on decision-making, few deal with escalation and fewer still approach the topic in a manner accessible to a wide audience including practising managers and policy-makers. This book is intended to fill that gap by drawing attention to the risks of escalation. The issue is important because unwarranted persistence means loss. Waste can never be justified. It becomes a public issue when the bill is ultimately paid by society, as it so often is, and as happened with Taurus.

This book reveals how a combination of ambition, power, greed, and conflict ruined Taurus. Whereas journalism is concerned with story-telling and analysis, academic research goes one step further and tries to relate events to theories of decision-making. Case-studies of escalation are rare. The book is therefore likely to be of interest to undergraduate and postgraduate students of management and decision-making as well as specialist academics working in the field. IT specialists and project managers may also find it instructive.

The aim is to reconstruct the decision process with the following questions in mind:

1. Why did the Stock Exchange proceed with a design which some observers said was a nonsense?
2. Why was an opportunity to cancel the project in 1991 not taken?
3. How was the decision to cancel the project reached?
4. Was cancellation a wise decision?

The theoretical framework and approach to research are described later in this book. It is sufficient to note here that a key issue

explored by the present study is whether persistence is the product of decision errors, or whether cases like Taurus are more
appropriately thought of as dilemmas whereby decision-makers
grapple as best they can with a multitude of uncertainties.

Structure of the Book

The first chapter sketches the conceptual foundations of this book.
The discussion falls into two parts. Section 1 describes various
theories which attempt to explain irrational persistence. Section 2
outlines an alternative viewpoint which argues that persistence
with projects such as Taurus may be an economically prudent
response to difficult circumstances. Chapter 2 describes the
research methodology.

The next three chapters trace the background to Taurus.
Chapter 3 comprises a very brief historical introduction to the City
of London and the Stock Exchange. Chapter 4 traces the origins of
the Taurus project with reference to the stock-market crash of
October 1987 and the subsequent settlements crisis. Chapter 5 is
concerned with the deliberations of the Siscot Committee, which
designed Taurus, nicknamed 'the Mad Hatter's tea-party'.
Chapter 6 describes Peter Rawlins's failed attempt to halt the project in early 1990 before anything had been built. Chapter 7 analyses the first phase of the escalation process including the
unsuccessful attempt to halt it.

Chapters 8 and 9 cover the period from 1990 to autumn 1991,
when Taurus was being built. These two chapters describe how
deadlines slipped repeatedly and costs rose, as issues marked in
the prospectus 'to be decided later' returned to haunt the project.
Chapter 10 analyses the mid-phase of the escalation process. It is
a theoretically significant juncture because many of the people
interviewed for this book suggested that Taurus should have been
cancelled in 1991. Indeed, it very nearly was.

Chapter 11 describes the final months of Taurus viewed through
the eyes of the market and the Taurus monitoring group. Chapter
12 covers the same period as experienced by the chief executive.
Chapter 13 analyses the decision to withdraw. Chapter 14 discusses the key theoretical and empirical implications arising from
the present study.

Readers interested in why Taurus failed will find the descriptive chapters most relevant. I hope though that the analytical sections contain something of value to practising managers and policy-makers. To make the text as readable as possible I have confined the more abstruse academic issues to the notes contained at the end of each chapter. Readers seeking to obtain an overview of the book are directed to Chapter 14.

This account makes no claim toward establishing 'the truth' about Taurus if, indeed, there is such a thing. An account which is real and accurate from one observer's standpoint seems like fiction to another. My task has been to represent as many different perspectives on Taurus as I can, for it is the conflicting rationales and realities, the misunderstandings, the arguments 'this way or that way' which form the very essence of decision-making and escalation.

The case of Taurus is extremely complicated and raises many complex theoretical, empirical, and practical issues. For that reason, it is dangerous to try to summarize the findings in one 'sound-bite'. With that caveat, if I were asked to state in a nutshell what causes escalation, the answer would be 'everyone behaving rationally'.

Taurus was a tragic failure. Much of the subsequent media commentary portrayed many of the participants as bungling idiots guilty of monstrous negligence. This is unfair and misleading, for it ignores the critical impact of forces beyond the decision-maker's control and eclipses the sustained ingenuity, commitment, and sheer hard work invested in the project by so many people. One technical manager I interviewed spoke with tears in his eyes when he said:

That's the sadness that's left. We did so much that was good. Then it got wiped out in a day.[9]

This is the story of how so much that was good came to be wiped out in a day.

NOTES

1. Interview, Peter Rawlins, Oct. 1993.

2. Ibid.
3. Interview, Peter Rawlins, Oct. 1993.
4. Telephone interview, Richard Waters, July 1993.
5. Ibid.
6. Interview, member of Stock Exchange technical team, May 1994.
7. Interview, member of Stock Exchange technical team, May 1994.
8. Interview, member of Stock Exchange technical team, Nov. 1994.
9. Interview, member of Stock Exchange technical team, June 1994.

ACKNOWLEDGEMENTS

On 11 March 1993 I was rushing through the Sidney Jones Library of the University of Liverpool when a headline in the *Financial Times* caught my eye. The headline read, 'City May Scrap Trading Scheme'.

I was very busy and thought little of it at the time. It was only some weeks later, when I suddenly remembered what I had seen, that I jotted a note in my organizer and decided to investigate. I was subsequently fortunate in obtaining funds from the University of Liverpool and latterly the Economic and Social Research Council to enable me to research Taurus. I applied for three grants that summer. Taurus was the only successful application. Without that support there would have been no book, a reminder of how momentous decisions can turn upon a caprice of fate.

I thank everyone who helped with the study. Michael Keighley and Eva Pias De Olivera, my research assistants, provided a sound and orderly foundation for the work. Dr Martin Beale assisted with some of the technical issues. David Musson, my commissioning editor, went beyond the bounds of duty in supplying references, material, and personal introductions which I might otherwise have missed. I also thank Emeritus Professor Frank Land for his encouragement and for his help in locating potential informants. Chris Thomas of the Bank of England Library and the staff of the Guildhall Library were most co-operative in providing access to their respective collections. My colleagues in Liverpool have been a constant source of good humour and consideration.

The present analysis owes an intellectual debt to the work of Michael Bowen. I have built upon his ideas, both published and those generously contributed in private communications. Professor Elizabeth Chell and Professor Morton Davies also read parts of the draft and made many helpful suggestions. An earlier version of Chapters 1 and 2 was presented at the Risk in Organizations conference in May 1995 sponsored by the Economic and Social Research Council. Parts of the analysis were rehearsed at the Programme on Information and Communication Technologies seminar in October 1994, an event also sponsored by the Economic and Social Research Council. I thank Professor Graham Loomes and Professor Bill Dutton for their respective invitations to participate. I am also grateful to Professor John Hayes for the opportunity to test some of my ideas at a meeting of the Research in Organization Behaviour Group of the School of Business and Economic Studies at the University of Leeds. I am also indebted to anonymous referees for their comments on my earlier research papers, which encouraged me to persist with the topic of escalation.

Research is almost as risky an endeavour as building a large-scale IT project. There are no guarantees that the mountains of interview transcripts and other documentation so painstakingly gathered can be welded into a coherent framework. When academics describe the research process as cycling continuously between data and theory, what they may really mean is, 'It was like one of those toys you bash with a hammer. You bash one peg down; another one flies up at you. Bash that peg down again; another one flies up!'

I thank the significant others in my life for their warmth, support, and companionship. The study took a little longer than I expected. Like building Taurus itself, there was always another piece of work, always another dimension that had to be investigated. Indeed I often found myself parodying one of my informants:

' "Are we any closer to the end?"
"We-ell, not really, because the end keeps moving." '

The Stock Exchange and Coopers and Lybrand declined to co-operate on the grounds of incurring potential legal liability. I am all the more grateful, therefore, to those who gave their time, (and often their hospitality) to recount their involvement in the long history of Taurus and for supplying me with copies of notes, reports, and other unpublished documentation. I owe special thanks to those respondents who read parts of the account and those who suggested possible themes for analysis.

The contributors include Hugh Armstrong, Michael Baker, Paul Bradbrook, Ian Cormack, Paul Dunk, A. E. (Frank) Francksen, Crispin Gascoigne, Sir Nicholas Goodison, Richard Grayson, John

Gubert, David Hanson, George Hayter, Anthony Hilton, Philip Hooker, Mike Jones, Pen Kent, Jeffrey Knight, Brian Ludlow, Patrick Mitford-Slade, Michael Newman, Andrew Palmer, John Powell, Denis Preston, Peter Rawlins, the Rt. Hon. John Redwood, MP, Tony Smith, Richard Waters, Bill Widdis, and David Wyatt. Some people assisted on condition that their identities be protected. I am equally grateful to them.

I emphasize that no criticism of any individual, group, or organization is implied by the text. My purpose in researching and writing has been to try to understand what the decision-makers did and why so that others may learn. Many of the people I spoke with knew that the exercise would evoke painful memories. They co-operated in the express hope that something useful might emerge from a tragic episode. I hope they feel I have done justice to that objective.

Liverpool
5 November 1995

CONTENTS

LIST OF FIGURES

CHRONOLOGY

1970

Heasman Committee recommends streamlining of London's equities settlement procedures.

1979

Director General of Fair Trading proposes to refer the Stock Exchange's rule book to the Restrictive Practices Court. Talisman implemented.

1980

Wilson Report on the functioning of the City published.

1983

Stock Exchange announces its intention to abolish fixed commissions. Referral to the Restrictive Practices Court withdrawn.

1986

May: Stock Exchange embarks upon Taurus, a computerized system for equities settlement. The three-year, £6 million programme is expected to save 1,700 jobs in the City and to cut transaction costs by 70 per cent.
October: 'Big Bang'; the Stock Exchange abolishes fixed commissions and single-capacity dealing and introduces automated trading systems. Taurus now due to be implemented in 1989.

1987

October: Stock-market crash. Settlements crisis reveals almost one million unsettled share bargains worth £13.4 billion.

1988

Development of Taurus 1 accelerated.
November: Siscot Committee formed.

1989

March: Taurus 1 abandoned. Stock Exchange criticized for spending five years and £6 million of members' money on the prototype. Siscot considers no fewer than seventeen Taurus designs.
August: John Watson appointed Taurus project director.
November: Peter Rawlins takes up the post of chief executive of the Stock Exchange. He tries to stop the project from going ahead.

1990

March: Taurus prospectus published. Time-scale for implementation: October 1991. Development costs £45–£50 million. Projected savings to the City £225 million over three years. Technical team holds its first meeting with Vista corporation.
May: The Stock Exchange announces that it will reduce the number of committees from over 100 to no more than fifteen.
July: DTI issues a consultative paper on the legal implications of Taurus. Contract with Vista signed.

1991

January: Launch of Taurus delayed from October 1991 to first half of 1992 because of unforeseen regulatory implications.
March: DTI demands a compensation fund for private investors and insists company membership be voluntary.
April: Dispute over who should regulate Taurus. Stock Exchange hints at the possibility of further delays.
May: £100 million compensation fund agreed with the DTI. Stock Exchange to regulate Taurus. May 1992 'pencilled in' as new start date for Taurus. John Watson tells the press, 'On the building of systems we are 95 per cent of the way there.'
August: Difficulties in developing and testing Taurus software described by John Watson as a 'hiccup not a disaster'. Stock Exchange commissions a review of the project.

September: Stock Exchange Council abolished and replaced by a company-style board. Board approves new budgets and time-scales for Taurus. Stock Exchange announces Taurus will miss May 1992 implementation date because of software writing problems. Taurus now expected to go live 'some time next year'.

October: Stock Exchange announces May 1993 as the new implementation date for Taurus. Projected final costs of Taurus £80-90 million.

November: Project consultants Coopers & Lybrand insist that significant Taurus milestones are now within the direct control of the Stock Exchange.

December: Proposal for thirteen-digit personal identification numbers for investors dropped. Legal framework for Taurus resolved.

1992

January: Andersen Consulting appointed by the Stock Exchange to examine options for contracting out trading and settlement systems. Contract reported to exclude work on Taurus.

February: Legislation for Taurus receives parliamentary approval.

May: Reports of possible further delays to Taurus because of problems with the IBM security package.

June: Taurus regulations published. The media report 'Taurus costs soaring' as development costs reach £47 million. The Stock Exchange announces that it anticipates spending a further £25 million on Taurus.

July: Marks and Spencer postpone shareholder vote on Taurus membership.

August: Press reports claim that Taurus may increase the cost of share-dealing.

September: Chairman of Stock Exchange describes Taurus as 'much awaited' rather than 'long-delayed'. 'Taurus will soon emerge,' he tells reporters; '. . . many superlatives spring to mind.'

November: 'How the hell can I tell?' says John Watson when pressed by newspaper reporters to name a date when Taurus will go live. Costs of Taurus reach £60 million.

1993

January: Press reports claim Taurus is unlikely to appear before spring 1994. Costs now estimated at £80 million. Latest delays thought likely to make final figure higher still. The original cost–benefit analysis is now said to be far out of date. The media further report that the most complicated part of the system (take-overs, rights, and issues), which usually account for 80 per cent of the problems in stockbroking packages, will be the last to arrive.

8 March: Taurus Monitoring Group decides to declare a crisis.

10 March: The *Evening Standard* reports that Taurus is about to be abandoned.

11 March: Taurus is abandoned. Peter Rawlins resigns as chief executive of the Stock Exchange.

1

What Causes Escalation?

ESTRAGON: Let's go.
VLADIMIR: We can't.
ESTRAGON: Why not?
VLADIMIR: We're waiting for Godot.

(Samuel Beckett, *Waiting for Godot*)[1]

In 1993 an investor called Jim (a pseudonym) bought 1,400 shares in a company known as Spring Ram. Spring Ram manufactures kitchen and bathroom fittings. The shares cost £1.45 each, making a total investment of £2,030. Jim's decision was influenced by two factors. First, the name 'Spring Ram' was familiar. He passes one of their outlets *en route* to work. Second, the shares were strongly recommended by the journal *Investor's Chronicle*. *Investor's Chronicle* is owned by the *Financial Times*. It enjoys a reputation for integrity, 'written by journalists not salesmen'. Jim said, 'I thought I'd play dangerously. I decided to take a risk and it looked like a good one. The *Investor's Chronicle* said so *twice* [Jim's emphasis] in one week.' The day after Jim purchased the shares, the price plummeted from £1.45 to 80p. The following week it rose to £1.20. Within days, however, a profits warning appeared and the share price fell to 48p. Jim's original investment of £2,030 was now worth only £672.

The Crash revealed that the firm's previous performance owed something to its accountancy procedures. For example, sales were recorded when customers placed orders and not when they actually took delivery of goods. Depreciation charges had been modest. Development costs had been treated as assets. 'How anyone can make a profit out of kitchen furniture in the middle of a recession when no one's buying houses is beyond me,' said Jim, 'but that's with hindsight.' When asked why he had not sold the shares Jim replied, 'What—at 48p when I paid 145p! If it [the company] sinks without trace so be it.' Jim said that he would only sell if he was desperate for money:

The annual report suggests next year will be better. Bear in mind there are some new key players in there. Both the *Financial Times* and *Investor's Chronicle* were saying Prudential (the company who had acquired Spring Ram) are determined to make it work. I'll give it a year.[2]

Despite the optimistic predictions, one year later the shares were worth only 37p. With only £517 of his original £2,030 left, Jim finally decided to cut his losses.

As Jim's experience shows, decisions can go wrong. Had Jim sold his shares when they fell to £1.20 he would have avoided the worst of the loss. He would still have been better off had he sold when the price appeared to stabilize at around 48p per share.

At least Jim's shares were still worth something when he finally sold them. Another investor who bought shares in a company which subsequently completely collapsed wrote to the *Financial Times* for advice. The letter said, 'Is my share certificate worth anything or should I frame it?' The reply read, 'Your share certificate is almost certainly worthless. Unless it is particularly artistic, framing would merely be throwing good money after bad.'

Harsh counsel perhaps, but from a financial standpoint, sound. Past investments are irrelevant to decisions about the future. The correct response is to invest in whatever option promises the highest return on investment. That may mean abandoning a successful investment in favour of one promising a higher rate of return.[3] In practice, decision-makers may do nothing of the sort, preferring, like Jim, to hang on to their investments in the hope of recovery though at the risk of compounding their losses. Persistence in the face of a stream of losses is known as escalation.

The purpose of this chapter is to sketch the conceptual background to the present study. No one knows for certain what causes escalation. This chapter outlines the main theories suggested by researchers. The discussion falls into two parts. The first describes possible social-psychological explanations of escalation. The second describes an alternative school of thought known as decision dilemma theory.

MONEY SUNK AND LOST

Escalation is defined as persistence with a decision well beyond the point where any sensible person would give up.[4] One theory of escalation is that decision-makers become emotionally attached to their investment. Jim, for example, is riveted to the £2,030 originally committed ('What—at 48p when I paid 145p!'). Clinging to the past in this way is irrational because it prevents Jim from seeing the situation for what it has become, that is, £672 left to invest.

Jim is exhibiting what is known in the escalation literature as a 'sunk cost' effect. It is thought that the more a person has invested in a venture, the more likely they are to persist with it.[5] For example, it is thought that people are more likely to sit through a bad play if they have paid £25 for a ticket than if they have paid only £1. Such behaviour is illogical because, assuming no refunds are available, the money is beyond recall. Why compound the loss by spending three hours or so feeling bored if the time can be put to better use?

PROSPECT THEORY: THE PSYCHOLOGY OF IRRATIONAL RISK PREFERENCES

Jim eventually accepts his losses but it takes him over a year to adapt. Decision-makers are thought to be highly vulnerable during the period of adaptation because loss may make people all the more inclined to take big risks.[6] Imagine a day at the races, for example. You have lost £200 on unsuccessful bets. You now meet a friend who offers you a choice between a sure gain of £100 or an even chance to win £200 or nothing. Mindful of the initial loss, you may reason that the problem is a choice between a 50 per cent chance of losing £200 and a sure loss of £100. This is known in the literature as a framing effect. Framing effects prevent the decision-maker from transposing the problem, that is, a choice between a 50 per cent chance of £200 and a sure gain of £100. In other words, the theory predicts that, obsessed by the lost £200, you might well pass over the gift of £100! Framing effects are thought to explain why betting on long shots is most frequent just before the last race.

It is also thought that people are apt to postpone unpleasant possibilities. The risk of a large loss some time in the future is believed to be preferable to a small but certain loss now. Moreover, risks which are judged to be highly unlikely may be ignored altogether. This can be disastrous, as many 'Lloyds Names' discovered to their cost. Although warned that they were financially liable 'down to their last set of cufflinks', many prospective Names regarded the advice as a formality because at the time losses were virtually unknown in Lloyds 300-year history.[7]

The sheer pain of loss may encourage people to behave irrationally. For instance, the anguish of losing a £10 note is thought to be much more acute than the pleasure experienced in finding a £10 note. This may explain why people resent paying a surcharge to use a credit card but will happily pay cash in order to obtain a discount of the same amount.

It is believed that distress is less acute if losses are incurred gradually. This is because people are thought to be less sensitive to the cumulative impact of a series of gradual changes than to one large change. For example, piecemeal increases in taxation tend to engender less protest than one big rise, even though the total increase is the same. Decision-makers are also thought to be affected by the magnitude of change. For instance, the difference in value between £100 and £200 seems greater than the difference between £1,100 and £1,200.

Such irrational preferences are potentially escalatory if they obscure the reality of a situation. For example, a vendor selling a house may lose sight of the sum total of concessions if these are extracted one by one. Likewise, a plaintiff may go to court for £100 on a contract involving £200 whereas they would accept the loss of £100 on a contract worth £1,200.

RESPONSIBILITY THEORY

Whenever things go wrong usually one of the first questions to be asked is 'who is responsible?' Another possible clue to escalation was suggested by a series of experiments which showed that decision-makers who were told they were responsible for an unsuccessful decision seemed more inclined to persist than those who inherited the problem, especially where subjects believed that their jobs were at stake. Researchers concluded that failure tempts decision-makers to persist in the hope of eventually turning matters round, thus enabling them to prove to themselves and to others that they were right after all.[8]

KEEPING UP APPEARANCES

In western culture leaders are ideally quick-thinking, resolute, and decisive. This stereotype is thought to be conducive to escalation because those who take time to think, and who change their minds frequently, are popularly perceived as weak and vacillating. Leaders may also find themselves trapped by their own public personae. For example, former prime minister Margaret Thatcher cultivated a reputation as a hard unyielding person, which made it difficult for her to reverse unpopular policies, notably the introduction of a poll tax.

Although in theory entrepreneurs' sole concern is to maximize profits, it is thought that some business decisions are driven more by emotion than reason. The Forte family's long quest to acquire the Savoy Hotel is potentially a case in point. The Savoy, like many luxury hotels, generates only modest profits whereas the Forte organization has always placed great emphasis upon achieving a high rate of return. Journalists have speculated that the real motivation for acquisition may be wounded pride:

None of the insults traded during the takeover battle of the 1980's have been forgotten and few have been forgiven. It was not just Mr Shephard's assertion that stewardship of Savoy hotels could not be entrusted to 'a vast combine which, among other things, runs service stations on the main arterial roads.'

What rankles more was Sir Hugh's remark to Mr Forte after Forte's initial failure to win control that 'I've always thought Italians make good hotel *managers*.'

Although Forte in his autobiography claims, 'I don't need the Savoy to crown my career. I have enough already of which to be proud,' the article points out that thirteen years is a long time to pursue something one does not need.[9]

Imagine being invited to bid in an auction. The prize is a £1 coin. There is no reserve price; it is possible, therefore, to acquire the coin for as little as one pence. There is one special rule, however. That is, the second bidder must pay the bid price. Would you participate on this basis?

The auction is a trap. Yet whenever I have conducted it with MBA students it has never been difficult to persuade people to enter the game. Moreover, invariably two unfortunate students find themselves locked into bid and counterbid as the price of the coin rises well beyond its face value.

Price wars between garages, supermarkets, and airlines are believed to be driven by a form of 'dollar auction' mentality. People sometimes become involved because they fail to see the long-term consequences of their actions. Once trapped, bidding is thought to be motivated by unwillingness to lose face, or even by desire for revenge. Desire for revenge may be powerfully conducive to escalation because of the lengths to which people will go in order to restore their sense of self-esteem. Literature and opera are replete with examples of characters who have destroyed themselves in order to avenge some real or imaginary slight.[10]

GROUPS AND ESCALATION

Many decisions are made by groups as distinct from individuals acting alone. Groups are thought to be more prone to escalation than individuals because group membership leads to a diminished sense of responsibility which in turn encourages 'gung-ho' attitudes to risk-taking.[11]

KILL THE MESSENGER

History suggests that it is rarely profitable to be the harbinger of bad news. Persistence in the face of mounting failure is thought to be facilitated by the way in which we respond to information. Decision-makers are said to be extremely adept at deceiving themselves and others into believing that things are not as bad as they seem or that given a little more time and/or a little more money matters will soon improve.

One way in which decision-makers are thought to rationalize failure is diverting blame away from themselves. A study which analysed a large sample of company reports found that bad news was consistently blamed upon factors outside the company's control such as currency fluctuations and the world economy whereas good news was consistently attributed to the directors' skill and diligence.[12]

Psychologists also believe that decision-makers tend to pounce upon facts and figures which support their preconceived ideas whilst ignoring contradictory evidence. Such biasing may occur unconsciously. For example, there is evidence which shows that executives tend to file material which justifies their decisions whilst disconfirming analyses and extrapolations are more likely to be destroyed.[13]

'IT COULD BE YOU.'

Decision-makers can be manipulated into risk-taking. For example, the popular cartoon character Andy Capp begs his wife Flo for money to place a bet on a horse. When she demurs Andy insists that the horse is a 'dead cert'. Flo then asks him where they went for their holiday last year. 'Yer mother's,' replies Andy.

'Where did the bookie go?' asks Flo.

'Bermuda,' says Andy.

'Think about it,' retorts Flo.

Since the only certainties in life are death and taxes, what convinces people like Andy Capp that a gamble is a 'dead cert'?

Significantly, Andy is picking the horse. Perceived control is believed to be conducive to persistence even when it is manifestly absurd to believe that one can control the situation. For instance, there is evidence that people will pay more for a lottery ticket if they can choose it themselves than if someone else chooses it for them. This explains why manufacturers of fruit machines incorporate 'nudge' and 'hold' buttons. Such devices encourage players to feel they are pitting their wits against the tyranny of chance. Likewise dice players typically throw hard when seeking high numbers and softly when seeking low numbers.

Amusement arcades are designed to encourage playing. Strobe lighting and continuous pop music enable players to suspend reality. Metal trays are used to ensure coins fall with a satisfying clatter. Language and visual images can also be deployed to encourage risk-taking by conjuring up an attractive vision of the future. Investment banks promise 'pure growth', 'pure performance', 'heaven from penny shares', 'the rewards of the stock market: none of the risks'. The aim is to detract attention from hard statistical data and small print which might, for instance, show that investment in the stock market is rarely risk-free.

A related technique is to make the vision seem as if it is almost a reality. The chances of winning the jackpot prize in the UK National Lottery are millions to one against. Yet the advertising slogan is designed to create the very opposite impression: 'It could be you.' Likewise football pools entrants are asked to indicate whether they would prefer no publicity in the event of winning. Such a question makes the prospect of 'scooping the jackpot' seem real indeed. Owners of fairground machines pile coins close to the edge. It looks as if just one coin will knock the whole heap over. Instead, the coin just pushes the heap tantalizingly closer, driving the decision-maker to try again.

The survival of sea-side fortune tellers defies logic. The explanation appears to be that people seek certainty and are therefore attracted to those who promise it, especially if the news is good. The more convincing they sound, the better. Andy Capp, for example, is captivated by the prophecy of a 'dead cert'. Likewise Macbeth is stirred by the exalted language, 'That shalt be king hereafter.' Yet the statement actually promises nothing. Too late Macbeth recognizes the 'scam'.

Even the more apparently sober advertisements are actually carefully crafted. For instance:

Investment for high rewards can never be risk free and some of our recommendations don't work out. . . . The impact of . . . disasters can be mitigated by operating a twenty-percent stop loss rule. We have found from long experience that when a share price drops by 20 percent after we have profiled the company that they are best sold. . . . If losses are confined to around 20 percent while profits are unlimited the odds on overall success are greatly improved.[14]

This all sounds very reasonable. An atmosphere of candour is created by the admission that some investments fail. The aim of such a disarming statement is to gain the prospective investor's confidence. The next step is to create a sense of control via the 'stop loss rule'. The advertisement then trades upon the company's expertise by attempting to persuade the reader that the risk of a 20 per cent loss is reasonable whilst dangling the possibility of glittering returns reassuringly couched in the language of professionalism.[15]

Professed expertise is potentially a powerful technique of manipulation. It is thought that people will act upon an expert's advice even though they are almost certain that the person giving it is wrong. For instance, there is evidence that where a project is in doubt, an expert report recommending continuance can be decisive even though a good case for abandonment exists. Besides, expertise is sometimes more apparent than real. Domestic property valuations, for instance, can vary enormously from surveyor to surveyor. This is because they are based on guesswork informed by local knowledge potentially available to any layperson. Expert power derives its strength from the recipient's belief that the expert is serving their interests and not the expert's own. Yet experts are not invariably neutral. The popular fictional barrister Horace Rumpole, for example, is urged by his clerk to spin out the more lucrative cases.

WHEN SUCCESS BREEDS DISASTER

Nothing succeeds like success, because success breeds confidence which may develop into overconfidence. For instance, a letter once appeared in a newspaper from a man whose wife had won £50. 'She immediately went out and spent £500 of her winnings,' said the husband. 'I dread her winning the National Lottery.'[16] The husband's fears were possibly well founded. Overconfidence may lead to unwarranted persistence because it encourages people to suspend critical analysis. Those who have experienced repeated success are believed to be particularly vulnerable because they become imbued with a sense of infallibility which means that they cannot conceive of the possibility of failure—even when it actually happens. Unscrupulous others can foster overconfidence by allowing their intended victims to experience success. For instance, card-sharpers sometimes deliberately lose a few games in order to encourage players to raise the stakes.

Similarly, people who believe they can perform a task well tend to do better than if they expect to fail. The danger, however, is that such perceived efficacy may lead them to focus upon the parts of the task that they can easily accomplish. Consequently they may, for example, accept a brief without properly considering those aspects of the task which they are unqualified to perform.

When National Lottery 'scratch cards' were launched in the UK some players were observed returning again and again to buy more cards. Near misses too are potentially conducive to persistence. One theory is that a near miss produces a similar excitement to actually winning. Another possibility is that failure by a narrow margin produces such frustration and regret that the person feels compelled to try again.[17]

DECISION DILEMMA THEORY

The problem with social-psychological theories of escalation is that if we pursue the foregoing propositions to their logical conclusion, then we would all be gambling addicts, because the literature implies indefinite persistence. Yet resources are finite. There are limits to how many lottery cards people can buy, and how often they can afford to repair an old car. Likewise, no one can stand at a bus stop or wait on hold on the telephone for ever.

The literature further assumes that loss is experienced as failure and disappointment. Yet if that were invariably true, how do venture capitalists and commodities traders survive in business? How do we explain the behaviour of people who walk away from fruit machines after one or two turns, or who confine themselves to one bingo or lottery card per week?

Jim resists the temptation to buy more shares in Spring Ram to show he was right. Nor does he cling to his investment in perpetuity. He waits a year to give the price a chance to recover. Seeing that it has remained stagnant for this period, he sells. Was that unreasonable when transaction costs (brokerage fees currently ranging from £9 to £36 plus half a per cent stamp duty per bargain) are considered?

An alternative school of thought exists in the escalation literature known as decision dilemma theory. Decision dilemma theorists argue that the real problem decision-makers face is uncertainty. It can be very difficult to know how things are going to turn out, especially in the early stages of a venture as feedback is likely to be sketchy. Moreover, when problems develop it may be sensible to give a strategy a chance to work. The end result may be failure but that does not necessarily mean that the decision-makers have behaved foolishly. Persistence can only be described as absurd where the decision-maker ignores information which clearly indicates that further investment is useless. Most of the time, it is argued, the decision-maker's information will be equivocal.[18]

Samuel Beckett's play *Waiting for Godot* encapsulates the predicament of decision-making. The script depicts two tramps waiting for a man known as Godot. Twice in the play at evening time, a messenger arrives with the news that although Mr Godot will not come today, he will surely come tomorrow. But Godot never comes. Several times during the play the tramps determine to leave only to change their minds. The play ends with the two tramps resolved:

ESTRAGON: Yes, let's go. [*They do not move.*]

How are we to judge whether the decision to carry on waiting for Godot is correct or not? By the time the play finishes no one is any wiser as to whether Godot will ever come at all, or whether he has come and gone unnoticed. Social-psychological theorists might suggest that Vladimir and Estragon persist because they are convinced that Godot will arrive. Yet the text of the play suggests that the decision turns upon a complex calculation. One factor is prospective reward. Vladimir and Estragon hope that Godot will grant them a favour. Second, there is the presumed proximity of the reward; Godot, the messenger promises, will surely come tomorrow. Vladimir and Estragon also weigh the costs of withdrawal, for they expect Godot will punish them if they leave.[19] The issues are finely balanced. Estragon concludes, 'Don't let's do anything. It's safer.'

According to decision dilemma theorists, many of the cases cited in the literature as examples of irrational persistence actually reflect decision-makers' behaving cautiously in difficult circumstances—America's involvement in Vietnam, for example. Likewise what appears as escalation can actually be decision-makers taking a long-term view of their investment. This particularly applies to so-called 'long-haul' projects such as bridge building, tramline construction, and sewerage schemes. Such projects rarely go entirely to plan. The long time-scale of such enterprises increases the probability of unforeseen contingencies especially if the project involves working at the boundaries of knowledge. The technology associated with such projects is typically inflexible, which also restricts the decision-maker's options. Then there is the sheer cost of removing the works. It is no light undertaking to rip up, say, a light-railway project. Whereas components and materials may be resellable before processing begins, once in process they are virtually useless for any other purpose. Only when they re-emerge in the form of a finished product do they once more hold value. Moreover, until the work is finished, there is no income to mitigate the effects of setbacks.[20]

Resources are finite: once funds are committed to a project it may be very difficult to switch to a venture offering a higher return on investment, especially if the scrap value of an existing project is low and/or closing costs are high. For example, it has been suggested that the American steel industry is locked into old-fashioned, relatively costly technology because of previous heavy investment.[21] Economists argue, 'The more a manager has invested in a project early on, or the larger and later the payoffs, the wiser it is to stay in the project.'[22] No one has seriously suggested closing down the Channel Tunnel project, for example, despite all the difficulties, though the company did suggest that if the final cost had been known at the outset they might never have embarked upon it!

It has been argued that the empirical evidence for irrational persistence is open to interpretation. People taking part in experiments may have opted to persist because their information was insufficient to justify withdrawal.[23] Besides, the evidence is conflicting. The results of some experiments suggest that decision-makers actually behave very sensibly. They persist for a while and then withdraw if their efforts seem futile.[24] Moreover, many of the studies pointing to irrational persistence were conducted with students with little or no business experience. When qualified professionals were supplied with the same data they made very different decisions, that is, they were more inclined to give up when faced with negative feedback.[25] Likewise evidence is beginning to emerge which suggests that decision-makers may not be entirely riveted by sunk costs. Recent studies have suggested that the level of project completion is more important. Decision-makers appear to be more inclined to proceed with a project that is 90 per cent complete than one which is only 10 per cent complete regardless of the amount of money invested.[26]

Most of the research has been conducted using experiments. The small corpus of case-studies of escalation in organizations has suggested that persistence may be highly political. Moreover, actions which may seem bizarre may actually mask a very careful balancing act whereby decision-makers incur losses in one sphere in order to realize gains in another. For example, they may tolerate or even seem oblivious to an incompetent employee because that person's presence is strategically important.[27]

WITHDRAWAL

The collapse of Spring Ram's share price prompted Jim to review his investments. His portfolio included a tranche of shares in a company known as Cable and Wireless. He felt anxious because Cable and Wireless were then relatively unknown. He discussed the situation with his broker. 'We quite like Cable and Wireless, sir,' the broker advised. Mindful of his previous experience, however, Jim decided to switch his shares to BT, an established 'blue chip' company. BT's shares have since risen modestly in line with the stock market. The share price of Cable and Wireless, however, has more than doubled!

What explains Jim's unfortunate decision? Most of the literature has focused upon the possible reasons for escalation. Little is known about the factors which might prompt decision-makers to abandon a particular course of action.[28] Withdrawal is important because it is the point at which losses are stemmed if the decision was ill-advised, or gains are forgone if the decision was sound.

Broadly speaking the social-psychological theorists suggest that withdrawal becomes more difficult as time goes on because an accumulation of investments, psychological, social, and material, bind the decision-maker. For example, pension arrangements may make it difficult to change an employer. Organizations may incur obligations to subcontractors and other vested interests. A whole infrastructure may have been created around the project:

All the rules, procedures, and routines of an organization as well as the sheer trouble it takes for managers to give up day to day activities in favour of serious operational disruption, can cause administrative inertia . . . Sometimes it's just easier not to rock the boat.[29]

Decision dilemma theorists predict that withdrawal actually becomes easier as time goes on, as information becomes more readily available, patterns emerge, and so forth. For example, time may reveal an employee's incompetence, or demonstrate that a marriage is failing to live up to expectations. Moreover, the theory predicts that a stream of negative feedback will eventually destroy the decision-maker's commitment to the venture. It becomes clear, for instance, that a misdemeanour or other disappointment is not an isolated incident but part of a pattern.

The evidence for both propositions is sparse and largely tangential. Alternative investment opportunities seem to blunt escalation, possibly because they highlight the opportunity costs of persistence. Opportunity costs are thought to be particularly relevant when projects are at the early stages of development. Good organizational control procedures are thought to curb escalation, especially if they require decision-makers to confront their options periodically. Likewise, a system of checks and balances may prevent organizations from assuming 'avoidable risks'.[30] It has been suggested, for example, that the collapse of Baring's bank in the UK in 1995 was caused by weaknesses in the bank's control structure which enabled an employee known as Nick Leeson to conceal trading losses until they reached catastrophic proportions. Some banks employ so-called 'weasels' to identify traders who break the rules.[31]

A recent field study of a solicitor who decided to enter into partnership has suggested that information may be a necessary but insufficient condition for withdrawal. The arrangement was clearly a disaster from the senior partner's viewpoint virtually from day one. However, it was only when an outsider complained that the senior partner felt justified in dissolving the arrangement. In other words, withdrawal may depend upon the decision-maker's ability to convert their information into power.[32]

RESEARCH AIMS

Clearly there are plenty of possible explanations for escalation. The literature basically reflects two schools of thought, however. One regards persistence in the face of negative feedback as the product of decision errors. The second argues that technically it is impossible for decision-makers to err in ill-structured situations.

The issue is important because both schools of thought suggest that decision fiascos are inevitable, but for different reasons.

Social-psychological theory depicts decision-makers as driven to persist at all costs. Decision dilemma theory implies they are helpless victims of circumstances. Decision dilemma theorists suggest that when projects begin to go awry there may be little that decision-makers can do but wait for market forces to exert themselves. Social-psychological theorists predict that decision-makers deliberately try to prevent market forces from curbing persistence.

The aim of the present study is to explore these problems by means of a case-study of a decision in the context of a complex organization. The case concerns the Stock Exchange's decision to commission Project Taurus and its subsequent decision to cancel the project four years later whilst it was still being built.

The central concern in studying the sequence of events is to understand how and why organizations become involved in decision débâcles, and why they persist once matters seem to be turning out badly. Do decision-makers allow feelings of pride and fear of failure to corrupt their judgement or are they just sometimes unlucky? Or, is there another, more complex explanation for their seemingly bizarre behaviour?

NOTES

1. (Becket, (1986: 15).
2. Interview, private investor, April 1994.
3. More correctly known as utility maximization. In theory it is irrational to accept anything less than maximal returns; see, for example, Simon (1957, 1960).
4. The definition of escalation is derived from Staw and Ross (1987a). It may be defined more formally as persistence in a course of action beyond a rationally defensible point. The concept is potentially applicable to any form of investment. Friendships and romantic associations are discussed in Rusbult (1980a, b); career decisions in Becker (1960) and Drummond and Chell (1992). Gambling behaviour is discussed by Fisher (1990) and Griffiths (1993). Armstrong et al. (1993) discuss the relevance of escalation to marketing operations.
5. For a discussion of the 'return on investment' rationale, see Northcraft and Wolfe (1984). Potential sunk cost effects such as 'foot

in the door' and 'low ball' techniques are discussed in Arkes and Blumer (1985). Other empirical studies of sunk cost effects include Garland (1990), Garland, Sandefur and Rogers (1990), and Garland *et al.* (1991). See however Conlon and Garland (1993) and Garland and Conlon (unpub. mimeo, n.d.), as they conclude that the level of project completion may be more important than sunk costs in decisions about whether to persist. The issue is also discussed in the following chapter.

6. Whyte (1993).

7. Prospect theory is outlined in a suite of papers by Kahneman and Tversky (1979, 1982, 1984) and Tversky and Kahneman (1981). Applications of the theory appear in McNeil *et al.* (1982). The link between prospect theory and escalation is articulated in Whyte (1986, 1989, and 1993). Bazerman (1994) and Fiegenbaum and Thomas (1988) also discuss the issue.

For accounts of the machinations surrounding Lloyd's Names see Mantle (1992) and Raphael (1995).

For some related experiments see Barton *et al.* (1989), Dunegan (1993), Garland and Newport (1991), Harwood *et al.* (1991).

Brockner (1992) reviews the competing claims of responsibility theory, prospect theory, and decision dilemma theory. Although Brockner argues that responsibility theory is the most promising explanation, this conclusion is based almost entirely upon experimental studies. Further, evidence adduced as contradicting decision dilemma theory could equally be interpreted as supportive of it. For example, in one experiment individuals reported feeling '*less* confident as their degree of entrapment heightened' (p. 52). This observation is entirely consistent with decision dilemma theory, which suggests negative information (perceived entrapment in this case) destroys commitment to a decision.

8. For discussions of responsibility theory see, for example, Staw (1980, 1981), Staw and Ross (1987*a*, 1989), Brockner (1992).

The touchstone paper concerning the effects of personal responsibility is Staw (1976). The experiment was conducted as follows. Respondents (usually undergraduate business students) were asked to imagine themselves as financial executives with power to allocate research and development funds. Respondents were then shown the financial history of a fictitious company and asked to choose between funding the consumer department or the industrial products department. Respondents were asked to explain their rationale briefly in writing.

Next, respondents received figures showing either an upsurge or a decline in each division's performance. Respondents were then asked to make a second investment decision. This time respondents were allowed to allocate monies exactly as they chose between the two divisions.

Respondents received different feedback about their initial decision. Some learned that their chosen division had outperformed the division not chosen. Others learned that their chosen division had performed worse than the division not chosen. Further, half of the respondents were assigned to a so-called 'high-responsibility' category whereby both investment decisions were made sequentially. The idea is that half of the subjects are responsible for a decision which was either successful or unsuccessful. The remaining half were assigned to a so-called 'low-responsibility' condition. 'Low-responsibility' subjects are only asked to make the second allocation of funds. They are told that the first apportionment was made by someone else.

The greatest allocation of funding occurred where subjects were responsible for an unsuccessful decision. The results were interpreted as substantiating the self-justification theory of escalation and for the idea of escalation itself. The very decision to allocate funding to an apparently poorly performing division was seen as evidence of decision-makers' propensity to throw good money after bad.

Similar results have been obtained in a number of studies. Bazerman *et al.* (1982), for instance, observed experimentally that subjects responsible for unsuccessful promotion decisions allocated rewards and biased performance evaluations more favourably than subjects not responsible for the decision. Likewise Schoorman's (1988) field study found that supervisors concurring with hiring decisions biased their evaluations positively, whereas dissenting supervisors biased their evaluations negatively. Fox and Staw (1979) explore the link between job insecurity and self-justification.

Possible links between personality factors and escalation are explored by Brockner *et al.* (1986), Sandlands *et al.* (1988), Singer (1990), and Schaubroeck and Williams (1993).

9. For the story of Forte and similar quests to acquire flagship hotels see Skapinker (1994), and also Forte's (1987) own account. Dixon (1976) contains an interesting exposé of military leadership.

10. For empirical studies of the social impact of escalation see, for example, Brockner *et al.* (1981) and Brockner *et al.* (1984). Teger (1980) describes the dollar auction. Kim and Smith (1993) discuss the psychology of revenge.

11. Bazerman *et al.* (1984) observed that groups as well as individuals escalate their investments when they are responsible for an unsuccessful decision. Citing Heider they speculate that since group membership may encourage people to see themselves as a unit,

high-responsibility group members may feel committed both to the group and to the decision.

Groups which have succumbed to 'groupthink' are believed to be prone to an 'illusion of invulnerability', which may drive them on in an escalatory fashion and lead to 'collective rationalization' of their decision (Janis 1972). If this supposition is correct, cohesive groups may be especially vulnerable to escalation.

Whyte (1989, 1991, 1993) argues that groups exacerbate individual tendencies to escalation. See also Darley and Latane (1968), Leatherwood and Conlon (1987), and Mynatt and Sherman (1975).

McCarthy *et al.* (1993) observed a greater propensity to escalate where entrepreneurs are in partnership than when acting alone.

12. Staw *et al.* (1983).

13. Staw and Ross (1978) suggest that individuals may process information differently after failure as distinct from success. Such differential processing, they suggest, may explain persistence. See also Borrgida and Nisbett (1977), Brockner *et al.* (1986), Caldwell and O'Reilly (1982), Conlon and Wolf (1980), Nisbett and Ross (1980), Northcraft and Neale (1986), and O'Reilly (1980).

For possible evidence of unconscious biasing towards retrospective rationality see Conlon and Parks (1987).

14. Drummond (1994c).

15. Manipulation tactics are described by Drummond (1991b) and Schwenk (1986). Drummond (1991a) discusses the problems decision-makers encounter in obtaining useful and reliable information. Singer *et al.* (1991) suggest how framing effects and other biases can be manipulated in buying and marketing contexts. For example, insurance companies project vivid images of an earthquake to engender anxiety and to make such an event seem more probable than it really is in order to sell policies.

See Wrong (1979) for a discussion of expert power. For a less formal treatment of the subject and examples from practice see Drummond (1991b). Schwenk (1988) examines the impact of devil's advocacy on escalation.

16. *The Times*, 1995.

17. Perceived control, gambling behaviour, and the psychology of the 'near miss' are discussed by Griffiths (1990) and Langer (1975, 1983). See also Fisher's (1993) most interesting study of behaviour in amusement arcades.

Gist and Mitchell (1992) explore the relationship between perceived efficacy and task performance. McCarthy *et al.* (1993) observe that the strongest predictor of decision commitment amongst entrepreneurs is the individual's belief that they can outperform others.

Other related empirical studies include Brockner *et al.* (1986) and Sandlands *et al.* (1988). Griffiths (1990) explores the link between success and overconfidence in gambling. The discussion draws upon prospect theory.

For non-empirical discussions of the link between overconfidence and success see Janis (1989), Neustadt and May (1986), and Schlesinger's (1965) commentary on the Bay of Pigs fiasco.

18. Bowen (1987). For a graphic illustration of some of the issues raised by Bowen, see Shilts's (1988) account of the spread of the Aids epidemic in America.

19. Escalation and entrapment are explored in Brockner and Rubin (1985) and Rubin and Brockner (1975). Becker (1960) discusses the potential impact of 'side-bets' on decisions to persist.

20. The risks and economics of 'long-haul' projects are discussed in Northcraft and Wolfe (1984). Bowen and Power (1993) explore the difficulties of managing projects involving sophisticated and untested technology. Collingridge (1992) examines the link between project scale and failure. The analysis is based upon some interesting case-studies, such as 'high-rise' housing construction programmes launched in the UK, albeit using mainly secondary sources. For a more specific discussion of IT failures see Saur (1993). Staw and Ross (1987*a*) discuss the possible impact of closing costs and salvage value. Garland and Conlon (unpub. mimeo, n.d.) speculate that tangible projects such as buildings are more likely to receive continued support than a less tangible project such as an electronic network.

21. Schwenk and Tang (1989). The authors conclude that a decision to switch to another technology 'hinges on the optimal timing of adopting the new technology which is determined by the gains in waiting and the additional marginal cost in the delay period' (561).

22. Northcraft and Wolfe (1984: 233).

23. Bowen (1987) argues that the interpretation of experimental evidence in favour of responsibility theory is potentially flawed. Some such studies did, however, ask decision-makers briefly to outline their decision rationale. The results are consistent with sunk cost effects but the decision may not have been irrational. For instance one subject reported, 'I had already invested so much it seemed foolish not to continue' (cited in Brockner 1992: 46). Conceivably it would have been difficult for respondents to know whether continuance was justified given the limited information available.

24. For example, Goltz (1992), Hanatula and Crowell (1994*a,b*), McCain (1986), Singer and Singer (1986*a*).

25. See Brody and Lowe (1995), Garland *et al.* (1990), and Jeffrey (1992).

26. Conlon and Garland (1993), Garland and Conlon (unpub. mimeo, n.d.).

27. Drummond (1994*a*). Political influences in escalation are also high-lighted in Drummond (1994*b*) and evident in Ross and Staw (1986, 1993).
28. Drummond (1995), Simonson and Staw (1992). Most of the research has been concerned with testing the various prescriptions for limiting escalation, for example, Barton *et al.* (1989), Ross and Staw (1991), Simonson and Staw (1992).
    Staw and Ross (1987*a*) suggest that the relationship between esca-lation and de-escalation is basically one of opposites.
29. Staw and Ross (1987*b*: 71). Staw and Ross (1987*a*) contains a more for-mal discussion of the impact of organizational forces upon escalation.
30. Studies linking control and proactive decision-making as a means of reducing escalation include Heath (1995), who suggests people only escalate when they fail to set a budget, or expenses are difficult to control. Hantuala and Crowell (1994*a,b*) identify importance of return rates, possible alternative investment opportunities, and other structural factors as determinants in persisting with a failing course of action. Bateman (1983) and McCain (1986) stress the importance of alternative investment opportunities. Kerman and Lord (1989) observe that specific performance goals are conducive to withdrawal when decision-makers are faced with questionable results. The evi-dence pertaining to confronting options is derived from Brockner *et al.* (1979) and Rubin and Brockner (1975). Other possibilities for lim-iting escalation include limit setting (Teger 1980), and awareness of the likelihood of entrapment (Nathason *et al.* 1982). For a review see Ross and Staw (1991).
31. The reference to 'weasels' is discussed by Acker (1995) in the context of agency theory. For a fuller, more formal description of agency the-ory see Harrison and Harrell (1993).
32. Drummond (1995).

2

Researching Taurus

In the beginning there was Mendel, thinking his lonely thoughts alone. And he said: 'Let there be peas,' and it was good. And he put the peas in his garden saying unto them 'Increase and multiply, segregate and assort yourselves independently,' and they did and it was good. And now it came to pass that when Mendel gathered up his peas, he divided them into round and wrinkled, and called the round dominant and the wrinkled recessive, and it was good. But now Mendel saw that there were 450 round peas and 102 wrinkled ones; this was not good. For the law stateth that there should be only 3 round for every wrinkled. And Mendel said unto himself 'Gott in Himmel, an enemy has done this, he has sown bad peas in my garden under the cover of night.' And Mendel smote the table in righteous wrath, saying 'Depart from me, you cursed and evil peas, into the outer darkness where thou shalt be devoured by rats and mice,' and lo it was done and there remained 300 round peas and 100 wrinkled peas, and it was good. It was very, very good. And Mendel published.[1]

The purpose of this chapter is to explain the research methodology. If there is such a thing as truth, three things are said to undermine it. One is perspective, the second is evidence, and the third is interpretation.[2] As regards perspective, unlike Mendel some researchers approach their subject deliberately devoid of hypotheses, preconceived research strategies, and conceptual categories. The argument is that such devices distance the researcher from reality when they should be moving closer. In practice it is very difficult to rid oneself of prior knowledge and ideas. Nor is it necessarily helpful, for research never disproves or destroys a theory. It either supplants it with a better one or modifies and develops existing models and conceptions.

The present study was guided by the propositions of social-psychological theory and decision dilemma theory outlined in

Chapter 1. To recapitulate, the basic research question was whether persistence in a failing course of action results from decision errors or is basically an economically prudent response to difficult circumstances. More specifically it was expected that escalation would either be characterized by irrational behaviour stemming from fear of failure, or that it would be a function of the decision-maker's information. Conversely it was expected that withdrawal would result either when the costs of persistence overrode social and psychological pressures or when such pressures weakened. Alternatively, withdrawal would result when decision-makers' information clearly indicated that further investment in the project was futile.

Such guiding propositions are not formal hypotheses but rough maps. They enable the researcher to know 'what to look for' whilst remaining vigilant for other potential possibilities.[3] As the research progressed it became clear that parts of the story did not seem to fit with either school of thought. Faced with such 'cursed peas' it was necessary to find a framework capable of doing justice to the story. All theory is bounded by assumptions. Sometimes the assumptions are so obvious that we fail to see them for what they are, that is, assumptions, no more no less.[4] For example, the eminent scientist Stephen Hawking realized that research in his field had been constricted by the assumption that time moves forwards. By recognizing that time might also move backwards, Hawking was able to conceive different hypotheses for testing which subsequently led to the discovery of 'black holes'.[5]

In the present study, an important bounding assumption seemed to be the idea that escalation is a concrete entity, something which can be traced to specific causes, just as typhus, for example, is associated with overcrowding and poor sanitation. Much of the literature utilizes a single conceptual lens, focusing upon the immediate causes of escalation without really explaining what escalation is or considering the broader context. The approach to analysis in the present study is summarized in Figure 2.1.

Three conceptual lenses were used to examine the case of Taurus. The first was a 'wide-angle' one. It considered Taurus in the context of the City of London and the Stock Exchange's role in the City. The perspective may be termed 'radical', that is, it attempts to get to the root of the story. This paradigm is concerned

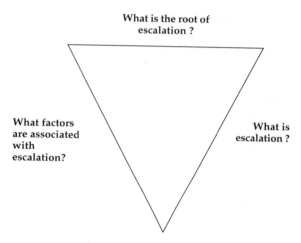

FIG. 2.1 A multi-paradigm approach to analysis

with the deep structural factors which may influence action. The assumption is that all systems produce contradictions. Contradictions generate tension and tension produces change. Moreover, decisions are made, or not made, because someone ultimately benefits from them.[6] The second conceptual lens examined escalation at the meso-level. The basic question for analysis at this level was 'what is escalation?' This analytical paradigm basically assumes that reality is something people create for themselves. The third lens examined the immediate causes of escalation. What factors drove decision-makers to persist? How did these come into play and how did they interact with one another?

By itself, each side of the triangle is capable of providing only a partial understanding of Taurus and escalation. The argument is that when all three perspectives are triangulated, they offer a richer more holistic picture than would have been extracted by using a single lens to explain escalation.[7]

THE SINGLE-CASE APPROACH

In 1483 King Edward V, aged twelve, and his brother, aged ten, were removed to the Tower of London by the order of their uncle and protector, then Duke of Gloucester. Shortly afterwards, they disappeared. They were never seen again. Two hundred years later, two skeletons were discovered in a chest buried at the foot of a staircase near where the princes had been detained.

It was presumed that the princes were murdered by their uncle, who subsequently became King Richard III. Some historians disagree, however, naming King Henry VII as the probable culprit. In 1955 the teeth of the two skeletons were examined and thought to correspond with the ages of the princes when they were last seen alive in August 1483, playing in the Tower gardens. The date of the princes' death is important because Henry Tudor was out of England in August. Forensic scientists could not be sure of course that fifteenth-century children developed in the same way as twentieth-century children. Accordingly, another fifteenth-century skeleton whose age at the time of death was known was examined. The development of the teeth corresponded exactly with what would be expected today, thus suggesting that the princes did indeed die in August 1483.[8]

In a world accustomed to the statistical survey and random sampling, reliance upon a single case to explain escalation might seem dangerous. Yet as the tale of the princes illustrates, the role of deliberate selection of a single case has its purposes. In order to study escalation, an example of escalation is required! Conversely, to study more than one instance may be wasteful. As much can be learned about smallpox by studying one case as by studying fifty. The only justification for multiple-case analysis is if the other cases exhibit different features.[9]

Whereas a statistical survey seeks to reach universally applicable conclusions (smoking increases the probability of developing cancer, for example), the aim of a case-study is to explore and to illuminate. The value of a case-study is its ability to encompass a wide range of variables, to probe delicate and otherwise inaccessible situations, and to see how the various pressures and counter-pressures interact with one another. A case-study aims to suggest directions for future research by identifying new possibilities.

The principal objection to case-study methodology is the alleged propensity to bias arising from subjectivity and lack of control. Quite apart from the fact that experiments are extremely subjective in the selection of variables studied, it is precisely the ambiguity, secrecy, and confusion of decision-making processes in large complex organizations that the researcher is interested in studying. Part of the purpose of research is to convey to the reader what it means to managers and employees to be involved in a decision débâcle.[10] For example, a member of the technical team described how he and his colleagues found themselves severely hampered by a decision taken early on to include private investors in the system, which it was now too late to reverse:

The thing that really screwed Taurus up was that if you wanted to get rid of paper for one you had to get rid of paper for all. I think that was a mistake . . . We often wondered why the hell we were bothering to do this for private individuals.[11]

EVIDENCE AND TRIANGULATION OF METHOD

In 1952 a doctor stood trial for murder. It was alleged that he had poisoned an elderly patient with heroin and other dangerous drugs. One nurse after another testified to having seen the lethal injections administered. When the prosecution concluded its case, the verdict seemed a foregone conclusion. Fortunately for the doctor, his defence lawyers had taken the trouble to discover and examine the drug books maintained at the nursing home. The books made nonsense of the nurse's evidence.[12]

The foregoing story illustrates the dangers of relying upon a single source of evidence. Researching Taurus is like trying to reconstruct the performance of a play. Everyone, actors and audience, saw something different according to where they were at the time. Recollections fade, become mingled and confused. Parts of the script are missing. The researcher's task is to produce as full and reliable an account as possible. Just as it is useful to utilize multiple conceptual lenses to examine a story, it is also desirable to utilize multiple and independent sources of evidence. If data from three different origins yields the same answer to a question then the researcher can be fairly sure that the evidence is reliable.[13]

This account of Taurus was compiled from three principal sources, namely newspaper accounts, interviews with witnesses, and documentation. Taurus was well documented by the quality press and in specialist journals covering the financial services industry. The researcher began by reading and summarizing the newspaper accounts in order to obtain a 'feel' for the story, to identify potential witnesses, and to provide the basis for interview questions.

The key categories of potential witnesses were the chief executive of the Stock Exchange; members of the technical team, including staff seconded from Coopers and Lybrand; members of the Siscot Committee, which devised the Taurus design; and members of the Taurus monitoring group and earlier project groups, which formed the link between the external market and the Stock Exchange. Other respondents provided valuable background information, including details of project Talisman, the highly successful precursor to Taurus, and the crisis caused by the Government's threat to refer the Stock Exchange to the Restrictive Practices Court.

Both the Stock Exchange and Coopers and Lybrand declined to co-operate, as part of a policy of press silence on the subject of Taurus. The policy was apparently motivated by fear of possible litigation. Certain key witnesses from both organizations did co-operate, however, on the strict condition that their identities be protected. Of all the people I approached, only two declined to be interviewed. Both were formerly members of the Stock Exchange technical team. They felt that the memories were too painful for them to discuss. Both Stock Exchange employees and staff seconded from Coopers and Lybrand are identified in the text as members of the Stock Exchange technical team.

Potential interviewees were approached by letter or telephone as seemed appropriate. Interviews took place mainly in respondents' homes or at their place of work though some had to be conducted in locations away from the City. Discussions ranged from approximately forty-five minutes to three and a half hours, the most usual being around one and a half hours. Interviewing ceased when accounts became heavily repetitive—a clear sign of saturation. The interviews took place between June 1993 and December 1994. Telephone discussions were also conducted with a range of more peripheral observers, including people working in banks and brokers' firms preparing for Taurus, journalists, and consultants.

Research colours the researcher's life. To give just a few examples of what it involved, I vividly remember occupying the green leather armchair in Peter Rawlins's study. He spoke for over three hours with barely any prompting,—lucid, cogent, every word relevant. I am reminded of his hospitality by the occasional clink of a wine glass audible on the tape.

February 1994 saw me sitting by the log fire in the centuries-old manor house at Stanton Harcourt, Oxfordshire, sharing a whisky with Crispin Gascoigne, watching the snow sweep across the countryside.

I can still visualize the glittering chandeliers of the Bank of England, the antique clock in Pen Kent's office striking four. Tea was served by a liveried attendant in delicate china cups.

The scene shifts to a sweltering Saturday afternoon in June, sipping lime juice in Tony Smith's garden. A plane is circling overhead, waiting to land at Heathrow. We raise our voices as a neighbour starts up his lawn-mower.

Next follows an interview with a leading figure of the financial services industry. The office is clad in red brocade adorned with sumptuous paintings. 'If you switch that wretched thing off', he says, pointing to my tape recorder, 'I'll tell you why Taurus failed.' Half an hour later the notes of 'why Taurus failed' are being dictated into a tape recorder whilst standing on the platform of Bank tube station on the dingy Northern Line. It was a good interview, well worth a cold beer on the train home.

The last interview was in London in December 1994. My respondent, formerly a member of the Stock Exchange technical team, now working for an American investment bank, went to considerable trouble to explain with the aid of a white board. On the way out I asked him how he liked his new employers. 'Very American,' he replies. I remember being struck by the white lights of the huge Christmas tree in the foyer; brilliant incandescence. What place such enchantment in a firm so 'very American'?

Interviews were tape-recorded and afterwards transcribed. Two named witnesses declined to be tape-recorded. Three others asked for the tape to be switched off at various junctures. (In one case the reason was nothing to do with Taurus but concerned the person's tax affairs!) None of the confidential witnesses agreed to be tape-recorded though all but one allowed notes to be taken. Notes and mental recollections were dictated into a tape recorder immediately after the interview.

Every witness was approached with a prepared list of questions. Interviews began by asking the respondent to describe their career and then their involvement in settlement and Taurus. The substantive questions were suggested initially by newspaper accounts but increasingly by findings from previous interviews and initial analysis of the data.

The interview aimed to be comprehensive, probing minutiae as well as asking the apparently more fundamental questions. Established 'facts' were also probed, partly because of the familiar caveat about not believing everything that appears in newspapers, but also because such exploration might yield new perspectives and insights. For instance, I asked Patrick Mitford-Slade, the chairman of Siscot (and other respondents), what type of settlements system the Stock Exchange might have built given a free hand. The purpose of the question was to test for possible embryonic schemes which never saw the light of day for some reason. No such schemes were mentioned but it prompted some respondents to recall the Stock Exchange asking a similar question, that is, what would the market do if the Exchange went ahead and built a system regardless of their views? The answer was apparently unequivocal: the Exchange would be left with a worse 'white elephant' on its hands. This information seemed to suggest something about the political atmosphere surrounding Taurus.

The list of questions was only to guide the interview. Respondents were encouraged to tell their own story. Throughout the interview the key probe was 'what does this person know, and how did he/she come to know it?'[14] Since information is thought to play a crucial role in escalation, considerable stress was placed upon identifying what was known, what was unclear, and what was assumed at critical junctures. For instance, the legal ramifications of Taurus proved to be a major obstacle. It was important to try to establish what research was undertaken beforehand. Likewise, what technical advice did the decision-makers receive, and equally significant perhaps, what information did they seek?

The documentation consists of consultants' reports, the Taurus prospectuses, market briefings issued between 1989 and 1993, letters and memoranda, diaries and workbooks. Most of the material was obtained by asking witnesses to delve into their filing cabinets. I also had access to the Bank of England's holdings on the subject. Missing from the suite of papers is a full set of the minutes of the Stock Exchange committees.

The policy analyst Graham T. Allison citing the political scientist Richard Neustadt, notes, 'If I were forced to choose between the documents on the one hand, and late partial interviews with some of the principal participants on the other, I would be forced to discard the documents.'[15] Interviews certainly breathe life into research whereas documents are often carefully crafted for posterity. Documents can be useful, however. For instance, in the present study the Taurus briefings issued by the consultancy firm Coopers and Lybrand confirm the succession of changes to the design and substantiate the suggestion made in interviews that the commercial imperative for Taurus was declining even as the system was being built. Conversely there are things which documents cannot reveal: for example, the background to the 'leaked' news of impending cancellation which appeared in the *Evening Standard*.

THE APPROACH TO ANALYSIS

Analysis, in the parlance of the financial services industry, is what adds value to research. Unlike dealing with, say, an attitude survey, no clear and definite coding format exists whereby the researcher can compute results. In the present case data gathering and analysis proceeded in a cyclical fashion. Information was read, reread, played, replayed, analysed and re-analysed many times as preliminary ideas and patterns suggested themselves. In turn, emergent possibilities formed the basis for further enquiry and analysis.[16] The overarching question for analysis was 'why persist with the project?'

At each stage of analysis the evidence was considered line by line. Although this method is highly time-consuming, it forces the researcher to consider everything.[17] Such a technique provides a safeguard against becoming hypnotized by the more vivid aspects of the data.[18] Contrast, for example, the quiet language of a member of the technical team describing the evaluation process which resulted in the choice of the Vista software package with the more colourful recollections of a colleague:

The assessment of where and how the documentation of Taurus mapped onto Vista functionality was carried out by the Stock Exchange design team. The basis for mapping was the discovery of a reasonable congruence between the top-level Vista specifications and the corresponding product.[19]

Vista said, 'We'll do a survey analysis routine, we'll look at the detailed requirements you've come up with so far, map it on to what our functionality is, then we'll decide what it is we have to do, with your guys of course, and then we'll come up with how much it's going to cost you.' We-ell, blimey, that was a nightmare . . .[20]

The second quotation attracts attention because it suggests 'a nightmare'. Yet analysis must accord both due consideration. The first statement is confirmed by other data: there was a formal appraisal of Vista. The second statement reflects differences of opinion amongst members of the technical team about whether the software package was suitable for the Stock Exchange's purpose. It also corroborates the suggestion that the package was evaluated whilst the design was still fluid: 'We'll look at the detailed requirements you've come up with so far'.

The fieldwork yielded a mass of paper. In order to cope with the volume, a system of key words was used: 'Talisman', 'G30' ('Group of Thirty'), 'Vista', 'Taurus monitoring group', 'Siscot', and so forth. Every item of data was assigned one or more key words. For instance, the following excerpt was assigned the key-words, 'Taurus monitoring group', 'progress', and '1991':

There was lots of progress. Every meeting lots of progress from where you were in the last meeting. However, when you sat back and said, 'Are we any closer to the end?'
 ' We-ell, not really.'[21]

Computer search facilities were utilized to retrieve and order the data.

INTERPRETING THE DATA

What seems theoretically relevant in analysis depends largely upon the conceptual lens employed. The advantage of employing three lenses is that facts which might otherwise be dismissed as insignificant can be accounted for. For example, one fact which seemed insignificant initially was the resignation of the Stock Exchange's chief executive Jeffrey Knight from his post in 1989. This 'pea' hardly seemed relevant to establishing the causes of the Taurus débâcle. Viewed through a wide-angle lens, however, this single, apparently isolated, event becomes interesting. The chief executive was moved out at the insistence of the big City firms. This corroborates media speculation that the Stock Exchange was under pressure from the securities industry. That in turn goes a long way toward explaining the Stock Exchange's determination to build Taurus.

Analysis is a creative as well as an ordering process. What we see and how we see it depends upon the questions asked and the researcher's willingness to play with the data. In the present study 'big' facts such as the choice of the Vista software were imagined to be insignificant whilst 'tiny' facts such as a breakfast briefing on Taurus were deliberately magnified to test the effect upon the story line. The technique was particularly valuable in the present study because it reduced the preconceptions suggested by press accounts. Inverting the sense of proportion suggested that although the choice of Vista was severely criticized after the project collapsed, the decision was perhaps less important than had been suggested. There would have been difficulties regardless. Conversely, dwelling upon a seemingly insignificant breakfast briefing highlighted the sheer complexity of Taurus. I could see why the market was becoming worried.

Small discrepancies are also highly important in analysis.
In the present case the emergent story line seemed to be that the impetus to Taurus stemmed from the stock-market crash and subsequent settlements crisis. Nicholas Goodison disagreed with this idea, however. 'I don't remember a time when we did not think that it would be sensible to revise the settlement system,' he said.[22] By allowing that tiny but discordant observation to 'nag' her, the researcher was alert to a remark made by a banker interviewed a few days later: 'It was the Stock Exchange's project,' he said; 'why should we bother?'[23] These two fragments of evidence suggested that the market saw Taurus as a Stock Exchange project primarily for the benefit of the Stock Exchange, and that the Stock Exchange was indeed regarded with hostility in some sectors of the financial community. Viewed in this way, the 'root' of escalation was the changed balance of power in the City following deregulation in 1986.

Another important question in interpreting the interview data was 'what is this person telling me?' Analysis aimed to extract themes from a disjointed mass of words. For example, a consistent thread evident in the transcripts of members of the Siscot Committee, which designed Taurus, was the pursuit of interest by the various constituencies of the securities industry. This became an important building block in deriving the metaphor of the tragedy of the commons. Likewise, various members of the Taurus monitoring group responsible for linking Taurus with the external market seemed to be suggesting that they had little confidence in official information. This point led to the idea of escalation as an attempt to maintain the dominant viewpoint.

Another technique employed was to ask different questions of the data. For instance, what exactly did the Board of the Stock Exchange abandon on 12 March 1993? Project Taurus, yes, but also a much-vaunted dream to deliver an integrated securities market. The decision also disposed of an unpopular chief executive. Which losing predicaments did the Stock Exchange extricate itself from—Taurus, or the whole issue of settlement? Was cancellation a devious and cynical ploy to remove the chief executive?

Much of the story is told in respondents' own words. The aim is to maximize the reader's access to the data, to show how a particular interpretation was reached, and to enable the reader to consider alternative possibilities. I have identified respondents by their role in the project except where it is essential to quote named individuals. Certain job titles have been slightly modified to protect the respondent's identity.

Using respondents' own words also makes for a better story and consequently a better understanding of the phenomenon of escalation. For example, mere narrative reads, 'In 1980, with Talisman installed and working, the Council of the Stock Exchange decided to switch IT resources from settlement into other areas.' How much more of the atmosphere of conservatism and internal politicking is revealed, however, by Crispin Gascoigne's recollection of a decisive moment in the council chamber, when someone said:

Gentlemen! We cannot possibly at this stage spend any more money on Mr Gascoigne's projects. We must put our dealing house in order. He's had it all too good for too long. Let us have a turn.[24]

Far from being abashed by such impressionism, I only wish I could convey more.

NOTES

1. This quotation is cited in Broad and Wade's exposé of fraud and deceit in scientific research (1982: 33). Apparently many scientists never report their failed experiments. Others are said to doctor their data in order to 'sharpen up' the results. According to the authors not a few reported studies are entirely fictitious.
2. The source of this remark is unknown but is probably Martin Gilbert.
3. For a discussion of the role of guiding propositions in research see Bryman (1988) and Yin (1989).
4. For a lucid discussion of the role of assumptions in theory testing see Bacharach (1989).
5. Hawking (1988) contains a vivid account of the results of discarding assumptions. White and Gribbin's (1992) account of Hawking's life and work also contains insights useful to the social scientist.
6. The paradigms utilized in the present study are derived principally from Burrell and Morgan (1979). The approach is also informed by Allison (1971), Morgan (1990), Morgan and Smircich (1980), and Murray (1992).
7. The argument for a multiple-paradigm perspective is contained in Gioía and Pitre (1990). Basically the idea is that triangulation of paradigms achieves the same effect as triangulation of methods. This implies asking the same question of the same set of events ('why persist?', for example), using different conceptual lenses. The present study utilizes three such lenses, namely the functionalist, to examine what causes escalation; the interpretive, to convey what escalation is; and a quasi-radical perspective to examine the roots of escalation. Although Gioía and Pitre argue for the bridging of multiple paradigms via the axis of structuration, this approach (as the authors acknowledge) is beleaguered by the incompatible assumptions underlying respective paradigms. Gioía *et al.* (1989) attempt to put some of their ideas into practice by studying the same phenomenon from two perspectives, the functionalist and the interpretive. Hassard (1991) studies different phenomena in the same organization. See also Parker and McHugh's (1991) reply to Hassard.

   Frost (1980) contains a discussion of potential approaches to studying organizations from a 'radical' perspective. Willmott (1987) examines management theory from a radical perspective, arguing that conceptions of the manager's role such as negotiator, figure-head, and disturbance handler (Mintzberg, 1973) mask managements' real purpose, which is to uphold the *status quo* whereby labour is exploited. Likewise Holloway (1991) argues that the problems selected for organization behaviour research are inherently biased towards maintenance of industrial order.

In the present study no attempt is made to formally bridge the three paradigms. The aim in utilizing a multi-paradigm approach is to explore the dimensions of escalation predicaments by exposing the data to different conceptual lenses. The approach is informed by Allison's (1971) account of the Cuban Missile Crisis.

8. For a fascinating account of the 'mystery of the princes' see Drewett and Redhead's (1990) account of a televised courtroom 'trial' of King Richard III and Tey (1988).

9. Mitchell (1983) details the argument for the single-case approach. Basically the methodology is appropriate where logical cogency is required and statistical generalizability is not. The purpose of a case-study is illuminative rather than representative, intended to guide surveys and experiments through its ability to encompass a wide range of variables and to penetrate inaccessible and delicate situations. For a comprehensive discussion of the case-study method see Yin (1989, 1993).

    Eisenhardt (1989) delineates the rationale for multiple studies and offers some methodological guidance. See however Dyer and Wilkinson's (1991) reply to Eisenhardt. They argue that Eisenhardt's ideas are too rooted in functionalism, too concerned with causal analysis at the expense of getting close to the phenomenon being studied. According to Dyer and Wilkinson such an approach yields only modest advances. The most significant contributions in the social sciences, they suggest, have resulted from single-case studies published in book form. Publishing in research papers, it is argued, prevents in-depth examination and extrapolation because of the space restrictions.

10. The role of qualitative methods in social sciences research has been the subject of extensive discussion. The present study was influenced by Dyer and Wilkinson (1991), Light (1979), Rosen (1985), Van Maanen (1979*a*, *b*, 1988), and in particular, Mintzberg's (1979) impassioned denouncement of the arrogance of some of the quantitatively orientated schools of management research. According to Mintzberg, if we want to know why decision-makers behave as they do, we should start by asking them. His views are particularly pertinent to the phenomenon of escalation as so much of the research in this field is experimental.

    For a discussion of the risks of bias in experimental research see, for example, Becker (1967) and Lawler (1985). Webb *et al.* (1966) argue that the solution is not to argue the superiority of one method over another but to utilize multiple methods.

11. Interview, member of Stock Exchange technical team, May 1994.
12. For a fascinating account of the unfortunate doctor's trial see Bedford (1989).
13. Becker (1958) argues for using multiple sources of data. Yin (1993) explains the mathematical basis of triangulation.
14. The approach to interviewing witnesses is partly derived from Trevor-Roper's (1972) investigation of Hitler's fate.
15. Allison (1971: 181).
16. The idea of cycling between theory and method is based upon Glaser and Strauss (1967). Yin (1989) argues that a case-study should be replicable in principle. I have tried to achieve that aim by making the steps of research and the process of analysis as transparent as possible.
17. Line-by-line analysis was based upon the method advocated by Turner (1983).
18. The various techniques of playing with the data and caveats about attention to vividness originate mainly from Mills (1959). Other sources include Kets De Vries and Miller (1987), B. Turner (1994), and Yin (1989). The style and methods of interpretation are informed by Ackroyd and Crowdy's (1990) study of an abattoir, Roberts's (1973) observations of life in a Salford slum, Rosen's (1985) observations of an organization's annual celebratory breakfast, Quaid's (1993) exposé of job evaluation techniques and Young's (1989) study of a sewing factory.
19. Bill Widdis (personal communication, July 1995).
20. Interview, member of Stock Exchange technical team, May 1994.
21. Interview, member of Taurus monitoring group, June 1994.
22. Interview, Sir Nicholas Goodison, Aug. 1994.
23. Interview, senior official, UK clearing bank, Aug. 1994.
24. Interview, Crispin Gascoigne, Feb. 1994.

3

'Time, Gentlemen, Please!'

'Why does a broker never hold meetings on a Wednesday?'
'Because it would ruin two weekends.'

(old City joke)

London: 18 May 1994. A grey morning, raining softly. I am standing in one of the City's narrow alleyways, known as Tokenhouse
Yard. The yard takes its name from a seventeenth-century house
that once minted tokens for London's merchants. The tokens, or
farthings as they were called, were the foundations of our modern
day monetary system.[1] Apart from the whiff of cigar smoke and
the surveillance camera, the warm enclosed feel of the buildings is
probably little different from the days when the tally brokers and
stockjobbers first thronged the streets and alleyways, eager to
capitalize on the opportunities that were opening up in the
embryonic securities industry.

Shares, or equities as they are sometimes known, represent
partial ownership of a company. They were invented to enable
people to lend money without violating the medieval laws of
usury, which were still in force in the eighteenth century. A stockbroker is someone who buys and sells shares (sometimes known
as securities) on behalf of others in return for a commission.
Stockbroking, or stockjobbing as it was originally known, was
first practised mainly as a sideline. Clock-makers, corn-factors,
wine and hop merchants, mattress manufacturers, and ware-
housemen all tried their hand at it. Such unregulated oppor-
tunism tainted the new profession with an unsavoury reputation
which died hard. As late as the 1950s the joke was that anyone asking a taxi driver for the 'thieves' kitchen' was automatically con-
veyed to the Stock Exchange!

When street trading was outlawed by the City authorities, the
brokers and stockjobbers removed themselves to the coffee
houses. Coffee houses provided work stations when offices were

rare. They functioned as centres of news and business intelligence when telephones, fax machines, and E-mail were unknown. There could be found auction notices, news sheets, and price-current lists, including 'The Course of the Exchange and Other Things', which detailed prices of commodities and some shares—a precursor of the Stock Exchange Daily Official List.

Coffee houses were also places of warmth and refreshment. In a world cosseted by central heating and other comforts, it is difficult to imagine just how cold, bleak, and biting seventeenth-century London could feel. The flaring lanterns of Garraway's, with its cosy mahogany boxes and sanded floors, were doubtless a welcome sight on days when the River Thames froze solid. The Fleece and Sun in Threadneedle Street was apparently highly recommended, serving 'Guinness of Dublin or Lane of Cork in its "native element," in "a bright, clean pewter pot" '. Traders brought their midday beef or mutton to 'the cook presiding over the gridiron with full instructions as to its being well done or underdone'. A surcharge of threepence was levied for ' "bread, cookin, and taters" '.[2]

Eventually coffee houses specialized in the type of business transacted. Insurance underwriters tended to gather in Edward Lloyd's establishment, whilst Garraway's and Jonathan's became best known for stockjobbing. The problem with coffee houses was that they were open to all manner of persons including rogues and undesirables. The more prosperous traders therefore began to seek their own premises, typically raising funds by subscription. The result was the formation of a conglomerate of clubs which was to characterize the commercial heartbeat of the City of London for the next two hundred years.

DECADENCE AND DECAY

The club structure offered considerable business advantages. The City of London's pre-eminence as a world financial centre is said to owe much to its reputation as a safe place to trade. The reputation was fostered by a tradition of shared values amongst club members, sustained by a network of exclusive cartels supported by nepotism and arranged marriage—hence the notion of the 'old City family'.[3]

The corollary of shutting others out, however, is to lock one-self in. 'Clubs, like families', notes David Kynaston, 'are capable of renewing themselves; but they still remain clubs.'[4] Historically competition amongst club members was ' "considered respectable only within comfortably agreed limits" '.[5] Shielded by seemingly insurmountable entry barriers, partners could afford to view management as something for Midlands industrialists. Hobson describes the atmosphere in the City in the 1950s:

If a director was in the office before 10 a.m. it was assumed the bank was going bust, and normal directional hours in the 1950's were from 11 a.m. to 4 p.m. The directors . . . took dry sherry before lunch in the Partners' Room where they all sat together.[6]

Siegmund Warburg described the establishment's reaction to a newcomer, a Jewish newcomer, and one who spoke with a foreign accent at that:

I remember some people in very good houses talked very nastily behind my back: 'Do you know this fellow Siegmund Warburg? He starts at the office at *eight o'clock* in the morning'. This was considered contemptible. . . . They looked down upon me with the utmost snobbism.[7]

Although Warburg showed that High City arrogance was ultimately no match for energy, ability, and dedication, even so, tradition and complacency died hard. In 1967 the dress code for brokers still specified a top hat or bowler.[8] Indeed, as late as 1981, one of the duties of the deputy governor of the Bank of England was to drop a penny into the upturned top hats of the Government brokers whilst they were closeted with the governor on their daily visits to the bank.[9]

Despite its stuffy lackadaisical image, the club can be wilful if its interests are at stake. The power of the establishment is rarely made visible but it exists none the less and can be ruthless. Expulsions from the club are seldom made public but they do happen: 'We understand each other. You're going. You're on a short time-scale . . . couple of months, get someone in to replace you and you're off. Understood, gentlemen?' At the lower echelons power is intensified by the disparities of wealth between partners and salaried professionals. Both parties may have been to Oxbridge but only one is likely to own a yacht. Many houses still operate on highly authoritarian lines. An Exchange employee remarked, 'When they get in their dining rooms and decide that something will happen . . .'[10] The sentence was left unfinished.

'SUBSCRIBERS ONLY'

Although stockbroking never achieved the same status as merchant banking, it became an exclusive occupation none the less. Although in theory the doors of the Stock Exchange were open to all 'honourable men', in practice, entry was largely reserved for what Anthony Sampson called the 'public school proletariat'.[11] In 1967 the entrance fee alone was 1,000 guineas, more than most manual workers earned in a year. A nomination to membership might cost anything from around £100 to £2,000. Partners moreover were required to possess assets over liabilities of at least £5,000.[12] Significantly, luxury-car manufacturers Bentley and Rolls-Royce considered it worth while to advertise in the Stock Exchange Year Book. In 1971 Graham Greenwell, senior partner of stockbroker Greenwell & Co., summarized the culture of the organization when he protested to *The Times* against the admission of women. The Stock Exchange, he argued, was not ' "an institution which exists to perform a public service" but a private gentlemen's club'.[13]

Although stockbrokers prided themselves on their role as investment advisers, theirs was scarcely an intellectually demanding profession. Before deregulation in 1986 (hereafter referred to as 'Big Bang') a broker, or an authorized representative, would enter the Stock Exchange with a sheaf of orders and buy and sell from one of the jobbers' pitches located on the floor of the Exchange. Jobbers (now known as market makers) held books of shares specializing in particular sectors of industry. Under the Stock Exchange's rule book, stockbrokers were forbidden to make markets and jobbers were forbidden to deal directly with clients, a system known as dual capacity. Commissions were fixed and contracts were verbal. Trading relied upon mutual trust, epitomized in the slogan 'My word is my bond.'

Orders were often finished within the first hour of trading, especially during the long periodic lulls in the market. Time then hung heavily, especially amongst the jobbers confined to their pitches for the rest of the day. Boredom frequently found relief in horseplay. A football might be introduced on the floor of the Exchange, or a dozing jobber's newspaper set alight to general enthusiasm. Hats were a frequent target of fun. One jobber who treated himself to an expensive purchase provoked his colleagues into secretly swapping it for an identical hat two sizes larger. At going-home time the said jobber was 'mystified to find that his new hat descended to his ears'. The next day the joke was repeated, only this time the original hat was restored, the inner band carefully padded with paper, 'So, when the jobber donned the article at the hour of departure, it perched precariously on the top of his head.' So it continued, day in, day out, until the unfortunate victim anxiously sought medical advice about his apparently shrinking and swelling head![14]

Advertising was forbidden but found expression none the less in the more colourful personalities. Legends abound: one man, for example, was said to have proclaimed his presence by serenading colleagues with tunes played on a cornet.[15] Another sported a huge red rose in his buttonhole. Beppo, an apparently superstitious jobber in the oil market, invariably absented himself on Friday the 13th, which became known as 'Beppo's Day'.[16] Another, known as 'Banger Bennet', used to drum up trade by creating cacophony at his firm's stand, changing all his prices up and down. Colleagues were driven to distraction, fearful that 'Banger' knew something they did not.[17]

Otherwise, jobbing and broking seems to have been a prosaic if lucrative existence. Much of the work consisted of routine form-filling, prompting a broker in the 1890s to complain, ' "Stockbroking . . . is a non-creative, uninspiring occupation. It is a living, not a life." '[18] Little seems to have changed over the years. A member of the Stock Exchange professional staff described a typical stockjobber in the 1970s and early 1980s:

He would know the way the business was done but he wouldn't have much ability to see the way the business could be done or the way outside influences were going to affect his business and the Stock Exchange. He would see the Stock Exchange as a club, would enjoy their lunches and dinners, consume the port and the fine wines copiously, and might even contribute to decisions on what was stocked. Occasionally he, and perhaps one or two of his brethren, would go and see the chairman to make a case about something and they would say that was life.[19]

If brokers and jobbers were a mediocre fraternity, what of the Stock Exchange's all-powerful ruling council presiding over the securities industry? Council membership was time-consuming and unpaid, tempting firms to nominate their more dispensable partners. A former broker whose partnership was part of a marriage contract describes how he came to be involved on the council: 'Flogging stocks and shares—boring. I was useless at it so it was suggested by my partners that I might serve the firm better on the council.'[20]

Like any caricature, the image of an organization composed of public-school dullards presided over by worse dullards is partly accurate and therefore partly inaccurate. A few 'barrow boys' mingled with the blue-blooded firms. Likewise the ruling council attracted some highly capable individuals. A former employee paid this tribute to one of the more distinguished councillors: 'He had an intellect that stood out in that place. But then you might say, "It would, wouldn't it?"'[21]

THINK THE UNTHINKABLE

During the 1970s the Stock Exchange became the focal point for mounting tension within the City. The heyday of broking for wealthy private clients was drawing to a close. In 1957 only 18 per cent of UK shares were owned by institutions. By the late 1970s that figure was approaching 60 per cent. Fund managers were beginning to challenge the practice of fixed commissions.

The challenge grew steadily more aggressive after the New York Stock Exchange abolished its system of fixed commissions in 1975. The resultant 'shake-out' of firms saw the emergence of a new breed of investment banks, imbued with a fierce work ethic, hungry for a share in the world market, and impatient with the self-protecting division of labour in the City with its separation into discount houses, merchant banks, brokers, jobbers.[22] Above all, they were determined to secure a share of the UK equities market.

The Stock Exchange was equally determined to preserve its privileges. Other forces were undermining the cartel, however. Business was beginning to bypass the organization. No legal requirement exists to buy and sell shares via an intermediary.

Willing parties can exchange them privately. During the 1970s such exchanges were beginning to occur on an increasingly large scale. Brokers were already engaged in the practice of 'put throughs', whereby buying and selling transactions were matched within their own offices, merely using the jobbers to check prices. For their part, jobbers were conducting institutional business surreptitiously.

A more tangible sign of discontent was the launching of a rival service known as Ariel (Automated Real Time Investments Exchange Limited) to handle institutional trades. Ariel's commission rates were cheaper than those charged by the Stock Exchange, which promptly reduced its prices. Although only a tiny amount of business was actually lost to Ariel, it was an ominous sign. The Stock Exchange had contributed little in recent years to the development of London as a world financial centre. Ariel showed the securities industry that the seemingly impregnable cartel was neither inviolate nor indispensable.[23]

Finally the Government intervened. In February 1979 it was announced that the Stock Exchange's rule book was to be referred to the Restrictive Practices Court. The announcement meant that the practice of fixed commissions, which sheltered the smaller and least efficient firms, might be declared illegal. That was only the tip of the iceberg. The entire securities industry was ripe for reform. Behind the scenes, the Bank of England was already urging the more progressive firms in the City to think the unthinkable. The 'City Revolution' had begun.

NOTES

1. Smith (1970) provides a fascinating account of the origins of the names of the streets, alleyways, and many of the buildings of the City of London.
2. This account of the early history of equities trading is drawn mainly from Morgan and Thomas's (1962) detailed and scholarly account of the Stock Exchange and David Kynaston's (1994, 1995) masterly history of the City of London. The reference to Garraway's and the Sun and Fleece is from Kynaston (1994: 144).
   Secondary sources include Addison (1953) and Hodges (1988) on

the origins of markets generally, and Barty-King (1977) and Rees (1972) on the City's commodity markets. Mortimer's (1969 edn.) eighteenth-century 'how-to-do-it' guide to stockbroking also contains some interesting insights. For more recent accounts see Jenkins (1973) and Long (1978). The latter contains some atmospheric photographs of the floor in the 1960s and 1970s which graphically convey the seedy race-course image. The book also contains a picture of the first woman allowed on the floor, dated 10 March 1973.

3. Hilton (1987) contains some critical insights into the workings of the City immediately prior to 'Big Bang'. For example, the MP Sir Peter Tapsell was refused employment by a number of firms as he had not been to Eton and it would take twenty years to acquire the connections he would otherwise have brought. Baring's Bank apparently made him an offer conditional not upon examination results, but marriage to one of the Baring's daughters. Tapsell decided to seek his fortune elsewhere. See also Hobson (1991) and Webb (1987). For more cosy accounts of City practice see, for example, Hamilton (1968) and Industrial Welfare Society (1960). Contrast these with Lewis's (1990) account of the competitive pressures on a modern-day trader.

4. Kynaston (1994: 8).

5. Ibid. 19.

6. Hobson (1991: 90). The quotation contains a partial citation from P. G. Wodehouse's 'Psmith in the City' which conveys the sheer boredom of office work. Grossmith and Grossmith (1945 edn) captures a similar spirit half a century before the 1950s. The origins and development of merchant banking are reflected in Burk (1989), Cassis (1988), Chapman (1984, 1986), Roberts (1992, 1993), and Zeigler (1988). The Report of the Parker Tribunal concerning the raising of the bank rate (Parker Tribunal 1958) is regarded by many historians as the first exposé of the incompetence and complacency fostered by the club culture of the City of London.

7. Reich (1980: 177), in a rare and detailed interview with Siegmund Warburg towards the end of Warburg's life.

8. Kynaston's (1991) history of the broking firm Cazenove contains a photograph of Throgmorton Street on the day of devaluation in 1967. In the foreground two men are conversing; one is wearing a bowler hat, the other a top hat.

   Custom dictated that only Government brokers were entitled to wear top hats though according to Hobson (1991) some lesser brokers imitated the practice.

9. Durham (1992).

10. Interview, member of Stock Exchange technical team, May 1994.

11. Sampson (1962). The rules stated that the doors were to be open to all

honest members but closed for ever to dishonourable cheats (Morgan and Thomas 1962: 157).

12. Sampson (1962).
13. Cited in Hobson (1991: 198).
14. Members' enthusiasm for practical jokes is extensively detailed in the literature, including Kynaston (1994, 1995), and Morgan and Thomas (1962), and Sampson (1962). Cobbett (1986) contains many delightful anecdotes of day-to-day life in the Stock Exchange in the years leading up to 'Big Bang', including the tale of the hat.
15. Kynaston (1994).
16. Cobbett (1986).
17. I am indebted to George Hayter (personal communication) for the anecdote of 'Banger Bennet'.
18. Kynaston (1995: 309) citing Lawrence Jones of Helbert Wagg.
19. Interview, member of Stock Exchange technical team, Nov. 1993.
20. Interview, member of Stock Exchange Council, Nov. 1993.
21. Interview, member of Stock Exchange technical team, Nov. 1993.
22. See especially 'The City Revolution' (*FT* 1986), a forty-page supplement to the *Financial Times* detailing the background to 'Big Bang', and the Report of the Committee to Review the Functioning of Financial Institutions (Wilson Committee 1980). The tensions within the old City establishment are also described in Clarke (1979), Hall (1987), Hilton (1987), Plender and Wallace (1985), Reid (1988), Speiegelberg (1973), and Thomas (1986).
23. Thomas (1986).

4

The Scandal that Never Was

Settlement was invariably the province of Gladys sitting down there, God bless her. She knew what went on. Nobody else did.

(Peter Rawlins)

In October 1987, in one day alone, £50 billion was wiped off UK share values in what became known as the 'Crash of '87'. Restaurant bookings in the City of London were cancelled as dealers watched prices plummet on their screens. The world bull market was over.

A situation of near-panic then developed as banks and securities firms attempted to assess the situation. What were their assets, and what were their liabilities? More to the point, where were they? As one apologetic subordinate after another failed to find the answers, leaders left their desks and went to see for themselves what the problem was.

They were horrified by what they found. One year earlier 'Big Bang' had enabled the UK clearing banks and foreign investment houses to acquire most of the City's old broking firms. Accustomed to efficient electronic mass processing of transactions in their own organizations, the mess heaped in former firms' back offices was unbelievable. Paper was stacked in crates, piled high against walls, and strewn across floors. Locked in the confusion were almost one million unsettled share bargains worth about £13.4 billion.[1]

The settlement of share transactions involves two phases, clearance and settlement. The clearance system identifies the parties and what they owe. Settlement completes the process by ensuring that shares and payments are duly transferred to buyers and sellers respectively. Although both parties are contractually bound when the order to buy or sell shares is placed, neither money nor share certificates change hands until settlement day, that is, the second Monday following the end of a two-week account period. The system was slow enough at the best of times but in 1987, because of the exceptionally high trading activity following 'Big Bang', it almost collapsed. Patrick Mitford-Slade recalls, 'Bargains were remaining unsettled for months and months. People weren't able to get their share certificates; dividends were therefore getting into the wrong hands. It was total chaos.'[2] It was also to prove expensive. Compensation payments for lost dividends and payments for additional staff and so forth cost individual firms about £1 million each, and an estimated £200 million for the industry as a whole.

The Stock Exchange assigned an extra fifty accountants to deal with reconciliation alone. Task forces were dispatched to help firms cope. Meanwhile, continued daily trading compounded the situation. A member of the Stock Exchange's technical staff recalls:

The [computer] files were starting to get very big and it was taking more and more time to process them. As settlement became less and less effective people were starting to get nervous: 'How much capacity have we actually got?'[3]

People might well have been nervous. In the UK stock market private investors account for about 70 to 80 per cent of trades but only 20 to 30 per cent of the total value of transactions. The reverse proportions apply to institutional trades. They account for only 20 to 30 per cent of the market by volume, but 70 to 80 per cent of the market by value. In other words, mixed up amongst the 700,000 or so small transactions were millions of pounds' worth of institutional liability. What if an institution defaulted? If *A* cannot pay *B*, then how is *B* to pay *C*? The result could be a horrendous failure of the entire securities market. A broker recalls:

The Bank of England got very nervous[, for] as trades couldn't settle, market makers borrowed more and more stock. . . . If something went wrong, if one of those guys went broke, there would be a horrible systemic collapse.[4]

The risk was very real. Many of the new investment houses now trading in the equities market (Kleinwort-Benson, Warburgs, and Smith New Court, for example) possessed only a modest capital base 'racked up' to maximum utilization with no parent banks to come to the rescue if they overreached themselves. The broker continued:

They [one of the new securities houses] didn't have a vast capital base and they were pushers. They would use the whole lot. These guys would trade everything and everything. Give them luncheon vouchers and they would trade them.[5]

Nor did it help that many of the leaders of the new financial services industry barely understood the businesses in which they were now involved. The effects of 'Big Bang' had been far-reaching, creating new organizations supplying new and often complex products and services in a highly competitive environment. Already shaken by the stock-market crash, they now faced months of uncertainty as the mess was unravelled. In the midst of it stood the UK clearing banks, upon whom the risk ultimately fell. The banks make the payments on behalf of brokers and dealers to enable transactions conducted during the account period to be settled. The banks were potentially naked because the timing of settlement leaves a gap of a few hours between payment and delivery of stock. Purchases were similarly vulnerable because there is a gap of a few days between settlement, when money changes hands, and registration of shares in the purchaser's name. Were a firm to fall in the interim, the liquidators and not the purchaser would have a claim upon the stock. To coin a phrase, a few days, even a few hours, is a long time in the capricious world of high finance, where 'time equals risk'. It was clear to some highly influential people in the securities industry that only sheer luck had saved London from catastrophe.

TOO MANY 'SIDS'

The prime cause of the settlements crisis was a character known as 'Sid'. 'Sid' was the name given to a character used to advertise the Government's privatization programme. The character was intended to portray the man or woman in the street in order to emphasize the opening up of the stock market to private investors dealing in small packets of shares. Since the early 1980s, millions of 'Sids' had entered the stock market in response to the Government's privatization offers. In 1984, for example, there were almost five million share transactions. On 12 December 1984, in one day alone, there were over 44,000 transactions. The upsurge in trading volumes began to place an increasing strain on the share settlement system' culminating in the upsurge of activity stimulated by 'Big Bang'. The backlog revealed by the stock market crash had been accumulating for years.

The underlying cause of the problem was the settlement system itself. In the eighteenth century share pledges were celebrated over a glass of sherry to the toast of 'Who pays?'[6] Two hundred years later, in 1987, with the exception of the sherry, little had changed.

There were two reasons why this was so. First, buying and selling shares in the UK is complicated. It involves at least five parties: customer, broker, market maker, company registrar, and the Stock Exchange. Any attempt to reform the system is therefore potentially a major undertaking. Second, there was little incentive to interfere. The excitement of trading begins and ends with doing the deal. Settlement was perceived as an unprofitable chore. Significantly, the only capacity in which women were initially employed in the Stock Exchange was in the settlement department itself, relegated to the basement and then only in response to wartime emergency. Firms' back offices were typically located beyond the City in order to save on rental costs. Administration, including settlement, seldom loomed large in the average partners' meeting. Peter Rawlins said:

Settlement was invariably the province of Gladys sitting down there, God bless her. She knew what went on. Nobody else did. The chaps who had run the business up till then, they were all dealing partners in their partners' room. . . . [They] didn't get involved in the grubby business of what happened afterwards.[7]

The stock market crash changed perceptions by exposing the risk involved in unsettled share transactions. For the first time, the securities industry woke up to the fact that quadrillions of pounds were at risk day in, day out because of 'black holes' in the settlement system, holes which many senior managers in the industry hardly knew existed.

Apparently the root cause of slow settlement was paper. It was paper that was holding everything up. Influential figures in the City began saying to one another, 'If only we could get rid of all this paper we could speed things up and reduce our exposure to risk.' Taurus, they recalled, was meant to get rid of paper. Where was Taurus?

'GENTLEMEN! WE CANNOT POSSIBLY AT THIS STAGE SPEND
ANY MORE MONEY ON MR GASCOIGNE'S PROJECTS'

Where indeed was Taurus? Although in 1987 settlement was slow
and cumbersome, it was even worse before Project Talisman was
implemented in 1979. Before 1979 brokers and jobbers physically
delivered orders to one another's offices. There followed the
tedious, complicated, and expensive task of matching hundreds
of buying and selling transactions. Talisman acted as a clearing-
house. Instead of brokers and jobbers dealing directly with one
another, transactions were funnelled via the Stock Exchange.

Talisman was a major venture for the Stock Exchange. It
involved a huge capital investment and members were exposed to
unlimited liability. A vote of the entire membership was required
to authorize funds for development. Even then, difficulties lay
ahead. Convincing the provincial stock exchanges (now largely
defunct), for example, was hard work. Crispin Gascoigne, then
chairman of the Settlements Committee, recalls going to considerable pains to persuade a group of Scottish brokers. At the end of
the presentation he asked one of their number: 'Are you satisfied
now, Mr McTavish?'

'Och no!' McTavish replied.[8]

The most intractable opposition came from within the Stock
Exchange itself. Although jobbers were dubbed tradesmen by
brokers who saw themselves as professional investment advisers,
it was they who dominated the club. Some were unhappy about
conceding control over stock to the Stock Exchange. A war of attri-
tion was mounted. Every aspect of Talisman was questioned. For
example, doubts were raised about the viability of the tariff structure. The project was held up for months whilst consultants pored
over the documentation only to conclude, 'The structure is perfect, sir.'

The then chairman, Sir Nicholas Goodison, eventually succeeded in overcoming 'dead-body' sentiments by an appeal to the
common good:

One day a bevy of jobbers would come through the door objecting to a
particular aspect of Talisman. I would have to say, 'Look, that may be
your interest, but I ask you in the interest of the total institution, and of
the totality of the savings world, not to press that point.'[9]

'Talisman wasn't a particularly good system,' said a member of the Stock Exchange's technical staff; 'it had the merit of working. That was all.'[10] Talisman certainly worked. It ran day in, day out unfailingly, even at the height of the settlements crisis. It saved firms substantial sums of money. Moreover, during the 1980s bull market, Talisman was generating 50 per cent of the Stock Exchange's income. Grubby though the business of settlement might be, the Stock Exchange discovered it was clearly a money-spinner.

Talisman had streamlined the task of clearance but the task of reforming the settlement system was only half-complete. The technical team were keen to press on with the next stage, known as book entry transfer, which would eliminate paper from the system. Not so certain powerful factions on the Council. Talisman had dominated the agenda for over five years. Some members were no longer on speaking terms with one another, such had been the intensity and bitterness of the debate. 'Big Bang', moreover, was already in the air. Crispin Gascoigne recalls the decisive moment in Council, when someone else said:

Gentlemen! We cannot possibly at this stage spend any more money on Mr Gascoigne's projects. We must put our dealing house in order. He's had it all too good for too long. Let us have a turn.[11]

For the next six years the Stock Exchange was consumed by tumult following the Government's threat to refer the rule book to the Restrictive Practices Court in 1979. The lawyers rubbed their hands as the Stock Exchange prepared to fight its case. By autumn 1980 £1.5 million had already been spent on legal fees, with a court hearing estimated to last six months to a year yet to come. Meanwhile the membership was becoming bitterly divided over the issue. Fixed commissions protected the least efficient firms—usually the small partnerships. The larger, more aggressive firms saw international opportunities passing them by. Sir Nicholas Goodison, then chairman of the Stock Exchange, recalls:

Debate after debate was concerned with how could we allow our member firms to partake in international business without eroding the restrictive practices embodied in the rules of the Exchange, namely fixed commissions and single capacity. . . . Large numbers of the membership were very reluctant to change the framework . . . and they had the vote.[12]

Once the membership agreed to abolish fixed commissions it became clear that single capacity was doomed. The Council then realized that the entire trading infrastructure would have to be re-engineered. Accordingly, in 1983 the Stock Exchange launched nine parallel IT projects, all scheduled to go live on 'Big Bang' day three years hence. It was a huge and exciting challenge which culminated in a successfully synchronized 'switch-on' on Monday 27 October 1986.[13]

In the months immediately following 'Big Bang' the City's leaders concentrated on the task of cementing the international market. Former brokers and jobbers adjusted to a new culture whereby price rather than relationships became the new business imperative. 'Big Bang' ushered in a new era of remote screen based trading. The Stock Exchange had spent £3 million developing a new market floor in order to placate its more trenchant members. 'It lasted six weeks I think,' recalled Patrick Mitford-Slade ruefully.[14]

To some, Monday 27 October was the day when the fun went out of the City. A new work ethic began to supplant the 'port-for-lunch' culture. The citizens of the Surrey stockbroker-belt town of Haslemere insisted on British Rail timetabling a new train, the 6.44 to Waterloo, because the 7.15 was too late. Previously such early timings had been reserved for cleaners and security guards.[15] The cosy cartelized club that had embraced generations of City families was now only a memory.

'IT WAS FELT "NO, NO, WE REALLY COULDN'T GO DOWN THAT PATH."'

Meanwhile Taurus was forgotten. Nicholas Goodison said:

It didn't really occur to us to seriously launch into a huge project like Taurus while trying to resolve all these other issues.[16]

And don't forget that the pattern of trading intimately affects what is going to happen in settlement. . . . The Council reckoned book entry transfer would come, and was a good thing. But in '83 we were overtaken by the need to reform the market system and therefore it had to go on the back burner: Also it wasn't refined in time. You don't say 'yes' to go ahead with the big development until you have got a clear indication of what it is . . ., of what it is going to cost and so on. We never got to that point.[17]

In 1980 a City-wide group known as the Powell Committee had agreed the basis of a book entry system.[18] The system envisaged a central register of share ownership to be maintained by the Stock Exchange, a concept similar to the UK vehicle licensing centre based in Swansea.

Enthused by the City's new-found sense of urgency and commitment, the Stock Exchange worked hard on the project during 1988. By autumn the specification was complete. It weighed twenty-five kilos. Taurus 1, as it became known, would have required two huge IBM mainframe computers and 560 disc drives to store and process the 1,000 billion shares then in circulation. Computer technology has since progressed. In 1988 such requirements posed a formidable challenge and some doubted whether the idea was even feasible. Then there was the cost, an estimated £60 million, at least. A member of the Stock Exchange technical team who worked on the development recalls, 'That was thought to be a "No, no, we really couldn't go down that path." '[19]

Cost and technical feasibility were two problems. There existed a third. UK law requires listed companies to maintain a register of shareowners. Most companies employ registrars to undertake this task. By 1988 the clearing banks had bought up most of the registration business and invested heavily in it. The last thing they wanted was a central register, because it would render their own newly acquired registration business redundant. When the clearing banks awoke to the implications of Taurus 1, they acted fast.

THE OLD LADY

The Bank of England holds a position of high moral authority in the City of London which is respected even by those organizations for whom it has little or no statutory responsibility. Over the years the offices, with their antique furnishings, leather armchairs, and French clocks, have been the repository of many secrets.

Probably no one will ever know who said what to who about Taurus 1 during the autumn of 1988. Once it became known that the banks were lobbying against it, others hastened to make their point, some in favour, some against. Recognizing that its authority rests upon consent, the Bank of England is normally reluctant to intercede, short of a clear case of market failure. It prefers to act as a conciliator, bringing protagonists together and suggesting some possible directions.

The Bank applied its tried and tested formula to Taurus by acting as a catalyst for the formation of an industry-wide committee known as Siscot (Securities Industry Steering Committee on Taurus). 'I didn't do more than seemed to be enough, and what has proved to be enough in past,' said Pen Kent, the associate director who initiated Siscot.[20] Having brought the parties together the Bank retired, continued to encourage the parties to press on, but did not get involved in the technical design.

It was Siscot's understanding that a future design for Taurus must be achieved without seriously damaging any business interests. In November 1988 members of Siscot began applying themselves to the challenge. 'We recognized that if another bull market arose, we wouldn't be able to hold it with existing systems,' said a senior banker.[21]

NOTES

1. Settlement procedures and systemic risk are explained in depth in London Business School (1993b).
2. Interview, Patrick Mitford Slade, May 1994.
3. Interview, member of Stock Exchange technical team, Nov. 1993.
4. Interview, member of Siscot, Nov. 1993.
5. Ibid.
6. Morgan and Thomas (1962).
7. Interview, Peter Rawlins, Oct. 1993.
8. Interview, Crispin Gascoigne, Feb. 1994.
9. Interview, Sir Nicholas Goodison, Aug. 1994.
10. Interview, member of Stock Exchange technical team, Dec. 1994.
11. Interview, Crispin Gascoigne, Feb. 1994.
12. Interview, Sir Nicholas Goodison, Aug. 1994.
13. The new electronic trading system broke down for a short while on the first day as a result of overloading by traders curious to see how the new system worked.
14. Interview, Patrick Mitford-Slade, May 1994.
15. FT (1986).
16. Interview, Sir Nicholas Goodison, Aug. 1994.
17. Ibid.

18. London Stock Exchange (1982).
19. Interview, member of Stock Exchange technical team, Nov. 1993.
20. Interview, Pen Kent, May 1994.
21. Interview, senior official, UK clearing bank, Dec. 1994.

5

The Mad Hatter's Tea-Party

We started walking through water, then it became mud, then
it became honey, then it became glue, and in the end, it was
quick-drying cement.

(A member of the Siscot committee)

Committees are a way of life in the City of London. When the
thirteen members of Siscot began arriving at Cazenove's in
Tokenhouse Yard in November 1988, they expected that, like the
First World War, it would all be over by Christmas. According to
superstition, thirteen is an unlucky number.[1] A member of Siscot
recalls:

It was put across initially as a review of the design [Taurus 1] . . . rather
than a root-and-branch exercise. . . . It was a check that this was the right
solution or very nearly the right solution and won't want much more
than a bit of adjustment here or there. . . . It would have been around
Christmas of 1988 that the message had sunk in that people were not
going to be happy with that.[2]

Siscot was locked in conflict from the start. The Stock
Exchange's cherished and much-vaunted dream was to create a
superb electronic market-place.[3] The ambition sprang from a
review of the organization's strategy following 'Big Bang'.
Leading professional staff and more enlightened members of the
Council recognized that the 'club' had no divine right of existence.
Its survival, they decided, depended upon supplying member
firms with valued services more cheaply than those firms could
do it for themselves. Settlement was an integral part of the vision
of an electronic factory producing 'safely completed trades'.

Unfortunately for the Stock Exchange, other organizations in
the securities industry had similar ideas. By what right, they
demanded, did the Stock Exchange as central market authority
compete with its own member firms? The controversy dominated

the early meetings of Siscot. The clearing banks demanded to know who would own Taurus. The institutions were determined that whoever owned settlement, it would not become the property of the clearing banks. 'We would have better risk,' acknowledged an asset manager, 'but boy would we pay for it.'[4]

Conflicting priorities were another source of tension. In theory everyone wanted to improve efficiency and reduce risk. In practice, however, the securities industry earns a significant element of its profits from non-value-adding activity. The brokers wanted to preserve their role as intermediaries. Likewise the custodians who administer the paperwork associated with share transactions on behalf of traders earned a substantial proportion of their living from the *status quo*. Likewise the banks were unwilling to reduce risk at the expense of their registration business. 'If the system collapses', said a senior banker, we're all up the swannery anyway.'[5]

Participants soon learned that the operant principle was to fight one's own corner regardless of the common good. One exasperated member of Siscot said:

The participants of the committee were anxious to grind their own business angle and blow anyone else. There was just no willingness to recognize there is a major risk involved in slow settlement.[6]

Another remarked, 'As far as I could see his [another member's] brief was, 'You are retiring in about two years, chum. Make sure they are still debating the minutes by that time." '[7]

A basic step in designing computer systems is to review existing practices and procedures first.[8] Whilst some members of Siscot argued for a reappraisal of the whole settlement architecture, the majority wanted none of it. Once Siscot realized that Taurus 1 could not be modified to satisfy business interests, they started designing alternative systems around the securities industry as it stood.

'GOOD LORD! OH NO!'

Each sector of the industry had its own ideas about what should be done. A member of Siscot recalls:

When the Pru [Prudential Insurance Company] turned up and said, 'We have had a meeting with fifteen of our members and this is what we want,' it was very difficult for Siscot to say 'No.'[9]

Siscot did not say 'yes' either but examined no fewer than seventeen possible designs for Taurus. Hopes ran high amongst the technical team. Each time a new design was proposed, 'Oh that's very interesting. We quite like that proposal,' said Siscot. Then, as the implications dawned, 'Good Lord! Oh no!'"[10]

The Stock Exchange's preferred option was a system for institutional traders only known as Taurus 3. It could be built using tried and tested technology and would cost just £15 million compared with £60 million for Taurus 1. Moreover, it would achieve a substantial reduction of risk within six months.

There was a snag, however. Taurus 3 was based on nominees. Nominees are an efficient way of processing share transactions because the dealing broker stands surrogate for the true owners. For example, instead of writing for a share certificate when a client wishes to sell, the broker simply calls up the record of holdings on the computer screen and executes the transaction. Likewise, instead of corresponding with hundreds of shareholders, the company registrar needs only to deal with the broker.

Taurus 3 worked on the pyramid principle. Each listed company would have only one registered shareholder, known as Sepon. In turn, Sepon would hold up to 1,000 names, including the largest institutional shareholders and the banks and securities firms holding shares as nominees on behalf of smaller investors. The idea of nominees was anathema to listed companies. When Siegmund Warburg won the 'aluminium war' (see Chapter 4) one of the partners of a leading City house apparently told him:

You didn't do any good for the City with this transaction. No company director whose shares are publicly quoted can sleep well from now on, because he must always wake up in the middle of the night and wonder who will make a raid.[11]

Raids on companies are typically preceded by surreptitious purchases of large blocks of shares. Nominees provide handy cover for this purpose. The Powell Committee had originally rejected the institutional option precisely for this reason.[12] Siscot now faced the same problem. A member of the Stock Exchange technical team who assisted Siscot recalls:

People were getting very concerned that proposal would put tons of stock into nominees. Poor old companies would never know who owned the blasted things [sic] and they would be issuing Section 212 Notices left right and centre, which they do anyway. . . . There would need to be a way of breaking out who the hell was in those nominees.[13]

The proposed solution to the problem of identifying underlying share holdings was to combine Taurus 3 with another version of Taurus known as Taurus 8. Taurus 8 envisaged a nominee system with details of individual share holdings contained in sub-registers. The registers would be held by newly created functionaries known as 'Taurus Account Holders'. In practice Taurus Account Holders would normally be brokers or other authorized intermediaries. One member of Siscot was not impressed with the idea of welding the two systems together:

It used to be a bit of a joke at Siscot, you know, 'Here goes ——— again . . .'
    Poor old Patrick [the chairman], he used to look at me wearily and say, 'I suppose you have got something to say now,' . . . but I was pretty sure of my ground. I have been building systems for twenty-five years. I have made my share of mistakes and it allows you to see when things are going wrong.[14]

Taurus was driven by the institutions. What of the eleven million private investors holding share certificates? Seven million of those holdings were 'Sid's' privatization shares, which were seldom traded.[15] Why load this dormant mass onto an electronic register? Surely it would be more sensible to cancel those certificates gradually, as and when traded, for example.

In the early 1980s there were only about two to three million private shareholders. Even so, the Powell Committee had envisaged dematerializing them last, if at all. Likewise, Touche Ross, the firm of consultants acting as advisers to the committee, pointed to potential difficulties.[16] Siscot decided to incorporate private investors into the system regardless. It was argued that a dual system would result in fragmentation, reduced liquidity, and price differentials. Although such differentials exist anyway, no one wanted to advertise the fact. A retail broker said:

What nobody wants to see happen is a yellow strip for the professional market and a green strip for the retail market, because that immediately says to all the clients, 'You are a second class citizens. You might not have realised it but you are and here's . . . daily evidence.'[17]

Besides, it was thought that Taurus would only save money for the securities industry if it was mandatory. A member of the Stock Exchange technical team said:

The thing that really screwed Taurus up was that if you wanted to get rid of paper for one you had to get rid of paper for all. I think that was a mistake . . . We often wondered why the hell we were bothering to do this for private individuals.[18]

Although it was still unclear quite how private investors would be handled, Siscot decided to proceed with the combined Taurus 3 and 8 design,[19] despite the reservations of a minority. That, at least, was what part of the membership believed had been agreed. In April 1989, however, just as Siscot was about to seek formal approval for the design from the Stock Exchange Council, rebellion erupted in the press. A faction of the membership insisted that the agreement was only to examine the combined option more closely. Siscot was almost back where it had started.

'IS THIS REALLY THE RIGHT WAY TO GO?'

The rebellion was spearheaded by the listed companies, dismayed by the prospect of searching through dozens of subregisters in order to investigate suspicious transactions. By May 1989, another source of tension was brewing. Brokers were beginning to worry about the cost of maintaining subregisters and the possibility of continuous demands from companies for updates from their registers. One broker claimed it would be like bringing the M25 motorway down to one lane.[20] The tensions were accentuated when the consultancy firm Touche Ross was commissioned by the Stock Exchange to prepare a business case for Taurus. The consultants were allowed only two months and besides had no clear and definite design to appraise. Their calculations were based upon a questionnaire circulated to industry representatives. The inevitably vague phrasing of questions caused the consultant's alarm.

Previously the Stock Exchange had proclaimed potential savings of £100 million to the securities industry once Taurus was implemented. Touche's estimates suggested otherwise. According to Touche Ross, at best Taurus would save only £18 million a year, with a worst-case scenario of £6 million. The consultant's report concluded:

TAURUS must be considered in terms of its strategic value to the UK securities market. As a strictly commercial proposition, its viability has not been proved by the data collected.[21]

In fact Taurus was on the point of collapse. The technical team were becoming frustrated by the endless doubts and prognostications. One project consultant recalls:

What we wanted was visibility so we went round saying, 'How can we make this visible?' 'Oh well, what we'll do is we could consolidate it and whiz it off to the registrar periodically.' There was a great deal of argument about this. 'We-ell, the network's not there and it's an awful lot of data traffic and God can all the firms cope? Is this really the right way to go?'[22]

The *Financial Times* reported that some people in the market were predicting the conflict would kill the project.[23] Besides, was the Stock Exchange competent to build Taurus? The UK system of equities settlement is unique. The design had moved from a central database (Taurus 1) to a distributed database. Not only would there be a line of communication from Stock Exchange to broker or market maker, but between broker and broker and market maker and market maker. Building these links posed formidable technical challenges for which no complete blueprint existed. Project director Bill Widdis had his doubts too:

My main concern was that we should get more management attention focused on how we can recognize that this is one of the largest projects that the Stock Exchange would undertake. . . . I was probably underselling the scale of the project. I had grave concerns about why the Stock Exchange was doing it. Even in '87 I was saying this is a banking system. It should be undertaken as a financial services utility. The project was bigger than the Exchange.[24]

The *Financial Times* noted that the history of the project did not augur well.[25]

Although late 1990 was still officially the date for implementing Taurus, it was becoming difficult to see how this could be achieved. By the summer of 1989 Siscot had spawned a plethora of subcommittees to address the intricacies and implications of the proposed design. One re-examined the business case, another argued over how many primary registers would be needed, a third considered the implications of company take-overs, and so on. Members found themselves devoting hours of their time and their staff's time to the project in response to requests from the Stock Exchange: 'Do think about this, do read these regulations, do read this design book, do . . . give us feedback.'

Despite the extensive research, some issues received more attention than others. For example, private investors' holdings were kept in nominee accounts; how would they receive dividends, perks, company reports, and so forth? Some Siscot members thought the institutions were putting themselves first. One member said, 'Companies came second, "we hope they will be satisfied." As for private shareholders, "they will get what they are given." '[26] Private investors were only one problem. Many corporate intricacies such as transfers, rights issues and benefits, and the legal implications of dematerialization were still unresolved when Siscot disbanded. An asset manager recalls, 'People began to disappear into detailed working groups to deal with corporate actions and rules from which essentially they never emerged again.'[27]

'WE WERE ALL PROGRESSIVELY AMAZED AT THE WAY COSTS WERE BUILDING UP.'

The latest version of the design raised the costs of Taurus to an estimated £25 million. As far as the Stock Exchange was concerned the expenditure was justified though people in the securities industry were doubtful. One committee member recalls, 'We were all progressively amazed at the way costs were building up but it wasn't . . . our money.'[28]

In August 1989 the Stock Exchange ceded to market pressure by announcing it would hold only a 40 per cent stake in Taurus. It was only an agreement in principle, however, and did nothing to assuage the conflicts which were consuming Siscot.

Would the conflicts ever be resolved? The chairman of Siscot was clearly beginning to wonder. In September he reported to the Council of the Stock Exchange:

An early resolution of the clearing house issue is critical to the success of Taurus since I believe we shall never get full commitment from the industry until their money is on the table! Even then I fear that there will be many who, without some external pressure, will choose not to have their stock held in the system or, as companies, will continue to raise objections to the new system. If the full benefits of dematerialisation are to be achieved, Government assistance may become necessary at some stage.[29]

Siscot had reached an impasse. It was now for John Watson, recently seconded from the consultancy firm Coopers and Lybrand, to find a way forward. Members of the technical team cheered. John Watson had directed the successful Talisman project. His standing in the City was high. A Stock Exchange project consultant said, 'If anybody could do it, he could sort this bloody business out, one way or another.'[30]

'WHEN ARE WE GOING TO BUILD TAURUS? WHY CAN'T IT BE QUICKER?'

The stock market crash had prompted a highly influential group of bankers known as the 'Group of Thirty' to define international standards for equities settlement. Two crucially important recommendations required financial centres to implement three-day rolling settlement (known as T + 3) and delivery versus payment (DVP) by 1992. Rolling settlement avoids the risks inherent in the practice of the entire securities industry settling simultaneously. Short settlement cycles reduce the likelihood of default, and expedite rapid buying and selling. Delivery versus payment eliminates the chance of a trader ending up minus cash and minus shares.

The Group of Thirty had some powerful sponsors, including the governor of the Bank of England; Lord Richardson, a former governor; and John Reed of Citrop. Moreover, the proposed reforms were said to be incompatible with London's creaking paper-based system. Consequently the pressure for Taurus intensified. Bill Widdis recalls, 'There was always somebody saying "When are we going to build Taurus? Why can't it be quicker?" If I didn't hear it at least once I would have thought I had been asleep all day.'[31]

The Stock Exchange, encouraged by the Bank of England,

quickly committed itself to achieving the targets set by the Group of Thirty. The technical team decided to add those objectives to Taurus. The effect was like throwing petrol on the fire. A member of the Taurus monitoring group recalls:

Project definition was always the weakest part, and partially ambition drove it to be defined broadly by the project managers. They wanted to solve all the securities problems at once. The minute they had more ambition, the more people tried to influence. So as they responded to those influences . . . the thing just became more and more complicated.[32]

It was to become even more complicated as John Watson strove to achieve an agreement. Parallel registers, staggered nominee systems, a listed companies access service, and other trappings were added, modified, subtracted, and re-added and sometimes subtracted again as various sectors of the securities industry attempted to chisel further advantage for themselves.

By November 1989 a year had passed since Siscot first met. There was still no sight of an agreement, despite all the modifications and compromises. Now it was being reported in the press that brokers were worried about the costs of becoming account holders. The media gave the impression that Taurus was hanging by its fingernails.[33]

Finally, in December it was announced that two parallel systems would be built. One half of Taurus would consist of designated account holders, identifying all buyers and sellers daily to the registrar. The second half would consist of undesignated account holders, identifying buyers and sellers monthly to the registrar with a facility for supplying details overnight if required. In other words, the second part of the system reflected the *status quo* minus paper.

Some observers doubted the wisdom of this last-minute concession. An asset manager said, 'Every instinct in me told me that the moment you start compromising on any form of system specification you immediately rack up cost.'[34]

Indeed the final projected cost of Taurus was £50 million, £35 million more than the sum originally envisaged and not much less than the projected £60 million cost of the original Taurus 1. Three designs, Taurus 3, Taurus 8, and lastly, Taurus 7, had been welded together with all the additional facilities for companies to identify their shareholders plus provision for short-cycle rolling settlement and delivery versus payment bolted on. Would it work?

'Complex but do-able', said the technical team.

'A sign of troubled times to come,' commented the financial press.[35]

A WHITE ELEPHANT?

'Do-able' maybe, but was the whole thing worth doing? In 1989 Philip Hooker of Hoare Govett published an exposé of Taurus which was circulated amongst the market and the Stock Exchange.[36] The document argued that Taurus and the Group of Thirty recommendations were fallacious. Why go to such trouble and expense to minimize the risk of default in an industry where default was almost completely unknown? As regards achieving 'delivery versus payment', the report notes, 'In a market where trades can be settled without documents, there can be nothing to deliver.'[37] The report also argued that linking settlement costs to London's attractiveness as a business centre was a red herring:

In truth, investment managers usually take no notice of the settlement consequences of their investment decisions; they invariably appoint custodians to take care of any problems. It must be true that if settlement costs are higher in one market than in another, relative investment returns will be affected but, in practice, the effects are barely perceptible. Custodians may make a song and dance about settlement delays, but most investment managers carry on regardless.[38]

Instead of building a £50 million 'white elephant', Hooker argued, why not just pass legislation to achieve the necessary change? Privately, at conferences and seminars, many people in the securities industry told Hooker that they agreed with him.[39] No one was prepared to speak out publicly, however, for Taurus had become sacrosanct and vital, it was said, to London's continued pre-eminence as a world financial centre.[40] The Stock Exchange ignored the report, though according to Hooker it afforded the technical team some merriment: 'It's true!' they said.

NOTES

1. I have assumed some poetic licence here. Siscot started with thirteen members but the membership soon expanded.
2. Interview, member of Siscot, June 1994.
3. London Stock Exchange (1989c).
4. Interview, member of Siscot, Sept. 1994.
5. Interview, senior official, UK clearing banks, Aug. 1994.
6. Interview, member of Siscot, July 1994.
7. Interview, member of Siscot, Sept. 1994.
8. Daniels (1993).
9. Interview, member of Siscot, Nov. 1993.
10. Interview, member of Stock Exchange technical team, May 1994.
11. Reich (1980: 181).
12. London Stock Exchange (1982).
13. Section 212 Notices are a provision of UK company law whereby a listed company can identify its underlying shareholders. Interview, member of Stock Exchange technical team, May 1994.
14. Interview, member of Siscot, Nov. 1993.
15. London Stock Exchange (1993).
16. Touche Ross (1989b).
17. Interview, member of Siscot, Nov. 1993.
18. Interview, member of Stock Exchange technical team, May 1994.
19. London Stock Exchange (1989a).
20. The M25 is London's orbital motorway. It is frequently heavily congested even with all lanes open.
21. Touche Ross (1989a: 5).
22. Interview, member of Stock Exchange technical team, May 1994.
23. R. Waters, 'Taurus Plan Enters Critical Phase', *Financial Times*, (9 Oct. 1989), 10.
24. Interview, Bill Widdis, June 1994.
25. R. Waters, 'Taurus Plan Enters Critical Phase', *Financial Times*, (9 Oct. 1989), 10.
26. Interview, member of Siscot, Oct. 1994.
27. Interview, member of Siscot, Sept. 1994.
28. Interview, member of Siscot, July 1994.
29. Internal memorandum from the chairman of Siscot to the Stock Exchange Council and 'G15' (Group of Fifteen, a UK subset of the Group of Thirty), 4 Sept. 1989.
30. Interview, member of Stock Exchange technical team, Sept. 1994.
31. Interview, Bill Widdis, June 1994.
32. Interview, member of Taurus monitoring group, July 1994.

33. R. Waters, 'Taurus Plan Enters Critical Phase', *Financial Times* (9 Oct. 1989), 10.
34. Interview, member of Siscot Committee, Sept. 1994.
35. C. Wolman,' 'Taurus is a Sign of Troubled Times to Come', *Financial Times* (6 Feb. 1989), 6.
36. Hooker (1990).
37. Ibid.
38. Ibid.
39. Telephone interview, Philip Hooker, July 1994.
40. London Stock Exchange (1990a). The Taurus Prospectus read, 'The perceived inefficiencies and risk associated with settlement in the U.K. have proved a deterrent for international investors and have threatened the continued development of London as one of the world's leading securities markets' (p. 8).

6

An Opportunity Lost

I did try to stop it and could not stop it.

(Peter Rawlins)

Taurus had damaged the Stock Exchange. Although the design had finally been agreed, the Stock Exchange captured little credit for its endeavour. Peter Rawlins recalls, 'There was a general belief it had all gone on too long, all that arguing, and what was the Exchange there to do?'[1]

What indeed was the Exchange there to do now that its trading floor was redundant and a substantial part of its regulatory functions had been lost? Before 'Big Bang' the chairman of the Stock Exchange ranked close to the governor of the Bank of England at City functions. Now the Stock Exchange was no longer as influential. Moreover it seemed an anachronism in the new order. Three years had passed since 'Big Bang' had revolutionized the culture and practices of the equities market. Yet the Stock Exchange had carried on as if little had changed. According to legend a new employee innocently asked to see an organization chart, only to create paroxysms of laughter. Although the recent widening of membership had enlivened the ruling council, it was still said to be dominated by superannuated brokers. 'A load of dinosaurs . . .', remarked Peter Rawlins; 'they seemed to have been there for ever.'[2]

The general stagnation was reflected in the spiralling costs of the organization. Although the functions of the Stock Exchange had contracted dramatically, staff numbers had almost doubled. In accordance with time-honoured club culture, a committee had been established to scrutinize proposals for new appointments. Since the committee had no power to refuse such requests, however, it merely added to the ninety-plus committees already in existence and serviced by Stock Exchange professional staff.

Traditionally the Stock Exchange met rising costs by increasing membership fees. By 1989 this solution was becoming untenable. The ending of fixed commissions and the stock-market crash had reduced firms' profits. 'Big Bang', moreover, had resulted in voting rights being transferred from individuals to member firms. Member firms were unsympathetic. They saw the Stock Exchange as costing them a great deal of money and doing little to promote the financial services industry. In 1989 the new order made its presence felt when they secured the resignation of the Exchange's chief executive, Jeffrey Knight. Knight was replaced by Peter Rawlins, head-hunted by the Bank of England. Rawlins's brief was to implement a drastic programme of reform of an organization that had manifestly lost its way. He was asked, 'Would you do a job on the Exchange please?'[3]

Born under the sign of Taurus, Peter Rawlins was aged thirty-eight when he took up the post of chief executive. An Oxford graduate in English language and literature and an accountant by training, he was described in the media as bright, iconoclastic, and determined.[4] Part of his career in the City had been spent as personal assistant to Ian Hay-Davidson, formerly chief executive of Lloyd's of London. Hay-Davidson's tenure at Lloyd's was distinguished by his challenge to the Lloyd's establishment. Perhaps because of that exposure, Rawlins's understanding of the City club mentality, its mediocrity and fierce resistance to change, was as deep as his dislike of it. The press welcomed both the brief and the appointment. They wished him luck and suggested he would need it.[5]

The new chief executive was undaunted by the task ahead:

I had a variety of theories about how to make change happen and they had to do with asking the bloody stupid questions, 'Why are we doing this?' The answer that . . . 'Well this committee said that this is what we ought to do' wasn't good enough.[6]

There was plenty for Rawlins to do. He found over thirty projects, drifting and sponsorless, their origins lost in time. Then there was the budget. Hitherto the chief executive had merely added his signature. Rawlins decided to dispense with the 'rubber stamp':

This chap duly rolls up and presents his budget. . . . It turned out that he serviced about thirty-five marketing committees plus 100 market committees. His budget [£6.7 million] was the head count for a lot of chaps serving those committees. So I said to him, 'What happens if we stop doing all of this?' His jaw dropped . . .[7]

'THE ONE THING I WAS SPECIFICALLY TOLD WAS THAT I DIDN'T NEED TO WORRY ABOUT TAURUS.'

The new chief executive was at least spared the worry of Taurus. 'Taurus was nothing to do with my brief,' he said. 'The one thing I was specifically told was that I didn't need to worry about Taurus. Taurus was the one thing that was OK.'[8]

Rawlins quickly sensed, however, that Taurus was far from 'OK'. He had accepted the job of chief executive in summer 1989 though no public announcement was made until the autumn. Shortly after Rawlins had accepted, John Watson had been appointed project director and had been given authority to 'get the thing [Taurus] sorted out'.[9] The appointment was made without consulting the chief executive designate. To Rawlins it seemed ominous. One of his first acts on taking up the post was a request to see John Watson's contract:

It just rang bells. Taurus was one of the number of things that were trains disappearing over the horizon. . . . I remember distinctly thinking, that's rather odd, here's Rawlins has just been appointed, and actually the world is carrying on as if nothing is changing and will change.[10]

The new chief executive raised his anxieties with the chairman of the Exchange, senior members of the Exchange's ruling council, the governor of the Bank of England, and leading members of the banking community. The response was invariably discouraging:

I had all sorts of warning bells flying around in my head. I was writing to people asking them about Taurus, that it just wasn't ringing straight. The answer that came back to me was, 'Look, this has been a heartache for everybody way before you arrived, sunshine. Just leave that alone, that's now in good hands.'[11]

The chief executive still felt uneasy. Although Siscot had virtually disbanded, the negotiations and compromises on the Taurus design were still continuing behind the scenes. It seemed a strange way to manage an expensive and massive infrastructure project:

There were at least thirty committees connected with Taurus spawned by what I thought was over twelve years of debate. Most of them had nothing to do with the Exchange but they all seemed to have a bearing on it.

They were springing up all over the City . . . The committee of London clearing bankers had a committee on Taurus, so did the registrars, so did Snoops, and Jones. You add them up and everybody was giving input to Taurus.[12]

The question perplexing the chief executive was 'who was responsible for Taurus?' Was it a Stock Exchange project, a banking project, or a City project? No matter who the chief executive spoke with, the answer was always the same: 'Don't bother about Taurus. It's the one thing that's OK. Don't touch it please. Just let that happen.'[13]

'IT WAS OBVIOUS TO ME THAT IT WAS NOT THE RIGHT THING TO DO.'

'Everybody was being promised the earth,' recalls Peter Rawlins.[14] Yet Taurus was only a means to an end. It did not deal with book entry. It did not deal with rolling settlement. It did not deal with delivery versus payment. It simply computerized existing manual processes. 'Nobody would have chosen to do Taurus of itself because all it did was represent a lot of cost and not a lot of benefit,' said Rawlins. 'The benefit was what it allowed you to do having done it.'[15]

Was dematerialization worth doing in such a convoluted and expensive fashion? The chief executive shared the concerns of people like Philip Hooker (see Chapter 5). Taurus was becoming an end in itself, supported by the moral rectitude commanded by the self-appointed 'Group of Thirty'. Surely there were better ways of improving settlement:

It was obvious to me that it was not the right thing to do. It wasn't the wrong thing to do. . . . It just struck me it was an unholy compromise. It struck me that the original simple concept was being emasculated . . . it was going to be unnecessarily complicated, . . . unnecessarily time-consuming and much more expensive than it need be and, above all else, I thought it would not deliver the promised benefits.[16]

No one was interested. 'There was a sort of uncritical acceptance by people, most of whom hadn't engaged their minds to it,' recalls Peter Rawlins, 'about [sic] "Let's get on with this." '[17]

Settlement is a complicated business. Taurus was an immensely complex project. It would have taken considerable research and explanation to expose the weaknesses inherent in the design. The new chief executive was isolated, however: 'I didn't have the calibre of people when I arrived to analyse this with the heavy-hitting capability to get up on their hind legs and argue,' he said.[18]

Was Taurus even relevant? Two years had passed since the settlement fiasco of 1987. Much had happened in the intervening time. The chief executive said:

> The primary cause of the '87 fiasco was nothing so sophisticated as that we didn't have DVP [delivery versus payment] or rolling settlement. It was simply blind panic. The newly established managements of these big organizations, and they were getting very big, . . . didn't understand the business they were in. Well, it so scared . . . them that by the time I arrived, a large part of the problem had self-corrected. . . . Businesses in the City were getting their own house in order. . . . What I didn't fully appreciate at that time was how much of what was going on would have gone on anyway irrespective of Taurus. I thought and was led to under-stand that a lot of things were going on out there because of . . . Taurus.[19]

Besides, why should any one worry, with two prestigious con-sultancy firms overseeing the project? Coopers and Lybrand were supplying consultants to build and manage the project under John Watson's direction. Touche Ross were retained as project moni-tors. The chief executive was unconvinced, however:

> There was this curious belief that I found all around the City, this lem-ming-like belief by people who generally don't know what they are doing, that as long as you appoint a household name . . . to oversee it for you and they tell you it's OK, then it's OK.[20]

Anyway, who cared? The 1980s had been good years for the City. The economic recession of the 1990s was in the future. Taurus would certainly require investment but money was still plentiful. The chief executive found himself facing a brick wall:

> As long as the horizon that we were talking about was relatively short, as long as people were still making a certain amount of money, which by the time I arrived they still were (it soon changed), then 'OK.' . . . There had been twelve years' argument about whether this way or that way. People were tired, . . . they were arguing about it for ever. As long as they were protecting their patch, . . . this unholy compromise had come up. Honour was satisfied all round. 'Do the bloody thing.'[21]

With all its weaknesses, Taurus at least offered a way forward at long last. After Siscot's tortuous deliberations, no one wanted to start again, far less adopt the chief executive's idea:

My thesis was we should go back to Taurus One. . . . If we are going to have the system changed for Christ's sake let's do it properly so we build one central register. I said, 'Why don't we do this properly?' The great advantage was that nothing had been built at the time I was there. 'No, sorry Peter, we have had all those arguments. Great idea but no, we have been arguing about it for twelve years, forget it.'[22]

'KEEP OUT OF THIS PLEASE'

In early 1990 the building of Taurus began. As firms began to see what the system would look like, it was soon apparent that the design was far more intricate than anyone had imagined. Nor was it clear how the various subsystems would interlock. Would they interlock? Systems experts in the market reached for their telephones. When the answers from the Stock Exchange technical team left them no wiser, the new chief executive was asked to attend committee meetings of the various constituencies of the securities industry. Although members were seldom as forthright with Peter Rawlins as they were in private sessions, the chief executive was disturbed none the less. He decided it was time to exert some control, only to be thwarted again:

I was getting all sorts of reports left, right, and centre. I set up a Settlement Services Board which I did not sit on. I was asked to 'Keep out of this please' by the chairman and other board members.[23]

What was Rawlins to do? He had been told emphatically not to intervene in Taurus and there were other, more pressing problems awaiting his attention:

Costs were out of control. We had crumbling technology. We had not really taken account of what was happening post-Big Bang. We were still running an old jobbing shop except we didn't have a trading floor any more. . . . Very tenuous. . . . It [the business] could have walked out just like that.[24]

With so much else at stake, settlement was hardly a priority:

Day-to-day settlement nobody knew anything about outside the Exchange, but actually the Exchange ran it very well. Yes it was archaic. Yes it needed to be improved in terms of international capability, but it was fine.[25]

Accordingly the Chief Executive concentrated his attention elsewhere. As for Taurus:

There was a full-time partner of Coopers overseeing the project. Funds had been voted, budgets had been set, the parameters were away, we had monitoring committees, Christ knows what. I fought my corner for a while and thought 'Fine, if you are all happy with this that's fine. Let's get on.'[26]

NOTES

1. Interview, Peter Rawlins, Oct. 1993.
2. Ibid.
3. Ibid.
4. C. Leonard, 'Ruthless Enemy of the Status Quo', *The Times*, (19 Oct. 1991), 19.
5. 'New Boy at the Exchange,' *The Economist*, 313, (1989), 116.
6. Interview, Peter Rawlins, Oct. 1993.
7. Ibid.
8. Ibid.
9. Ibid.
10. Ibid.
11. Ibid.
12. Ibid.
13. Ibid.
14. Ibid.
15. Ibid.
16. Ibid.
17. Ibid.
18. Ibid.
19. Ibid.
20. Interview, Peter Rawlins, Oct. 1993.
21. Ibid.
22. Ibid.
23. Ibid.

24. Ibid.
25. Ibid.
26. Ibid.

7

The Origins of Escalation

Tell me, where *did* this camel come from?

(A banker)

The purpose of this chapter is to analyse the opening phases of the Taurus story. Since the seeds of the project's subsequent collapse were sown during this period, the central question for examination is how and why organizations become involved in decision débâcles in the first place.

According to the social-psychological literature escalation begins with bright but illusory prospects. Then, once a decision takes shape, psychological and social pressures induce persistence. Decision-makers may ignore questionable feedback early on in order to justify their initial enthusiasm for the venture. Since, however, relatively few material, social, psychological, or organizational commitments are likely to exist early on, decisions are thought to be fairly easy to reverse.[1] Decision dilemma theorists basically suggest the opposite. Initially commitment to a decision is likely to be high as decision-makers have yet to test their aspirations against reality. Moreover, feedback will probably be patchy and unreliable at first.[2] Accordingly, the researchers' guiding propositions for analysing the initial phase of the Taurus story were:

1. Commitment to a flawed decision occurs because decision-makers cannot reasonably foresee that their expectations will prove unrealistic.
2. To the extent that negative feedback is available, psychological and social pressures prompt decision-makers to ignore such information.
3. Since few resources have been committed early on, however, withdrawal is probable if it becomes clear that the decision-maker's expectations are misplaced.

A PLETHORA OF MYTHS

The focal decision for analysis in the present study is the Stock Exchange's persistence with Project Taurus following the collapse of the initial proposal to build a central register design known as Taurus 1. The 'decision-maker' is defined as the Council of the Stock Exchange advised by the chief executive. In order to understand the forces for persistence, however, it is necessary to consider the wider decision context, including the actions of players other than the 'decision-maker'. These principally comprise the Siscot Committee and the wider securities industry, sometimes referred to as 'the market'.

The decision to proceed with Project Taurus stemmed from a plethora of myths and competing myths dating back to the late 1960s. Myths, it was suggested earlier, are ideas which gain and lose acceptance over time. Acceptance is defined here as becoming institutionalized, that is, a particular viewpoint comes to signify the dominant community or organizational values. It becomes so deeply embedded as to be 'taken for granted', like some inviolate rule beyond individual discretion.[3]

Taurus sprang from the myth promulgated in the late 1960s that settlement was ripe for reform. It was not at that stage institutionalized: 'The council reckoned that book entry would come . . . .' The real impetus to Taurus was a crisis in the Stock Exchange immediately following 'Big Bang', which gave rise to the myth that IT-based services held the key to the Stock Exchange's survival. This myth was reinforced by the existence of a competing myth. Member firms attempted to denigrate the Stock Exchange for their own commercial advantage. Such developments were escalatory because they added to the pressure on the Stock Exchange to secure its 'market share' and improve its reputation by delivering Taurus: 'There was a general belief it had all gone on too long, all that arguing, and what was the Exchange there to do?'

A crucial assumption of the escalation literature is that decision criteria are objectively verifiable.[4] The present study suggests otherwise. Persistence in the initial stages could be interpreted as an attempt by the Stock Exchange to save face. Yet it was underscored by a clear and plausible rationale. Reputation is an important strategic asset, especially in the financial services industry.[5]

Settlement was potentially a lucrative business. Furthermore, as central market authority, the Stock Exchange had a responsibility to take the initiative in an industry-wide issue. Conversely the strategy was 'irrational' in that it ignored post-'Big Bang' environmental developments, notably the instigation of price competition and the new balance of power in the City. Viewed in this way, the decision criteria were simultaneously rational and flawed: 'It was not the right thing to do. It was not the wrong thing to do.'

The word 'crisis' means danger and opportunity. The settlements crisis produced another critically important double-edged myth. The Group of Thirty's recommendations facilitated the Stock Exchange's ambitions by elevating settlement to a commercial imperative. The reduction of risk and streamlining settlement were imposed by the Group of Thirty as a critical value of the securities industry, though such moves primarily benefited the institutional constituency. Treating the Group of Thirty's recommendations as 'holy writ' and capitalizing on the Bank of England's tacit support for these enabled the Stock Exchange to capitalize on its authority as market regulator to promote its own competitive ambitions. It did so by institutionalizing the Taurus myth. It achieved this by the creation of a project rhetoric.[6] Project Taurus became synonymous with achievement of the Group of Thirty's recommendations when it was only a means to that end.

The myth was double-edged because it increased the time pressure on the Stock Exchange to deliver Taurus: 'There was always somebody saying "When are we going to build Taurus? Why can't it be quicker?" ' The myth was also double-edged in that it was the source of a destructive tension. Systemic risk and international compatibility of settlement systems were important as far as institutional investors were concerned. They were not really an issue in the retail broking sector though dematerialization had its advantages. The latter found itself becoming involved in a venture which involved cost but was primarily for the benefit of the institutional constituency. The long arguments at Siscot were basically an attempt to impose a rationale upon a fundamental contradiction.[7]

Furthermore, although the Group of Thirty's recommendations were supported by a carefully reasoned case, it was questionable whether they were commercially sensible even for the institutional investors they were meant to serve. Philip Hooker exposed one potential flaw when he claimed, 'In a market where trades can be settled without documents, there can be nothing to deliver'.[8] Likewise, the cost of achieving rolling settlement rises exponentially the shorter the period becomes whereas the reduction in risk decreases exponentially. Some players in the securities industry doubted whether anything shorter than five-day rolling settlement was justified.[9] The majority of players, however, were acquiescent, unwilling to be seen as attempting to 'scupper' a project purportedly vital to London.

A crucial decision taken early on was to cancel the millions of share certificates owned by private investors. It was said to have been 'The thing that really screwed Taurus up.' Paucity of information does not explain that decision. The Powell Committee envisaged dematerializing private shareholders last, if at all.[10] Touche Ross reminded Siscot of the difficulties involved.[11] From a social-psychological standpoint such apparent recklessness might be interpreted as decision-makers' ignoring disconfirming information.[12] The evidence suggests, however, that they considered the matter very carefully. The choice was based upon an assessment of the cost implications and the political climate. The issues were finely balanced. In retrospect it was the wrong decision taken for the right reasons.

THE TRAGEDY OF THE COMMONS

The escalation literature assumes that a course of action flows from a 'decision'. The word 'decision' means 'to cut',[13] thus implying a clear choice between options. Alternatively, the literature suggests that decisions are the product of incremental drift, sometimes known as 'decisionless decisions'.[14] Events in the present study are more akin to the metaphor of the potter fashioning a lump of clay than to a clear and precise decision 'to cut' or decision by default.[15] The difference between metaphor and the data, however, is that the metaphor envisages a single potter, shaping the clay, fashioning the design—changing from a jug to a vase perhaps, but basically the potter is in control of events. The present study exemplifies the significance of multiple influences upon the decision-making process. In the present study, the potter (the Stock Exchange) was bombarded with different views about how the clay should be fashioned. It was the organization's responsiveness to 'this way or that way' that corrupted Taurus. So far, it has been argued that there are no absolutes in decision-making. If we suspend that idea for the moment, the rejection of Taurus 3 marks the point where rationality began to unravel. Taurus 3 was logical in that it stood to achieve a substantial reduction in risk within six months using tried and tested technology. It would also have secured a central role in settlement for the Stock Exchange.

Escalation at Siscot resulted neither from paucity of information nor from members behaving irrationally but from everyone acting logically according to their circumstances. Everyone at Siscot fought their own corner because their primary duty was to their employers and not to the Stock Exchange. A useful metaphor here is the tragedy of the commons. The commons were stretches of land offering unrestricted grazing rights. Logic dictated that each peasant graze yet another beast. Eventually the cumulative effect of everyone pursuing their own interests was that the land was ruined. Ultimate ruin was inevitable because it was inherent in the policy of unfettered grazing rights.[16] In the case of Taurus, the seeds of ultimate collapse were contained in the contradictory policy sanctioned by the Bank of England, of preserving business interest in the face of an inherent conflict of interest. The resultant 'free-for-all' led to the design becoming exceedingly convoluted.

Although tragedy was inherent in the policy of the commons, destruction was not inevitable. The same applied to Taurus. Someone might have said, 'Stop! This is becoming ridiculous.' Prospect theory predicts that the risk of a large future loss is preferable to a smaller but certain immediate loss.[17] That would suggest that Siscot agreed to take a chance with a bad design rather than start again. Whilst the group was certainly approaching exhaustion ('people were tired, they were arguing about it forever'), there is no evidence that this option was seriously debated and framed as a choice between risks.

Taurus was designed by a group. Groups are thought to make riskier decisions than individuals. One possible reason for excessive risk-taking is a phenomenon known as 'groupthink', that is, a false consensus arising from members' reluctance to upset the cosy atmosphere which sometimes develops in groups. Another is known as 'risky shift', that is, a reckless choice resulting from a diffusion of responsibility.[18] There is no evidence that Siscot succumbed to 'groupthink' or 'risky shift'. If anything, Siscot was more likely to have collapsed because of the destructive tensions between the players. Moreover, there is no evidence that members' critical faculties were suspended. On the contrary, they examined no fewer than seventeen options and in considerable detail, metaphorically speaking, walking through 'mud . . . glue . . . and quick-drying cement'.

Nor is it likely that Siscot was motivated by a desire to 'end the pain' or sentiments of 'to hell with the consequences', which are thought to sometimes overtake groups.[19] On the contrary, members were deeply concerned about the ramifications of the various models ('We quite like that proposal'; 'Good Lord! Oh no!'). The present study does suggest an interesting insight, however. By about September 1989 Siscot had reached an impasse. Negotiations then passed to John Watson. Perhaps decision-makers try to 'end the pain' by delegating part of the problem. Such action is potentially escalatory because control weakens as the formal mechanism for communication and discussion begins to loosen. In the present study no member of Siscot claimed to have seen the final Taurus design. Although they knew the implications for their own business constituency, it was unclear precisely what had been decided informally.

Second, and more importantly, responsibility for a decision is thought to be highly conducive to injudicious persistence.[20] In the present study the opposite applies. Members' freedom of action was not the product of group dynamics but structural. Just as the peasant had no responsibility for the preservation of the land for the common good, Siscot members were responsible to their constituencies and not to the Stock Exchange. It was this perceived freedom from accountability for Taurus which resulted in escalation: 'We were all progressively amazed at the way costs were building up but it wasn't . . . our money.'

Another structural factor was the moral rectitude attached to the Group of Thirty's recommendations. A minority at Siscot thought the evolving design was unworkable. Likewise, many players in the market apparently shared Philip Hooker's view that Taurus was overelaborate and unnecessary. The banks had considerable reservations about Taurus from the start. All declined to press their objections publicly for fear of being seen to undermine the project. Power is defined here as the ability to produce 'intended effects.' Intended effects can emanate from unchallenged assumptions. The literature suggests that control can be subtly maintained by elevating an issue to such a level that the criticism of the dominant viewpoint becomes unthinkable.[21] Such repression proved escalatory in the present case because it prevented alternative viewpoints from influencing the debate.

Politics is defined here as the pursuit of interest in the face of scarce resources. Considerable attention is paid in the organizational literature to proactive political behaviours whereby interested parties compete with one another to block or achieve change. In such circumstances decisions typically turn upon political acceptability rather than technical merit.[22] The present study also shows how decisions may be shaped by passive political behaviours: 'There was a sort of uncritical acceptance by people, most of whom hadn't engaged their minds to it.' The club culture of the City was still very much in evidence despite 'Big Bang'. The less competent leaders of the securities industry had yet to awaken to the reality of systemic risk and long-term strategic implications of Taurus. They were content to pay lip-service to the Group of Thirty's prognostications, for in their minds settlement was still 'the province of Gladys'.

Managerial attention is a scarce asset. The present study suggests that low-status projects may be prone to escalation because they fail to command sufficient organizational resources to ensure that they are properly managed. Such projects may drift along, scarcely noticed yet incurring both direct costs and opportunity costs.

THE BALANCE OF POWER

A major reason for the project's subsequent collapse was that critical issues were unforeseen at the design stage. Decision complexity was also relevant. Siscot lacked the resources to investigate all the potential implications of Taurus. Indeed, many issues were still unresolved when Taurus collapsed: 'People began to disappear into detailed working groups to deal with corporate actions and rules from which essentially they never emerged again.'

A more theoretically significant question, however, is what factors determined the allocation of resources? Business interest coupled with freedom from responsibility was one consideration. Another was the balance of power on Siscot. The metaphor of the commons assumes that all 'peasants' are equally powerful. This was not the case here. Taurus was driven by the institutions. The retail-broking constituency was insufficiently puissant at that time (it subsequently changed) to force consideration: 'they will get what they are given.'

This is doubly suggestive. First, the promulgators of negative feedback may sometimes be insufficiently powerful to press their objections during the decision-making phase. Second, they may continue the contest elsewhere, as happened with Taurus (see Chapter 9). So what constitutes negative feedback? The present case suggests that there is no clear dividing line between the rational and the irrational in decision-making. It was sensible to postpone consideration of private investors in order to make progress on the institutional front—the biggest source of systemic risk, but unwise because of all the problems entailed.

What emerges here are the divided fortunes of a power struggle. The Stock Exchange was insufficiently powerful to force a system on the market, hence the policy of consultation. The institutions were sufficiently powerful to determine the foundations of Taurus but unable to get their own way entirely. The retail-broking constituency was powerful enough to insist upon two parallel systems being built but was unable to force full consideration of private clients' needs. Listed companies actually profited. Registrars were acquiescent but still dissatisfied. It was the effect of trying to combine conflicting rationales and the lack of responsibility which gave Siscot the appearance of a 'Mad Hatter's tea-party' and turned Taurus from a 'horse' into a 'camel'.

POWER AND RESPONSIBILITY

The foregoing analysis does not explain why the Stock Exchange as the ultimate decision-maker did not say 'Stop!' By early 1990 there was certainly an accumulation of negative feedback.

Taurus 1 had proved non-viable. Then Taurus 3 foundered. Subsequently, layer after layer was added to the design, adding to the cost and to the complexity. Twice during 1989 Taurus teetered close to collapse. Surely such an unremitting succession of failures would have damaged if not destroyed the Stock Exchange's commitment to Taurus?

Although in September 1989 the chairman of Siscot may have been preparing the Council for the possibility when he wrote, 'There will be many who, without some external pressure, will continue to raise objections to the new system,' and then raised the possibility of invoking Government intervention, there is no other evidence that the Stock Exchange contemplated giving up. Prospect theory might suggest that the making of concessions piecemeal was escalatory because it obscured the sheer magnitude of the changes to the design.[23] The difficulty with this explanation is that the major changes were clear and definite, that is, first Taurus 1, then Taurus 3, then Taurus 3 combined with Taurus 8, and so on.

According to social-psychological theorists, escalation is sustained by decision-makers' propensity to seek out and promulgate supportive information whilst ignoring negative feedback. Ostensibly this is just what happened: 'Everyone was being promised the earth.' Likewise the reservations expressed by Touche Ross concerning private investors and the commercial viability of the venture were apparently ignored.

There is no evidence, however, that the Stock Exchange deceived itself in the manner suggested by escalation theory. The promises reflected the organization's policy of accommodating business interest and maintaining support for the project. Social-psychological theory assumes that disconfirming information is accurate whereas decision dilemma theorists argue that all information is equivocal. The present study points to the symbolic significance of information in decision-making.[24] Touche Ross's analysis was commissioned months before the final outline was agreed upon.[25] The figures were bound, therefore, to be extremely tentative. More importantly, what do we mean in any case by the word 'ignore'? In their study of Expo 86 Ross and Staw concluded that the ever-changing attendance estimates which outstripped Vancouver's hotel processing reflect biased information processing. Their data, however, do not indicate what actually happened to the information.[26] Social-psychological theory implies that contradictory information receives a cursory glance before being pushed aside in the enthusiasm of the moment.[27] This was not the case here. The researcher saw the chairman of Siscot's copy of the report. It is heavily annotated, suggesting he read it very carefully. Moreover the margins are littered with question marks, exclamation marks, and his own calculations. The word 'rubbish!' is scribbled against one sentence.

According to decision dilemma theorists the data reflect the sheer difficulties which decision-makers experience in obtaining accurate information early on. Yet why conduct the exercise when the design was still being debated? Surely the real purpose of commissioning an analysis was to demonstrate to the securities industry that the Stock Exchange was mindful of their interests and adopting a commercial approach to Taurus? The production of a business case couched in the language of accountancy forms part of the ritual of decision-making.[28] It was an important step in institutionalizing the venture because it held the potential to bolster the perceived legitimacy of the venture.[29]

Likewise Taurus came to be surrounded by myopia, not through self-hypnotism, as implied by social-psychological theorists, but through the management of meaning. During 1989 and 1990 a rhetoric was created round the project which subsequently prefaced almost every major press article and seminar paper. The rhetoric elevated Taurus from the status of important, which it was, to vital, which it was not. It is thought that if people hear a message often enough, they begin to assume it is true.[30] Whilst that may have been true of the uncritical players in the securities industry, the more sophisticated players were sceptical. They kept their views private, however. The significance of the project rhetoric was not that people necessarily believed it, but that it helped to render Taurus sacerdotal and therefore safe from overt criticism.

Decision dilemma theorists equate rational behaviour with a concomitant relationship between information and commitment. That is, 10 per cent failure results in a 10 per cent reduction in commitment. The present study offers a new insight. The data suggest that the relationship between commitment and information is potentially curvilinear. Negative feedback has less impact upon a project which is regarded as important than one which is judged unessential. Extrapolating beyond the data, it may very well be that where a project is perceived as unimportant, decision-makers are more likely to say 'to hell with it' when problems arise.

The data further suggest that high perceived importance of a venture increases decision-makers' willingness to make concessions.[31] Social-psychological theorists might regard excessive compromise as irrational. Again, this presupposes that an objectively verifiable dividing line exists. In history many decisions which were judged successful were actually the product of considerable dilution and configuration. For example, the establishment of the UK National Health Service was facilitated by a concession allowing doctors to maintain private practice in addition to their National Health Service commitment. In the present case the Stock Exchange's rationale was clear. Taurus was strategically very important, hence the Stock Exchange's willingness to invest in it. Although the rationale seemed questionable to some observers, the rising costs of Taurus were not necessarily all that important (1) given a daily turnover of some £1 billion and (2) the long-term benefits of the venture. Although brokers' back offices had become more efficient since the settlements' crisis, the problem of systemic risk was still outstanding. Arguably what was another £25 or even £50 million given the quadrillions of pounds potentially at risk.

ORGANIZATIONAL AND PROJECT FACTORS

Persistence with a 'camel' cannot be entirely explained by politics. Escalation is thought more probable when players are operating at the boundaries of knowledge.[32] The present study bears out this notion. Settlement was an extremely intricate issue to begin with. Few of the decision-makers were IT experts and even the technical team were operating in uncharted waters. It is also believed that the risk of escalation is greater when the implications of a decision are not perceived at the outset.[33] In the present case, although some issues were ignored because of the power differentials between players, it was also true to say that some problems could not reasonably have been foreseen, notably the legal ramifications of dematerialization. The present study suggests a link between the two propositions. That is, operating at the boundaries of knowledge increases the possibility of escalation because it makes it more difficult for decision-makers to perceive what they are committing themselves to.[34]

Escalation theory suggests that control mechanisms are conducive to preventing escalation.[35] The present study indicates that the reverse is true. The absence or failure of such mechanisms is conducive to escalation because the flow of communication is impeded. In the present case, the decision to add rolling settlement and 'delivery versus payment' to Taurus compounded the complexity of the project. Although some respondents thought Taurus was 'techy-driven' the decision actually flowed from the Stock Exchange's public commitment to implement the Group of Thirty's recommendations. The pledge was made at the highest level, apparently without prior analysis of the technical ramifications. Thus committed, the technical team then opted for a 'Big Bang' approach. It is unclear what communication took place between the Exchange's senior management and the technical team. In accepting the challenge the technical team may have overestimated their ability to cope because of their previous successes with Talisman and 'Big Bang'.[36] The point is, if that was the case, then there was no 'fail-safe' device to stop them.

Furthermore, part of the decision-making occurred 'off stage'. The failure to impose firm control was escalatory because the decision parameters began to be obscured. A double danger existed because the reports, analyses, and other documentary trappings of decision-making imparted a false sense of certainty. In approving a project 'complex but not grossly so'[37] the Stock Exchange Council thought they knew what they were deciding. In fact, their knowledge was an illusion.

THE RELATIONSHIP BETWEEN POWER AND RESPONSIBILITY

Social-psychological theorists predict that withdrawal is fairly easy to accomplish early on in a venture because relatively few investments exist. A change of senior management, such as the appointment of a new chief executive, is also thought to facilitate withdrawal.[38] Since nothing had been built in late 1989 or 1990, theoretically the chief executive's introduction of negative feedback should have prompted withdrawal or at least a review of the project. Yet his impact upon the Stock Exchange's commitment at that juncture was negligible. How can this be explained, and what are the implications for escalation theory?

Contrary to the idea that decisions involve few commitments early on, the present study suggests that early on may be precisely the time when reversal is most difficult. The chief executive failed to change the dominant viewpoint, that is, that building Taurus was what should be done. It was suggested earlier that the perceived importance of Taurus outweighed negative feedback. Yet the chief executive was basically saying that the whole project was misconceived, convoluted, and unnecessarily complicated, incapable of delivering the promised benefits. Why were his reservations disregarded? More importantly, why was someone in such a powerful position unable to stop the project?

One possible explanation is that Peter Rawlins relied upon devil's advocacy—for example, 'why don't we do this properly?' Devil's advocacy appears to be only marginally effective in reducing commitment.[39] Furthermore, during the first few weeks of his appointment the chief executive was energetically questioning almost every aspect of the Stock Exchange's operations. Asking so many apparently 'stupid' questions may have blunted his impact as regards Taurus. Competing priorities may contribute to escalation if they distract decision-makers' attention. As Janis says, only the squeaky wheels get oiled.[40] The chief executive certainly had some extremely pressing issues to address, and might not therefore have pursued Taurus with sufficient vigour: 'Costs were out of control. We had crumbling technology. . . . We were still running an old jobbing shop.'

Such explanations are at best partial. Far from being ignored, the evidence is that the new chief executive's challenge disturbed the Exchange. Even if it was an exaggeration to say that there had been twelve years of argument about Taurus, the last eighteen months had certainly witnessed intense discussion, work, and argument on the part of the Stock Exchange and the securities industry. Who, apart from the chief executive, wanted to re-open the conflict? Likewise, Touche Ross were far from saying that everything was 'tickety-boo' but their reservations did not reach the chief executive's ears.

The timing of the chief executive's appointment is significant. Motivation is thought to increase as a goal nears completion. The

Stock Exchange's goal was to obtain an agreement to a new design for dematerialization following the collapse of Taurus 1. Moreover, the identification of a possible solution to a decision problem is thought to give rise to a paradox, that is, 'where there is way there is a will.'[41] Had Peter Rawlins taken up his post when Siscot was still floundering he might have been able to steer the discussion in a different direction. Instead he arrived just as months of debilitating conflict had ended: 'people were tired, they had been arguing about it for ever.'

The present study is consistent with the idea that paucity of alternatives is conducive to escalation.[42] The present study suggests a link between this factor, the nature of the decision process, and the level of dependency. Nobody was happy with Taurus, but although the chief executive's suggestion of reverting to Taurus 1 might have been a 'great idea' technically, it was a non-starter in that political climate. If twelve months' intense debate at Siscot had failed to identify a viable alternative to the hybrid solution about to be built, what likelihood was there of doing so now? Moreover, for the Stock Exchange to procrastinate at that point, after the expenditure of so much effort, might have provided the market with an excuse to withdraw not only from Taurus but from membership of the Stock Exchange itself.[43] Conceivably then, escalation is more probable where the decision-making process has been characterized by conflict and complexity; where the number of alternatives is limited, and where the organization is dependent upon external constituencies. The real danger, however, arises with the emergence of a possible solution, as it locks decision-makers into a specific course of action.

Although the forces for persistence were considerable, this still does not explain why the chief executive was unable to stop Taurus. Equivocal information was hardly the problem. What was lacking was the power to utilize it, that is, the 'heavy-hitting capability' to analyse the data and present a case. Such powerlessness was structural. John Watson is understood to have insisted upon complete autonomy over Taurus as a condition of accepting the job of project director, hence the instruction 'Keep out of that please.'

A key factor in explaining escalation at this juncture lies in the relationship between power and responsibility. The chief executive was basically saying what the more sophisticated players in the market already knew but chose to ignore and what the less sophisticated were indifferent to. What distinguishes them from the chief executive was their perceived accountability for the outcome. The present study suggests that escalation is most probable when those with most power to influence a decision have least responsibility for its outcome. In the present study this category is defined as the market overshadowed by the Group of Thirty and the Bank of England, followed by Siscot, and lastly the technical team.

A THEORETICAL SYNTHESIS

What emerges so far is the notion of escalation as simultaneously rational and irrational, bound up with power, politics, and opportunity, and influenced by the vagaries of project and organization. Let me now attempt to synthesize the findings into a coherent framework.

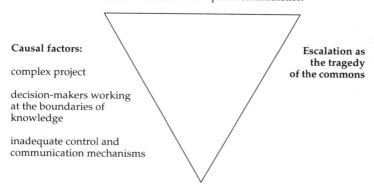

The root of escalation:

overarching influence of 'the great and the good'

means Taurus is built upon a contradiction

Causal factors:

complex project

decision-makers working at the boundaries of knowledge

inadequate control and communication mechanisms

Escalation as the tragedy of the commons

FIG. 7.1 The origins of escalation

The triangle depicted in Figure 7.1 represents the three analytical paradigms utilized to analyse the data.[44] The top of the triangle views the process at the macro-level. The question for analysis at this level is what is the root of escalation? Viewed from a 'wide-angle' lens, escalation emerges as the product of structural forces. Such forces dictate the dominant community values for their own material benefit. In the present case it was the unchallengeable but contradictory prescriptions of 'the great and the good' as represented by the Group of Thirty, the Bank of England, and the Stock Exchange in its capacity as market regulator which sowed the seeds of ultimate disaster.

The second side of the triangle examines escalation at the meso-level. The question for analysis at this level is 'what is escalation?' Viewed from this perspective escalation emerges as something which people create themselves. The image of the tragedy of the commons was invoked to describe the process. What appears as collective madness is traceable to the interplay between different rationales. Disaster is preventable but only if the various players are prepared to take responsibility for the common good. Since the assumption of such responsibility is illogical in the circumstances, everyone pursues their own interests. Viewed from this perspective, disaster results not from people behaving irrationally but from sheer logic. The 'Mad Hatter's tea-party' is an irony.

The third side of the triangle examines escalation at the micro-level. The central question for analysis at this level is 'what are the immediate causes of escalation?' Two factors are identified in the present study, project and organizational. The main project factors are the sheer complexity of the settlement and decision-makers working at the boundaries of knowledge. The main organizational factor concerns the Stock Exchange's control mechanisms. Communication facilities between the higher and lower echelons were inadequate. The balance between the chief executive's power and the chief executive's responsibility was highly asymmetrical. Such influences make escalation more probable because they obscure 'reality'. They are instrumental in lulling decision-makers into a false sense of security.

Each paradigm yields a partial perspective. Triangulated they provide a more holistic understanding of how and why organizations become involved in decision fiascos such as Taurus. The unchallengeable prescriptions of 'the great and the good' committed players to reforming settlement, which in turn locked them into Taurus. Once locked in, players responded rationally by fighting their own corners. The result was to corrupt the Taurus design and for certain critical issues to be under-researched. As the original simple concept of Taurus became increasingly convoluted, project and organizational forces conspired to obscure reality. Those players who realized what was happening were prevented from intervening because Taurus had become sacrosanct.

CONCLUSIONS

It was expected that escalation would result either from paucity of information or from social-psychological pressures. It was certainly true that the decision-makers could not possibly have foreseen some of the difficulties which lay ahead. Moreover, some of the risks were obscured by the sheer complexity of the project and certain organizational weaknesses. To that extent the data are consistent with decision dilemma theory.

It is also true to say that considerable hyperbole surrounded the project. Taurus was proclaimed as vital to London's continued pre-eminence as a world financial centre. Moreover, promises appear to have been made and certain disconfirming indications may have been disregarded. To that extent the data are consistent with social-psychological theory.

To explain the data in the present case, however, it is necessary to look beyond both perspectives and to probe beneath surface appearances. The key to understanding the origins of escalation lies in the balance between the power and the responsibility of those involved in the decision processes. Viewed in this way escalation emerges neither as the product of ignorance, as suggested by decision dilemma theorists, or as the product of irrational behaviour on the part of the decision-makers, as suggested by social-psychological theorists. Instead, what we see is the destructive logic of the situation beginning to unfold. It is the cumulative effect of everyone behaving rationally which makes the whole episode seem bizarre and results in the transformation of the 'horse' into the 'camel'.

It was also expected that withdrawal would be unproblematic early on because relatively few commitments would exist. Yet the project proceeded despite the introduction of potentially serious doubts and the fact that nothing had been built.

Again, the present study suggests that it is necessary to look beyond decision dilemma theory and social-psychological theory in order to understand how organizations become 'locked in' to highly questionable ventures. By the time the chief executive arrived, Taurus had already passed the critical juncture, that is, the project had become institutionalized. The chief executive was powerless against the massive forces sustaining commitment and shaping the design. Taurus had become linked to the destiny of the City itself. It was like a fly trying to stop a juggernaut.

Many players besides the chief executive saw that the project was an 'unholy compromise' and guessed that it might not deliver the promised benefits. Taurus went ahead because of the impact of the settlements crisis, the ambitions and competitive weaknesses of the Stock Exchange, and the irresponsible cynicism of the market. In early 1990 what choice was there other than to 'Do the bloody thing'?

NOTES

1. See, for example, Ross and Staw (1991), Staw (1981), Staw and Ross (1987a, b).
2. Bowen (1987).
3. Bacharach and Baratz (1963), Berger and Luckmann (1966), Bowen (1987) citing Hedberg and Jonsonn (1977), Meyer and Rowan (1978), Zucker (1977).
4. The point is implicit in both social-psychological theory and decision dilemma theory. It is derived from the assumption that decision-makers seek to maximize utility.
5. Kay (1993).
6. See, for example, Gowler and Legge (1983), Quaid (1993).
7. Devons (1961), Morgan (1986).
8. Hooker (unpub. mimeo, 1990).
9. London Business School (1993b) attempts to calculate the costs of various levels of systemic risk.
10. London Stock Exchange (1982).
11. Touche Ross (1989b).
12. Staw and Ross (1978), Bazerman (1994). See also Borrgida and Nisbett (1977), Brockner *et al.* (1986), Caldwell and O'Reilly (1982), Conlon and Wolf (1980), Conlon and Parks (1987), Nisbett and Ross (1980), Northcraft and Neale (1986), and O'Reilly (1980).

13. Drummond (1991a).
14. Becker (1960).
15. Mintzberg (1992).
16. Hardin (1968).
17. Kahneman and Tversky (1979, 1982, and 1984).
18. Janis (1972). See also Bazerman *et al.* (1984), Flowers (1977), and Whyte (1986, 1989, 1991, 1993).
19. Janis (1989).
20. Bazerman (1994), Brockner (1992), Staw (1980, 1981), Staw and Ross (1987a, 1989).
21. The definition of power utilized here derives from Wrong (1979). The idea of power stemming from unchallenged assumptions is derived from Bacharach and Baratz (1963, 1970), Lukes (1974), Martin (1977), and Schattsnieder (1960).
22. The definition of politics utilized here is derived from Miller (1962). For discussions of political behaviours in organizations and the sacrifice of technical efficiency for political expediency see, for example, Bacharach and Lawler (1980), Bower (1983), Burns (1961), Clegg (1981), Giddens (1979), March (1962), Mintzberg (1985), Morgan (1986), Pfeffer (1981).
23. Kahneman and Tversky (1979, 1982, and 1984).
24. Devons (1961), Feldman and March (1981), Meyer and Rowan (1978), Morgan (1986), Quaid (1993).
25. Touche Ross (1989a). The report was published in April, when Siscot was considering the combined Taurus 3 and Taurus 8 model.
26. Ross and Staw (1986).
27. See, for example, Bazerman's (1994) and Staw and Ross's (1987a) reviews of the literature.
28. Gowler and Legge (1983), Quaid (1993).
29. Berger and Luckmann (1966), Meyer and Rowan (1978).
30. Drummond (1991b).
31. Brockner and Rubin (1985), Rubin and Brockner (1975).
32. Bowen (1987), Bowen and Power (1993), Ross and Staw (1993).
33. Teger (1980).
34. See Bowen and Power (1993) for an interesting exploration of the two factors.
35. Hantuala and Crowell (1994a), Heath (1995), Jeffrey (1992), Kerman and Lord (1989).
36. Griffiths (1990), Langer (1975, 1983), Schwenck (1986).
37. Taurus as described in an internal memorandum from the chairman of Siscot to the Stock Exchange Council and the Group of Fifteen (a UK subset of the Group of Thirty), 4 Sept. 1989.
38. Ross and Staw (1993).

39. Schwenk (1988).
40. Janis (1989).
41. Cohen *et al.* (1972).
42. Bateman (1983), McCain (1986).
43. I appreciate that membership of the Stock Exchange is a legal requirement for firms to trade. Laws can be changed, however.
44. Burrell and Morgan (1979), Morgan (1980, 1983), Morgan and Smircich (1980). The idea of triangulation is based upon Allison (1971), Gioía and Pitre (1990), and Morgan (1990).

8

Building Taurus

It all looked marvellous in the prospectus.

(Patrick Mitford-Slade)

Settlement systems take a long time to build and are expensive. France has been working on hers since 1949. Japan spent £560 million and was dissatisfied with the result.[1] So, when the Taurus prospectus, published in March 1990, promised delivery of a comprehensive infrastructure within eighteen months at a cost of £45 million, the media were impressed. The *Financial Times* called the proposals lucid.[2] The costs and benefits analysis prepared by the consultancy firm Coopers and Lybrand was deemed a praiseworthy exercise.[3] Taurus promised to save the equities industry £255 million over ten years, plus the invisible benefits arising from enhanced confidence in the UK market. The project received a further boost a few days later when the government promised to abolish the half-per-cent stamp duty on share transactions when Taurus was implemented. The prospectus described the Taurus timetable as 'aggressive, deliberately ambitious' in order to galvanize the market into action by emphasizing the reality of Taurus.[4]

'WHY DO WE HAVE TO BUILD IT THREE TIMES?'

Just how ambitious was the timetable? Some respondents felt that it was driven partly by market pressure and the perceived need to do something *urgently*. One senior technical manager said:

I thought the project was going to go to rack and to ruin because the commitments made to the community were not being matched by the schedule of deliverables necessary to achieve those dates. We were not getting specifications for these things in order to build them. We were just getting instructions to build them. I said, 'This is not a viable way forward.'[5]

The Stock Exchange technical team had had their share of difficulties where previous projects were concerned. Consequently they
had refined their working procedures in order to allow more time to
be spent upon more detailed requirements phases of the projects:

When we started looking at Taurus we thought, 'OK we've done quite a
lot of development work now and we've had problems. We've not been
able to deliver things as quickly as we would like . . . We did quite a lot of
work analyzing why and decided that part of the difficulty was we
weren't getting the requirements right enough at the front end. So we
decided to spend more time getting the requirements straightened out so
that when we came to build, it would be fairly straightforward.[7]

In the event, however, the requirements never stood still for
long enough to enable the technical team to deploy their preferred
methodology.

Having obtained the market's commitment to Taurus, it was
vital for the Stock Exchange to retain it. The technical team therefore began constructing the outer parts of the system first. A member of the technical team explained the strategy:

Things had to come out to the market-place. You don't go into limbo. You
don't go behind locked doors and say two and a half years down the
road, 'Oh guys, got a system here. You know about it, this Taurus thing?'.
. . . The technicalities were doable—ultimately. It was a question of how
one went about it and the way we had to go about it seemed ridiculous.[8]

Besides, participants needed to build their own systems to link
with the Stock Exchange. Accordingly, the technical team began
disseminating information. The problem was that the design was
still being changed by the Stock Exchange project board. The
result was chaotic, as one programmer recalls:

More records came in, some went out, things on record changed, the
description of what the record was used for might grow. That process
happened too many times. . . . It used to drive us crazy. We felt we were
giving information too early . . . but people were very keen to see the
direction we were going, what the records might look like. There was
tremendous pressure to produce something.[9]

Once people saw what the records might look like, they then
wanted to change them, right down to the last detail such as the
number of characters per line or the number of lines in an address
box. The Stock Exchange's previous policy of consultation re-

bounded as constituencies began to interfere with plans. The problems were exacerbated when the market dropped the idea of owning a share in settlement via the Clearing House. With no stake in Taurus, the equities industry embarked upon a 'free-for-all'. No sooner had one modification been agreed in one quarter than another party demanded something different. A member of the Taurus monitoring group recalls:

There were multiple meetings at multiple levels with different constituencies who would have to interface with Taurus and were constantly impacting on its structure and design: 'We are the custodian community and we would need this sort of information. We are the registrar community and we would need this sort of information and we would input in this way.' So they [the technical team] were constantly saying, 'OK, well, we will have to recode and redo to cope with that.' Then software manufacturers would say, 'Ah but then you have to make this change and you have to make that change and you have to interface these things that are now from different suppliers.' So the complexity just grew and grew.[10]

'Why do we have to build it three times?' said an exasperated manager.[11]

As the Stock Exchange continued to revise its documentation, the Vista company was faced with the problem of trying to match the new requirements to the parts of the system they had already built. It was an intricate task to say the least.

'NOBODY STEPPED FORWARD AND SAID, "I DON'T REALLY
UNDERSTAND THIS." '

What was the Stock Exchange building? Taurus seemed to have no definable parameters or limits. One investment banker said, 'I kept asking, "What is Taurus?" and was never satisfied with the answers yet nobody stepped forward and said, "I don't really understand this." '[12]

Taurus was overseen by a series of boards. The Taurus monitoring group, as it became known, consisted of senior representatives of the equities industry. Their role was to see Taurus connected to the external market and to advise on priorities. The group met for just one and a half hours every month: 'Someone comes in and talks to you for most of the time. You ask a few questions and they go away again,' said one member.[13]

'All we were doing was hearing reports and throwing in concerns,' said another.[14]

'How do you control a group?' demanded a third. 'You formalize it, bureaucratize it, and give it lunch.'[15]

A typical discussion ran as follows:

We'd ask, 'How can you achieve that?' or 'Have you checked with your user group that they like that?' To which the answer was usually, 'Yes, don't worry about that. We have got that under control.'[16]

Despite such assurances, the monitoring group soon felt uneasy. For example, they received reports on software development, some of it being done 'in-house', some of it contracted out to various suppliers:

We said, 'How is all this going to come together?'

And they said, 'Well, we have an integration plan, and we have a testing schedule, and we have all these other things.' And they had a lot of them. Yet there was never a sense that the project was under control.'[17]

The City is a tightly knit community. A few members of the monitoring group had worked with some of the project team for a long time. The plans were taken apart and avidly discussed during Friday night drinking sessions after work. Time-scales were calculated, re-calculated, and debated. The results were disquieting. One member of the monitoring group said:

I drew some graphs quite early on, plotting planned deliverables against actuals. At one point the graphs weren't even converging. They were showing delivery at infinity. Even when they started to converge they were showing delivery in 1995.[18]

'IT WAS A CRUCIAL DECISION. IT WAS THE WRONG ONE.'

Taurus required an engine to drive the system. In computing the engine is known as the software. One possibility was for the Stock Exchange to commission a software house to write the necessary programs. This option was rejected because of previous unsuccessful experiences. Another possibility was for the Stock Exchange to undertake the task itself. This idea too was rejected because it would have required 150 to 200 staff and eighteen months to two years to complete the work. A member of the technical team continues the story:

So, what's the faster way of building it? You go off and you get a package. I thought, 'Oh yes, I don't believe there are such things upon the shelf to do the sort of things we do.' You've got to stop and ask yourself, 'Why?' . . . Take one transaction. It's between a market maker, a broker, it involves a client; that's three parties. It involves a registrar. That's four parties, and it involves the Stock Exchange doing some accounting, so it's got five parties. It may have Inland Revenue connotations too. . . . It is a very complex interrelationship, and those, when you model them, actually are where the difficulties lie.[19]

Indeed, there were no such packages available. The Stock Exchange initially examined about sixteen. Ian Cormack of Citibank (chairman of the monitoring group) and John Watson contributed suggestions. Only three seemed potentially viable. Even then none was a perfect fit. The evaluation team chose a package known as Vista. Vista is a good package. Some of the technical team felt, however, that it was inappropriate for the purpose. They argued that Vista was primarily a custody package and was never designed to drive settlement. They favoured building from scratch.

Bill Widdis disagreed; he felt it was nonsense to replicate work unnecessarily. Finally he put an end to the argument. It's my decision,' he said. Some of the technical team subsequently lobbied John Watson to countermand the proposal. John Watson reviewed it and decided to let it stand. Bill Widdis recalls:

He [John Watson] didn't know whether it [the decision to use Vista] was the right one or the wrong one. He thought that in principle it was correct to shorten the development cycle and to have the facility to supplement the system.[20]

The monitoring group was notified of the decision. A member describes the group's reaction to the proposal:

Like any board, the management comes along and says, 'We have spent six months in due diligence. We have looked at these different suppliers and we have ranked them in this order against these different criteria and we think these are the people to go with.' Unless you happen to know a great deal more than they do and can say, 'No, you have missed something very serious,' what tends to happen is you say, 'Well, OK . . . this isn't a capricious thing . . . you have actually gone to some effort and work and analysis, . . . and OK, you think this is the right thing to do.'[21]

The monitoring group asked the standard questions, such as 'Have Vista got the capacity to undertake the work, do you think they have got the competence? To which the answer was, "Yes, yes, we have checked all of that." '[22]

One member of the group felt the decision to utilize a package was wrong in principle:

I have been building systems for twenty-five years and you get a feel. . . . I was dead against buying American software and changing it because I believed that it would need to be changed far too much. All these off-the-shelf products are fine if you just tinker round the edges. If you have to re-engineer them to anything more than 20 per cent . . . you always have to travel.[23]

'It was a crucial decision,' said a member of the technical team. 'It was the wrong one.'[24]

'HOW LONG IS THIS PIECE OF STRING?'

The Vista package was initially supplied for a three-month trial period. The contract to purchase the package was signed in June 1990. The agreement provided for alterations to be paid for on a time-and-materials basis. Although Vista's daily rates compared favourably with UK consultancies, nevertheless the Stock Exchange would have preferred a fixed price because time-and-materials contracts make it difficult to control costs, 'a licence to print money' according to some managers. Vista declined to enter into a fixed price.[25]

The evaluation team estimated that the tailoring of Vista would take about a year and would cost approximately £1 million. When you try on a shirt or a pair of trousers it is easy to see what adjustments are required. A software package is a different proposition. There is nothing to see as such. It can only be understood by studying detailed engineering documentation. Vista's documentation was not what the Stock Exchange expected. Only one person, the programme manager, understood the workings of the whole system. The programme manager then suffered a heart attack, leaving the technical team to piece together the jigsaw with other Vista staff as best they could.[26]

As the technical team's understanding deepened, they realized that the software would require more alteration than was originally thought. A member of the team said:

Like all these things, they have a product which does a certain task. It has some similarities but when you examined it at any level of detail, it wasn't really there. Probing it more and more, we realized how way off beam this was going to be. . . . We said, 'What is Vista going to do out of this totality of an outline design we think we might have got?' We had to break it down into chunks: 'Well, Vista should be able to do all this,' and then we talked to Vista about various things and: 'Well, we can't do that. We don't handle it. Anyway it doesn't work very well . . .'[27]

Vista had done extensive and highly commended work in the UK. It was therefore assumed that they were familiar with the intricacies of UK practice. Not so, as Vista discovered to their surprise and as the Stock Exchange discovered to their cost. Although the language is similar the meaning can be different. For example, when a rights issue is made in the UK, share allocations are on the basis of 'two for one'. In other words, for every one unit of stock held, an investor receives two extra new shares. In America, however, 'two for one' means that for every one item of stock held, an investor receives only one extra share. Likewise, American dating structures for settlement are different from those in the UK. Time was lost before such errors were discovered. Then more time was lost explaining UK practice to Vista and repeating work. As 1990 wore on deadlines began to slip.

Such difficulties were trivial compared with those that followed. When the Vista package was evaluated substantial parts of Taurus were marked 'To be announced.' Moreover, parts of the system that were clear when the contract was signed had since changed. A Stock Exchange technical manager said:

You should never . . . buy a package unless you have firmed up on the requirements and preferably have a pretty damn tight design so that you are able to put a framework around precisely what you want them to do with their product. . . . At the time we had a set of high-level requirements but no real design of how the whole lot would be put together.[28]

Vista were willing to make adaptations but at what price? The budget for alterations was being rapidly eaten up by so many unforeseen developments. One member of the team recalls the looming sense of insecurity:

Vista would say, 'If you want to do it that way, we'll do it that way. Whatever you want, we can do it. It's not a problem!'
   And we'd say, 'Well, how long is this piece of string?'

'We-ell, as long as you wanna [*sic*] make it. Whatever you want, we can change it . . . it's not a problem.'[29]

Yet the alterations were a problem. The Vista Corporation was not a software house but an enterprise with one ready-made product to install. Accustomed to making minor alterations only, they were ill-equipped to perform the wholesale rewriting now required by the Stock Exchange. Software engineering requires elaborate working methods. Vista had no such mechanisms in place. Inevitably, deliveries were slower than expected.

There were problems in the Stock Exchange too. Bill Widdis retired from the Stock Exchange in early 1991. Thereafter the management of the interface between Vista and the Stock Exchange weakened: 'We started to get that nasty feeling that you had told them what you were after and it was coming back in a different way,' said a member of the technical team.[30] That was hardly surprising as there were four different groups of technical staff, each giving different instructions to Vista in accordance with their diverse views on how the package should be used.

Vista originally estimated that the project would require fifteen to twenty staff. By 1991 the number employed was over seventy, as faxes and E-mails were transmitted back and forth between London and New York, decisions made, countermanded, and changed again. A member of the technical team said:

Sometimes we would put an idea to them for evaluation and they would go and evaluate it and then build it. And then we would say, 'We are not going to go that route . . . because there is something not quite right about this.' . . . And then later on down the track you'd find that some of the old ideas . . . had resurrected themselves. It was like one of those toys you bash with a hammer. You bash one peg down, another one flies up at you. Bash that peg down again, another one flies up![31]

'THEY WANTED REGULATORY APPROVAL FOR SOMETHING THAT DIDN'T EXIST.'

As 1990 wore on, another problem emerged. Taurus proposed to remove paper from share transactions. In law, paper is important. Paper is the means whereby property rights are established and changed. Taurus involved supplanting share certificates, contract notes, and written registers by electronic transfer. It also entailed the creation of new parties to a transaction, known as account holders. What were the legal implications of all this?

This question had been a worry from the start. When Siscot concluded its deliberations, the legal ramifications of dematerial- ization remained a 'niggling doubt' according to Patrick Mitford- Slade, though when Peter Rawlins arrived he was advised that the legislation involved only 'five or six pages worth of mechanics'.[32]

The Taurus timetable assumed that the draft regulations for the new system would be published by October 1990. This deadline was critical because until the regulations were clear, the project require- ments could not be finalized. Initially the feedback from the consul- tation exercise was encouraging. In September 1990 informal reports from the DTI indicated 'A few problems but nothing insurmount- able.' That soon changed. The prospectus indicated that the precise legal framework had yet to be determined, 'some . . . details . . . may change' it said.[33] Parts of Taurus were marked 'To be announced'. Law is synonymous with precision. John Redwood recalls:

In the beginning they wanted regulatory approval for something that didn't exist on paper. . . . They hadn't thought through all the details about how it would work. We were constantly striving to get them to define all the details of the system. . . . You need to know every kind of transaction. It is no good saying you will sort it out later. So when, for example, the Stock Exchange were unable to explain the procedures for rights issues and nationality issues for large corporations, we could only send them back to consider.[34]

The issues, moreover, were extremely detailed and complex. A person buying shares, be it one or one million, acquires partial ownership of a company and is entitled to attend meetings, vote, receive dividends and perks, and so forth. Shares are a form of property and can be given away, sold, mortgaged, or otherwise disposed of.[35] Every last detail had to be legislated for. A member of the monitoring group recalls:

There were endless arguments about whether Scots Law had to change and whether the register could be kept outside the company . . . whether the register of companies incorporated in Scotland could be maintained on a computer in London. . . . Enough to try the patience of a saint.[36]

The abolition of certificates and the institution of company account holders to maintain records of share holdings on investors' behalf proved to be a more far reaching change than anyone had realized. Since investors would no longer hold shares, what would they receive? One thing was clear: 'You couldn't hack this one under existing company law,' said a member of the monitoring group.[37]

The lawyers eventually solved the problem by creating a new concept of ownership. Instead of owning shares outright, investors would now own an entitlement to shares. It was an extremely complex idea which no one really understood. For example, the Coopers and Lybrand briefing on the subject said:

> If investors do not hold the right of entitlement, what do they hold? Regulation 29 answers this question: investors hold an interest in entitlement, the entitlement itself being held by the controller *to the account* of the investor, or *account holder*.[38]

As to what an interest in entitlement meant in practice, readers were advised to consult with their lawyers.

The change from direct ownership to entitlement involved a complete revision of the existing regulatory framework. The lawyers of the Department of Trade and Industry (DTI) warmed to their task. There were regulations specifying arrangements for the issue of new uncertified shares. There were clauses covering the transition to electronic transfer of title. There were rules governing the approval and supervision of controllers and provisions for the compulsory transfer of entitlements from one commercial controller to another if the Stock Exchange considered that investors were at risk. There was legislation enjoining account controllers to ensure that the correct authorization code was quoted. There were requirements as to record-keeping and reconciliation and so on and so forth. The Stock Exchange felt the DTI was being pedantic in insisting upon legislating for every contingency. The DTI thought otherwise. The 'five or six pages of mechanics' blossomed into over 100 pages of intricate clauses and sub-clauses.[39] Meanwhile, as the days turned into weeks, the timetable slipped further and further.

'MY JAW DROPPED . . .'

Whatever the prospectus might say about Taurus facilitating wider and deeper share ownership, and how the needs of the private investor were central throughout the planning process, the reality was that Taurus had been designed first and foremost for the institutions. Research conducted at the time of the Powell Report in 1982 suggested that private investors would probably react favourably to dematerialization.[40] Even so, in January 1989 Touche Ross had urged the Stock Exchange to investigate private investors' attitudes towards dematerialization.[41] This issue was largely brushed aside, however, because the needs of the institutional sector dominated the debate.

From mid-1990 onwards letters began appearing in the press from private investors hostile to Taurus. Taurus, it was claimed, would result in increased costs and make trading more difficult. The proposed abolition of share certificates drew particular malevolence. Although Taurus would generate statements, in law the evidence furnished by such records would be secondary to the electronic transfer. Computer records are highly vulnerable to corruption and accidental eradication. Change, moreover, can be difficult to prove. The Stock Exchange's public relations department tried to counter the bad publicity by emphasizing the disadvantages of share certificates. Private investors were reminded that share certificates require safe keeping, and that they cost twenty-five pounds to replace if lost. No one was assuaged. 'At least if you have a share certificate you can hold it in your hands—like a £20 note . . . ,' wrote one observer; 'it's not the same as reading a statement claiming you own it.'[42]

The existing system required a signature on a transfer form and the production of a certificate before shares could be sold. Once such documents were abolished, and shares held in trust by a commercial account holder, what mechanism would prevent a fraudulent dealer from selling a client's shares without authority? How would a registrar know that an instruction to change a name on the company register was genuine? Institutional investors are less vulnerable to deceit in so far as they can treat such risk as a commercial matter and protect themselves accordingly. The DTI was more concerned for private investors because they had no option but to place their trust in an agency who they could know little about. Where were the safeguards for the private investor promised in the prospectus?

The precise and detailed security implications of dematerialization had also been marked 'to be decided later'. The DTI demanded that Taurus incorporate a system of personal identification numbers. A two-part code was envisaged. The first set of digits would identify the investor. The second part would comprise a unique random number created for specific transactions and known only to the investor. When an investor wished to sell stock it would be necessary to quote the full code, which would serve as a form of 'electronic signature'. The Stock Exchange was dismayed by this new complication. It would require active investors to maintain a series of codes each thirteen digits long. Peter Rawlins observed that such a safeguard was unlikely to 'go down a bundle' with those whom it was designed to protect.[43] Moreover, applying it to institutional trades would require fund managers to supervise thousands of codes and ensure that the correct one was used for each trade. 'Scope for the most almighty muddle,' commented Coopers and Lybrand.[44]

Personal identification numbers would reduce but not eliminate the risk of fraud and accidental erasure. Again, where were the safeguards promised in the prospectus? The Stock Exchange assured the minister that Taurus was risk-free. John Redwood played his ace: 'As it is risk-free you will therefore be happy to offer an indemnity,' he told the Stock Exchange.[45] 'My jaw dropped,' said Peter Rawlins. 'I said, "Are we trying to stay competitive in the world, or are we just trying to run a club?"'[46]

The minister was unmoved. His job was to protect the public interest. 'We have an old-fashioned settlement procedure that works. We couldn't have a new one in London that didn't work,' he said.[47]

The sum initially suggested was £250 million. The Stock Exchange first thought of insuring it themselves. When this proved impractical they consulted the market. The premium demanded was said to have been astronomical.[48] It hardly suggested that Taurus was risk-free. The chief executive returned to the DTI:

I [said] 'John, you know I can't pay the money for this.'
He was quite adamant. 'Unless you do, I won't approve the regulations.'[49]

The Stock Exchange found itself trapped by its own rhetoric. Meanwhile the retail stockbroking constituency had done its homework. Peter Rawlins said:

It was a very difficult thing to stand up and say to the world, 'Look, frankly we are not doing this for Mrs Snooks of 22 Acacia Grove and her 100 ICI.' We were not trying to put her out of business or make it difficult for her but we definitely did not have her as number one priority. ... Furthermore, Mrs Snooks had a lot of allies in the private-client stockbrokers who used to lobby hard the politicians: 'What is going to happen if Mrs Snooks' shares get ripped off?'[50]

Another bombshell awaited the Stock Exchange. As early as 1989 the DTI had said that Taurus should be voluntary. The Stock Exchange, however, had proceeded on the assumption that listed companies would be legally required to join Taurus. 'No,' said the DTI. The consultation process confirmed the department's original view. Taurus must be voluntary.

Now, in addition to all his other responsibilities, John Watson faced the prospect of making presentations throughout the UK in order to persuade shareholders to join Taurus. The chief executive was angry. The Government had previously allowed companies to change designation from 'Ltd' to 'Plc' without obtaining shareholder's resolutions:

Would they do that for Taurus? Would they hell! The Government said everybody has to have a choice here and if a company don't wish to get rid of share certificates, they don't have to.[51]

It was at this point that many of the people I interviewed said that the project should have been stopped.

NOTES

1. London Business School (1993*b*).
2. 'Taurus', *Financial Times* (10 Mar. 1990), 24.
3. Ibid.
4. London Stock Exchange (1990*a*, *b*).
5. Interview, member of Stock Exchange technical team, June 1994.
6. Interview, member of Stock Exchange technical team, May 1994.
7. Ibid.
8. Ibid.
9. Ibid.
10. Interview, member of Taurus monitoring group, June 1994.

11. Interview, member of Stock Exchange technical team, July 1994.
12. Interview, investment banker, July 1994.
13. Interview, member of Taurus monitoring group, June 1994.
14. Interview, member of Taurus monitoring group, July 1994.
15. Interview, member of Taurus monitoring group, Sept. 1994.
16. Interview, member of Taurus monitoring group, June 1994.
17. Ibid.
18. Interview, member of Taurus monitoring group, Nov. 1993.
19. Interview, member of Stock Exchange technical team, May 1994.
20. Interview, Bill Widdis, June 1994.
21. Interview, member of Taurus monitoring group, July 1994.
22. Interview, member of Taurus monitoring group, June 1994.
23. Interview, member of Taurus monitoring group, Nov. 1993.
24. Interview, member of Stock Exchange technical team, May 1994.
25. Interview, member of Stock Exchange technical team, July 1994.
26. Interview, member of Stock Exchange technical team, May 1994.
27. Ibid.
28. Interview, member of Stock Exchange technical team, Nov. 1994.
29. Interview, member of Stock Exchange technical team, May 1994.
30. Interview, member of Stock Exchange technical team, May 1994.
31. Ibid.
32. Interview, Peter Rawlins, Oct. 1993.
33. London Stock Exchange (1990) p. 17.
34. Interview, John Redwood, Nov. 1994.
35. Chalton (1990), Mercer (1991).
36. Interview, member of Taurus monitoring group, July 1994.
37. Interview, member of Taurus monitoring group, Nov. 1993.
38. Coopers and Lybrand Deloitte (1991), issue 4, p. 3; italics in original.
39. See DTI (1991).
40. London Stock Exchange (1982).
41. Touche Ross (1989*a*).
42. Goldstein-Jackson, K., 'The Hidden Costs of Taurus', *Financial Times* (31 Aug. 1991), 6.
43. Interview, Peter Rawlins, Oct. 1993.
44. Coopers and Lybrand Deloitte (1991), issue 2, unpaginated.
45. Interview, John Redwood, Nov. 1994.
46. Interview, Peter Rawlins, Oct. 1993.
47. Interview, John Redwood, Nov. 1994.
48. John Redwood (personal communication, Sept. 1995).
49. Interview, Peter Rawlins, Oct. 1993.
50. Ibid.
51. Ibid.

9

Chickens Come Home

It was slipping a hundred per cent . . .
(Member of the Taurus monitoring group)

The first public sign that Taurus was in difficulties came in January 1991 when implementation was postponed for six months, from October 1991 to April 1992. The delay was blamed upon the Department of Trade and Industry's failure to produce the regulations in time. The media reacted calmly: 'The market felt it was under extreme pressure to meet October: so there will be a measure of relief and recognition that this is a realistic action,' John Watson told the *Financial Times*.[1]

In May 1991 a reduced compensation fund of £100 million was agreed with the DTI and the draft regulations duly published. The following week the launch date for Taurus was again postponed, this time by one month to May 1992. 'On the building of systems we are ninety-five per cent of the way there,' said Watson.[2]

Yet even the revised timetable was to prove inadequate. The technical team did their best. Many worked long hours, struggling to maintain key project management disciplines, such as documentation and testing. John Watson's unavoidable absence was a blow to morale and efficiency. Although project meetings continued to be held, it was not the same as having John Watson regularly in the chair.

The building of Talisman had been overseen by a team of external monitors who reported regularly to the Stock Exchange Council. It had been intended that Touche Ross would undertake this task for Taurus but they had been sacked from the project a year ago as part of a cost-cutting exercise.

Chris Rees of Touche Ross wrote to the chief executive to protest against the decision:

I believe that our role is a valuable one, not only for the Exchange but also to reassure the wider investment community, given the great importance which the City and the Government attach to the project and given its size, complexity and chequered history.[3]

Observers too were dismayed. 'I didn't think Touche were adding much value but I quite liked their presence. . . . To have a resident whistle-blower was extremely important,' commented a member of the monitoring group.[4] 'Disastrous for a start,' said a member of the Council.[5]

In August 1991 the Stock Exchange announced a further delay of two months. This time it was attributed to difficulties with the software. John Watson told the press that the scale of the task had been underestimated: 'A hiccup and not a disaster,' he said; 'I don't expect it to happen again.'[6]

By September, however, the edifice was clearly under strain. John Watson came under intense pressure to announce a new date for Taurus. He committed himself to 'some time in early 1992'.[7] There were problems, however. External constituencies continued to demand changes to the design. The rate of delivery from the Vista Corporation was failing to keep up with the timetable. Added to that were the emerging problems with the technology. Taurus incorporated a high level of security, including encryption (transmission of messages in code) and non-repudiation (storing archives for seven years). The system, moreover, utilized 'tamper-proof' hardware, that is, machines which automatically switch off if, for example, an unauthorized person attempts to use a screwdriver to gain entry. No prototype existed; there were delays as manufacturers who were themselves in a learning curve delivered late. Added to that, a whole module now needed to be rewritten as a result of the DTI's consultation exercise. Even so, John Watson was given to understand that the requirements were 'virtually finished'.[8] 'And they virtually were,' said a junior programmer. 'The problem was, how virtual?'[9]

'THAT DOESN'T SOUND ABSOLUTELY RIGHT.'

Again the press reported that the market was responding calmly to the delays. Although there were calls for Watson's resignation, the *Financial Times* reminded everyone that it had been widely acknowledged that the original timetable was highly ambitious, adding, 'There is widespread if grudging respect for Mr Watson in the securities industry, and a feeling that if he cannot bring Taurus off the drawing board, no one can.'[10]

The software houses undertaking work for the Stock Exchange were undismayed by the delays and the recoding.[11] Likewise technical staff working in the banks and broking houses were pleasurably absorbed: 'We couldn't see how it would fit together,' said one employee, 'but we were enjoying working on the project.'[12]

There were signs, however, that the commercial imperative for Taurus was waning. Newsletters published by Coopers and Lybrand were continually exhorting the market to think through the strategic implications of Taurus, to attend to operational details such as staff training in new computer codes, and to familiarize themselves with the legislation: 'Do be sure someone in your organization reads through the Stock Exchange's weighty documentation very thoroughly,' they urge.[13] Systems designers were enjoined not to slacken their pace but in the same paragraph are warned, 'Beware the publication later this month of the revised system specifications, which we suspect will contain some significant changes.'[14]

Information technology plays an important role in sustaining competitiveness in the financial services industry. As far as the banks, brokers, and investment houses were concerned, Taurus was just one project amongst many and not necessarily the most vital. An investment banker said, 'To us, every Stock Exchange project has represented a cost and not always a lot of benefit.'[15] The resource implications of Taurus were formidable. For instance, share certificates would no longer serve as collateral for loans. Lenders would therefore need to search thousands of records in order to arrange new security. 'This is no easy problem,' acknowledged Coopers and Lybrand. 'Literally millions of shareholdings are held as collateral at the moment primarily by banks, and all these must be identified, verified, and recorded in the right commercial account.'[16]

Retail custody posed another problem. What of the many thousands of share certificates lodged with banks for safe keeping? What was to be done about the strongboxes lodged in vaults? The banks had no idea what the boxes contained. Would Taurus result in droves of customers suddenly dispensing with the service? One clearing bank (its holdings still on a manual register) conducted a pilot study to assess what was involved in contacting customers, organizing partial refunds, and so forth. Was it worth expending time and effort on Taurus when Coopers and Lybrand were advising, 'The following notes represent our understanding of the current position—but since the situation is very volatile, don't be surprised if things change soon!'?[17] Likewise Coopers and Lybrand observed that whilst there were advantages in joining Taurus early, those first in the queue would serve as test pilots requiring 'verve and fortitude'.[18]

A custodian described his reaction to developments:

You always get the feeling in the middle of a project that it's all going awry but you give it a chance. You let this restructure happen and that new project manager have a go. That was perpetual. . . . Looking back, our view was, 'Good, that's improvement.' But in the back of our minds, 'That doesn't sound absolutely right.'[19]

Despite an injunction from Coopers and Lybrand that: 'We strongly advise that you do not use the recent announcement to down tools,'[20] the delays and constant changes to Taurus tempted firms to do just that. As management teams asked themselves the question, 'Are we going to put resources into Taurus?', increasingly the answer was 'No. Let's wait and see.' Discreetly, one by one, firms began transferring their development teams onto other work.[21]

'THERE WAS ALWAYS AN ELEMENT OF HOPE . . .'

By now the Taurus monitoring group felt Taurus was far from sounding absolutely right. 'We were given nice timetables but they never seemed to be meeting any of the deadlines,' said a member of the group.[22] In June 1991, another member of the group wrote to the Stock Exchange to express his anxieties:

There were always new things being brought in because they had to be brought in. I felt the project wasn't being managed properly. I felt there were far too many consultants involved, that there weren't enough senior permanent staff with clear responsibilities.[23]

Asked why no one pressed their doubts, he replied:

There was always an element of hope that we are 50 per cent of the way there, we are now 60 per cent of the way there. Now the hundred per cent was shifting away. That was my worry. Whenever I see a project where the hundred per cent starts moving, that concerns me.[24]

The monitoring group began asking the technical team for more information. The table became festooned with sheets indicating progress since last meeting, issues open, plans for next month, and so forth. It made little difference because the real problem was the constantly evolving state of the project. A member of the group recalls:

You'd say, 'How many of these issues have you resolved?' And they would say, 'We have resolved all of them.'

And there was another page that was 'risks': 'What risks are you running?' There was a long list of risks . . . every meeting they'd come with this chart and that chart and they would say 'We have resolved all these issues, and now we have got another set of issues . . .'

So there was lots of progress. Every meeting lots of progress from where you were in the last meeting. However, when you sat back and said, 'Are we any closer to the end?'

'We-ell, not really.'

And that was really what was happening. . . . You knew people were working hard and they were getting work completed and putting it behind them and then they discovered there was a whole set of other things.[25]

Time and again the technical team reassured the group that everything was under control, despite set-backs. One member said, 'Perhaps I listened to him [John Watson] too much but I felt that with him in charge the project would succeed and without him it wouldn't.'[26] Another member of the group said:

It's easy to look back and say, 'Why didn't you see it all the time?' Well, most disasters look obvious in hindsight. When you are in the middle of it and your objective is to get to the end you take each issue and you try and deal with it, and then another issue and you try to deal with it, and another issue and you try to deal with it.[27]

Peter Rawlins was asked to attend some of the meetings. 'I hear your concerns . . .,' he told the group; 'thank-you for your contribution.'[28] Members were unconvinced. The chief executive seemed to be more interested in the restructuring exercise of the

Stock Exchange which he had initiated. 'It was very difficult to get him to focus on Taurus,' said one member. 'He always seemed to want to wash his hands of it.'[29]

'IS THIS STILL OK?'

Rawlins was a lot more uneasy about Taurus than appearances suggested:

> The boys were having trouble with the technology . . . The regulations were getting more and more complex . . . requirements being built which were nothing to do with the original specification. . . . Nobody is telling me there is any great problem but the time has gone. [So] I weighed in. I banged heads. I said, 'I have been here for a year now, where is it? This will not do!'[30]

Richard Wilson, a partner of Coopers and Lybrand, was asked to review the project. Rawlins said, 'I asked them, "Is this still OK guys? I am nowhere near this and it is worrying me." '[31] The review took about a fortnight to complete. It concluded that Taurus was still feasible but could not be implemented for May 1992. 'Forget it. You have missed it by twelve months,' Wilson allegedly told the Stock Exchange.[32] The review indicated that the earliest possible date for implementation was April 1993 and then only if no further problems developed.

Meanwhile the Stock Exchange Council had been dissolved and replaced by a board. The aim was to give the Stock Exchange a more commercial ambience. The former Council, described by Peter Rawlins as 'a load of dinosaurs', promptly formed a private dining club and designed their own dinosaur tie.[33]

As the 'dinosaurs' retired to the sidelines, the chief executive pondered what to do about the revelations contained in Wilson's report. Rawlins felt he had more important things to worry about than Taurus. According to one manager, the chief executive was not pleased: 'He [Rawlins] had hoped to go to his first board meeting with a strategy for the Stock Exchange. Instead he had to eat humble pie over Taurus.'[34]

The chief executive did indeed receive a frosty reception from his new board:

It was along the lines of what I came to call a 'sharp intake of breath syndrome'. . . . They [the board] rounded on me as chief executive: was I satisfied about these budgets, budgets to time as well as money? They were worried about how much more time because it was seen as an embarrassment. I said, 'Fellers we can stop this.' In my view the issue was not . . . is this the right cost or the right time, as to which there had to be respectively doubt, the question I said we should be asking is whether we should be doing this at all . . . is this the right project?[35]

The board returned to the issue of budgets and time-scales: 'Peter, are you satisfied?' they repeated.[36] Rawlins replied:

I said that provided the Government enacted legislation within promised time-scale, provided there were no further changes to the project, and provided there were no more problems with the technology, then yes, I was content. But, big provisos.[37]

The board accepted the chief executive's recommendation and approved funding until March 1993. Significantly, the next Coopers and Lybrand newsletter emphasized that immediate milestones were now within the 'direct control' of the Stock Exchange. The bulletin further notes the new date for completion was dependent upon a smooth run. Even then, the newsletter continues, the eight weeks allowed for final testing were almost certainly bound to prove inadequate.[38] 'I think the Exchange was hoping that it was going to go a damn sight better than their advisers were telling them,' commented another.[39]

Peter Rawlins had his doubts too. He had considered stopping the project. However, the various reassurances he had received and his preoccupation with other matters led him to act against his better judgement:

IBM came back and said, 'Don't worry, we will hack it.' The DTI said, 'Don't worry, we will enact these regulations, we won't slow it up any more . . . .' Coopers came back and said, 'It's fine.' On the strength of the answers I got, the decisions I took were correct. . . . Of course, with perfect hindsight I should have had the degree of probing I forced through at the end of 1992. . . . I can only put that down to the fact that at the time Taurus was frankly a pain in the bum, an irritation. . . . The other things I was doing were massive, pioneering . . . far more challenging. They needed every ounce of my intellectual and professional energy. So, that was one opportunity that I had, and I just didn't like the smell of it.[40]

NOTES

1. Barchard, D., 'Stock Exchange Delays Taurus Launch to Next Year', *Financial Times* (26 Jan. 1991), 5.
2. Dunham, R., 'Countdown to Taurus', *Accountancy* (May1991), 107.
3. Letter from Rees to Peter Rawlins, 22 Jan. 1990. Rawlins's reply (dated 25 Jan.) confirms the decision was made pending 'a generic piece of internal work aimed at developing appropriate policy guidelines governing the use of independent external monitors'.
   Touche Ross never returned to the project.
4. Interview, member of Taurus monitoring group, Sept. 1994.
5. Interview, former member of Stock Exchange Council, May 1994.
6. Dobie, C., 'Taurus Hit by Further Delays', *The Independent* (10 Aug. 1991), 15.
7. Interview, member of Stock Exchange technical team, Dec. 1994.
8. Interview, member of Stock Exchange technical team, Nov. 1994.
9. Ibid.
10. Waters, R., 'Man with a Bull by the Horns', *Financial Times* (18 Sept.), 11.
11. Interview, independent consultant, Apr. 1994.
12. Telephone interview, UK clearing bank employee , Apr. 1994.
13. Coopers and Lybrand Deloitte (1991), issue 2, unpaginated.
14. Ibid. issue 1, unpaginated.
15. Interview, investment banker, Nov. 1994.
16. Coopers and Lybrand Deloitte (1991), issue 1, unpaginated.
17. Ibid. issue 2, unpaginated.
18. Ibid.
19. Interview, custodian banker, Nov. 1994.
20. Coopers and Lybrand Deloitte, issue 2, unpaginated.
21. Interview, senior official, UK clearing bank, Dec. 1994.
22. Interview, member of Taurus monitoring group, July 1994.
23. Interview, member of Taurus monitoring group, Nov. 1993.
24. Ibid.
25. Interview, member of Taurus monitoring group, June 1994.
26. Interview, member of Taurus monitoring group, July 1994.
27. Interview, member of Taurus monitoring group, Apr. 1994.
28. Interview, member of Taurus monitoring group, Nov. 1993.
29. Ibid.
30. Interview, Peter Rawlins, October 1993.
31. Ibid.
32. Interview, member of Taurus monitoring group, Sept. 1994.
33. Patrick Mitford-Slade (personal communication, Nov. 1995).

34 Interview, former Stock Exchange employee, Sept. 1994.
35. Interview, Peter Rawlins, Oct. 1993.
36. Interview, member of Stock Exchange board, Sept. 1994.
37. Interview, Peter Rawlins, Oct. 1993.
38. Coopers and Lybrand Deloitte, issue 8, unpaginated.
39. Interview, member of Taurus monitoring group, Sept. 1994.
40. Interview, Peter Rawlins, Oct. 1993.

10

A Second Opportunity Lost

> There was nothing in the history of the project that would
> lead to such optimism.
>
> (A member of the Taurus monitoring group)

This chapter analyses events leading up to the decision made by
the board of the Stock Exchange in the autumn of 1991 to allocate
further funding to Taurus. This decision is theoretically significant because it was made in the light of clear knowledge that the
decision-makers' original expectations would not be met. The
decision is especially interesting because in retrospect, some people close to the project felt that it should have been stopped. The
focal questions for analysis are (1) why did the decision-
makers persist? and (2) was persistence a rational response to
circumstances?

According to the decision dilemma theorists withdrawal is
logical when it becomes clear that decision-makers' expectations
will not be met. In theory, then, it was absurd to persist with
Taurus beyond 1991.[1] According to the literature irrational
persistence is initially driven by decision-makers' unwillingness
to admit failure. Then as the difficulties become increasingly
apparent, continuance becomes a matter of maintaining appearances.[2] It is a matter of record that the project was not stopped in
1991 despite considerable negative feedback. Accordingly, the
researchers' guiding propositions for analysis at this juncture are:

1. Persistence is initially explained by information equivocality.
2. Once it becomes clear that expectations will not be met, persistence is dictated by psychological and social pressures coming
   into play sequentially.

Although the focal decision for analysis in the present study is
the board's decision to allocate further funding to Taurus, it is necessary to examine the rationale for a whole series of decisions

leading up to that point. The 'decision-maker' is defined as the Council of the Stock Exchange (latterly the board), advised by the chief executive. In order to gain a proper perspective, however, it is necessary to consider the actions of other players, including the market and the Taurus monitoring group.

FROM ABSOLUTES TO SHIFTING SANDS

In their experiments concerning project completion and escalation, Conlon and Garland cautioned that some of their extrapolations were extreme and therefore potentially unrealistic: 'A project that had consumed 90 per cent of its budget yet was only 10 per cent complete might suggest woeful mismanagement. Wouldn't such a project have been terminated long ago?'[3] The present case exemplifies the difference between experimental pen-and-paper exercises and real conditions. In autumn 1991, Taurus was nought per cent complete in that it was still eighteen months away. Moreover, it had consumed 100 per cent of its budget. It was obvious, therefore, that the decision-makers' expectations had not been met. Moreover, the emergent legal complexities, the objections from private investors, and all the technical problems which had been encountered augured badly for the future. According to decision dilemma theorists, withdrawal now becomes highly probable as intense negative feedback destroys commitment.

The theory contains a tautology, however. It suggests that persistence can only be described as irrational if the decision-maker's information clearly indicates that reinvestment will not meet 'the outcome standards of the future'.[4] A striking feature of the data at this juncture is that when it becomes clear that initial expectations will not be met, the decision-makers revise their expectations. The change occurs initially through a series of postponements and is ultimately sanctioned by the board approving funding until April 1993. Moreover, they do so in the knowledge that there is a risk that future expectations, that is, completion by April 1993, will not be met: 'big provisos,' the chief executive reminds the board.

Prospect theory might suggest that the decision-makers had lost sight of the absolute magnitude of change. Whilst that may have been true of shorter postponements, when the definitive decision was taken to reinvest in Taurus, the deadline for completion was a full eighteen months away at least. Prospect theory might also suggest that the decision-makers preferred the risk of future deadlines not being met to the immediate loss of cancellation or substantial modification of the project.[5] There is little evidence to support this proposition either. Cancellation was an acknowledged possibility but there was no significant discussion of the pros and cons by the board or at the lower echelons of the Stock Exchange.

Another possibility is that escalation was socially motivated. It is inconceivable, for example, that John Watson was unmoved by approbation he received, and this may have been a factor in encouraging him to proceed despite all the difficulties: 'If he cannot bring Taurus off the drawing board, no one can.' Yet it was the board and not John Watson who were the ultimate decision-makers. The board were said to have been embarrassed by the delays. There is little evidence, however, that the board's decision to persist was driven by a collective sense of shame. Indeed the board's acerbic reaction suggests that if anything, embarrassment came closer to producing withdrawal than persistence. Emotion, it seems, may act as a stimulant to action but it does not necessarily dictate what that action shall be.[6]

Besides, all of these explanations presuppose that the decision to continue with the project was irrational. Economists argue that the more invested in a 'long-haul' project such as Taurus, the more sensible it is to persist.[7] Since it was known from the start that the timetable was highly ambitious some adjustment would surely have been justified. What is interesting is that the adjustment appears to have been made without recomputing the cost–benefit analysis, and amidst signs that the commercial imperative for Taurus was declining. Does this mean persistence was foolhardy?

In order to make progress it is necessary to side-step the question momentarily and instead examine what was happening. Basically, the decision-makers' actions amount to a series of gambles. Some of these fail, thus compounding the difficulties. There is little evidence, however, that gambling behaviour is based upon overconfidence or an erroneous belief that the goal is close to realization, as suggested by the social-psychological literature.[8] Instead, the decision-makers appear to have been walking a tightrope between what was technically feasible and what the external market would tolerate. The decision rationale at various critical junctures represents a finely balanced political calculation.

A critical decision was the commitment to an 'aggressive' timetable: The Stock Exchange, because of its reduced influence in the market place following 'Big Bang' was forced to take due accord of the market's demands for an urgent solution to the settlements' problem. It was also unable to resist the market's insistence upon a highly complex design. Taurus was built upon a contradiction in that it was both urgent and extremely complicated. Those two factors, urgency and complexity, compelled the Stock Exchange to speed up the building programme.

Similarly the short time-scale was one reason for utilizing a software package instead of building from scratch. That decision in turn forced the Stock Exchange into an undesirable contractual arrangement. The decision to build the outward parts of the system first prompted further interference with the project, hence the spiralling complexity and constantly changing requirements which ate into the already precarious timetable. By tracing the sequence of decisions it becomes evident that each was a rational response to a previous decision. It is the cumulative effect of all these decisions which makes the decision-makers' behaviour seem bizarre.

The blaming of two major delays on exogenous factors, the portraying of shorter delays as a 'hiccup and not a disaster', and the repeated assurances to the Taurus monitoring group—'Yes, yes, we have that under control'—are indeed examples of impression management. It does not follow, however, that such behaviours were irrational or that they produced irrational persistence in the manner implied by social-psychological theorists. The claims were made mainly in response to interrogation by a potentially hostile market. Information is by no means a neutral entity. It is highly susceptible to manipulation and distortion. It was commercially necessary, therefore, for the Stock Exchange to be circumspect in its reports. Otherwise detractors might have used such information to undermine the project for their own business purposes.

The tactics adopted by the Stock Exchange were escalatory because they made it increasingly difficult to engage in the sort of open and constructive discussion which is conducive to problem solving. Instead the Stock Exchange became trapped in vicious circle.

THE GREAT AND THE GOOD

The favourable cost–benefit analyses generated by Coopers and Lybrand could also be interpreted as an example of biased information processing, that is, the Stock Exchange erroneously convinced itself that the project was financially more beneficial than it really was in order to justify proceeding with Taurus.[9] However, the analysis applied not to the Stock Exchange but to the market. The market's reaction is interesting. The media suggested that the figures were optimistic. It is thought that privately some players were sceptical about the assumptions. Yet no one protested publicly. The same applies to all the delays and changes to the project. Instead of demanding a review which might have saved much subsequent waste, the market limits its support for the project by covertly directing development resources elsewhere. Meanwhile, having failed at Siscot, the private-client stockbroking constituency continues the contest by lobbying the Government: 'What if Mrs Snooks' shares get ripped off?' The effect is to seriously undermine the project without appearing to do so deliberately.

At the macro-level persistence is explained by political correctness.[10] No constituency wanted to be seen to 'scupper' Taurus, so 'Nobody stepped forward and said, "I don't really understand this." ' Yet the situation is hardly one of collective myopia. Escalation theory is bounded by the notion of progressive investment in a deteriorating situation. The present study shows how escalation predicaments are capable of multiple meanings.[11] As the Stock Exchange escalates its involvement by committing more resources to the project, simultaneously withdrawal has begun.

ESCALATION AS INSTITUTIONALIZATION

The foregoing analysis leaves much unexplained. For example, why did the Taurus monitoring group apparently ignore reliable data showing delivery in 1995? Why did the technical team never step forward and suggest a rethink? Why did the chief executive recommend continuance despite his better judgement? Why did the board apparently side-step the vital question, 'Is this the right project?'

It is clear from the data that there are no definitive answers to such questions. Indeed, ultimately, not even the decision-maker knows why he or she acted in a certain way.[12] For example, in the present case the chief executive cannot fully explain his crucial decision to recommend further funding for the project. He says, 'I can only put that down to . . .'

If we step back from the detail there is a 'golden thread' running through the decision-maker's behaviour. The thread may be called 'institutionalization'. Institutionalization is defined here as a form of code. It is a shared expectation about what is appropriate behaviour in a particular set of circumstances. For example, in medical school students are taught 'correct' clinical practice. To break the code is to act in a manner which would be regarded by others as unthinkable.[13] Viewed from this perspective, Taurus owed its survival not to dissimulation or incompetence but to the observance of due diligence.

The Role of Management

One reason why Taurus survived was that the efforts of key players were concentrated upon trying to make the project work. Such behaviour is consistent with the managerial stereotype of 'getting things done' despite obstacles. One feature of institutionalization in the present case is that of manager as 'problem solver, negotiator, and fixer'.[14] For example, the monitoring group contribute to the debate on the legal implications and other changes affecting the project. The chief executive and the project director negotiate over compensation and security arrangements with the DTI.

The technical team likewise respond in an institutionalized fashion. They may have chuckled at Philip Hooker's report (see Chapter 5). Subsequently they were sometimes angry and frustrated: 'How long is this piece of string?' Ultimately, however, their job was to build the system, not to challenge whether it was worth building. Accordingly they concentrate upon solving the problems, coding and recoding, bashing one peg down, then another and another.

The board too discharges its duty in the proper manner. In UK company law a board member may be extremely stupid so long as they are honest.[15] Board members are not expected to delve deeply into complex issues. In the present case, the chief executive correctly emphasized that the new time-scale was heavily contingent: 'big provisos', as he puts it.

'Are you satisfied . . .?' the board replies.

The chief executive can only repeat, 'Yes, I was content. But, big provisos.'

Due diligence has been observed but the real problem ('Is this the right project?') has been side-stepped.

Institutionalized behaviour is escalatory because it leads to first-order thinking.[16] Attention is riveted upon solving the problem rather than questioning the problem itself. When one problem-solving strategy or control technique fails, decision-makers respond by applying 'more of the same', that is, they try another engineering technique, or demand more detailed information. Likewise the chief executive haggles with the DTI over the compensation figure at the expense of considering the problem as symptomatic of a deeper malaise. When events begin to contradict the 'nice timetables' the monitoring group responds by demanding more detailed information. The exercise is futile because it merely generates 'more of the same', that is, more charts and more explanations which are subsequently contradicted by events: 'Every meeting lots of progress. . . . However, when you sat back and said, "Are we any closer to the end?"

"We-ell, not really." '

The group then asks the chief executive to attend. Since the chief executive's job is to defend the project in public, the meeting falls far short of an open and constructive exchange. Inevitably it is reduced to ritual: 'I hear your concerns . . . thank you for your contribution.'

INSTITUTIONALIZED ACCEPTANCE OF AUTHORITY

Escalation is thought to result from a 'can-do' mentality on the part of decision-makers.[17] The present case suggests that what may appear as a 'gung-ho' attitude may be rooted in the institutionalized acceptance of the managerial prerogative.[18] Many members of the technical team were working long hours. They had been unable to utilize their preferred methodology. They had experienced the frustration of constant changes. The tasks which lay ahead were extremely difficult. Yet there is no evidence that subordinates rebelled. Consequently those in authority may have believed that the situation was more hopeful than it really was.

To some extent management creates the forthcoming decision débâcle. It is a speculative point, but it seems reasonable to suggest that if there had been a full and reasoned discussion about the problems in 1991, the project might have been cancelled with honour. Alternatively a realistic time-scale would have been determined. There would then have been no failure.

Institutionalization and Information

Institutionalization is also evident in the giving and receiving of information. In theory, information is the key to problem diagnosis. In practice decision-makers' information may lead them away from the truth rather than towards it.[19] For example, the information fed to the Taurus monitoring group satisfied all the symbolic requirements—'we were given nice timetables'—yet never really told the group what they most wanted to know. It was not just that the Stock Exchange was being cautious in its reports. The observance of due form reduced communication to a ritual: 'Someone comes in and talks to you for most of the time. You ask a few questions and they go away again.' The group responded in an equally ritualistic fashion, receiving reports, throwing in concerns, asking predictable questions which invited predictable answers. For example, 'Have you checked with your user group that they like that?' Both parties, supplier and receiver of information, are locked into institutionalized expectations about what is appropriate. No one anticipated, for example, that the technical team would reply, 'Yes, we have checked with the user groups and they raised the following reservations . . . and we wondered what you thought about it.'

When mistakes occur in organizations they are usually assumed to result from a breakdown in rationality. The present study highlights how decision debacles may be caused not by a *breakdown* in rationality so much as by *rationality* itself.[20] In approving the choice of Vista the decision-makers conscientiously considered the available options and chose the package which most closely matched the requirements. Although it was open to the monitoring group to express reservations about utilising a package, their attention was largely concentrated upon the three alternative packages set out before them. The process functions like a sausage machine. The documentation submitted to the group is prepared according to received practice. It is evaluated according to received practice. Note how the language reflects institutionalized expectations about what is appropriate in management, 'work', 'effort', and 'analysis'. The monitoring group asks all the right questions. The process is systematic and thorough; the epitome of good practice. Yet the decision is flawed in principle.

Knowledge is power but only if it is timely and apposite. Initially the chief executive was powerless to stop Taurus from going ahead (see Chapter 7). By 1991 the situation had changed. It is not powerlessness which explains the chief executive's actions at this juncture so much as his absorption with higher priorities. It is correct practice for managers to order their attention in accordance with organizational exigencies. The response to emergent problems is also correct, that is, the chief executive commissions a review of the project. The chief executive asks the rational question, that is, is Taurus still feasible: 'Is this still OK?' Another sausage machine is thus set running. The information generated by that investigation then forms the basis of a crucial decision. The whole episode is an example of textbook practice. The trouble is that the chief executive's information says nothing about the value of the project.

Players' most disquieting information was either intuitive or unofficial. For example:

—'There was never a sense that the project was in control.'
—'That doesn't sound absolutely right.'
—'I am nowhere near this and it is worrying me.'

Those feelings were disturbing because they contradicted received reports. As events subsequently showed, players' intuition was well founded. Yet for most of the time, they seem to have felt unable to act upon it. Players' reluctance to act reflects the dominant view of management as cerebral activity whereby detailed information gathering and analysis are the only acceptable bases for action.[21] To use a courtroom analogy, vague fears and disturbing senses are inadmissible in the decision-making process.

The same applied to unofficial data. For example, the graphs showing delivery at infinity and latterly in 1995 were based not on 'gut feel' but hard fact, 'taking the plans apart'. It could be argued that disquieting feedback was counterbalanced by the technical team's enthusiasm and ostensible confidence. Whilst the data certainly suggest that the audience may have been moved by charisma—'I felt that with him in charge the project would succeed and without him it wouldn't'—there is no evidence that the group were swayed in the way that the American Government was said to have received John de Lorean's presentations. Manipulation of information is thought to succeed because it detracts from hard statistical data.[22] In the present case the contradiction between the technical team's confidence and reality contributed not to escalation, but to anxiety.

This suggests an interesting possibility. John de Lorean's exercise in persuasion took place before the venture became a conspicuous loss-maker, whereas in the case of Taurus the prognostications were made in the face of slippage and other evidence of serious problems. Two plausible hypotheses suggest themselves. First, manipulation of information may only succeed where decision-makers have not yet experienced the sharp pain of failure. Second, manipulation attempts in the face of failure may accentuate the impact of negative information.

Returning to the issue, it is much more probable that players felt constrained because their information was unofficial. Decision dilemma theorists treat information as a neutral entity.[23] Information is a weapon.[24] The present case exemplifies the sheer power of received information over unofficial data—however reliable the latter. The tragedy of Taurus is that in organizations it is often better to be wrong for the right reasons than to be right for the wrong reasons.

The Impact of Organizational Factors

One theory of escalation is that persistence may eventually be dictated by the sheer weight of the corporation.[25] This would imply that by 1991 Taurus had become so organizationally embedded and so surrounded by vested interests that continuance was inevitable regardless of the Stock Exchange's interests. The data contain very little evidence for this proposition. Although some of the software houses were doing well out of Taurus, there is no evidence they exerted a force for continuance. Likewise, although the market had invested in Taurus, that interest was counterbalanced by the knowledge that the project was potentially detrimental to certain other business objectives. Besides, the market was already curtailing investment in the light of developments despite exhortations to the contrary, for example, 'Do not use the recent announcement to down tools.' Taurus certainly represented a major part of the Stock Exchange's organizational infrastructure. Yet almost two-thirds of the Stock Exchange establishment had or were about to be made redundant, so that can hardly have been a restraining factor. As far as the chief executive was concerned, such massive consumption of resources was a good reason to close Taurus down. Indeed, he tells the board, 'We can stop this.'

An Organizational Dichotomy

There were other organizational factors at work, however. Escalation theory is predicated upon the notion of a single venture. The present study highlights the impact of multiple and conflicting goals on escalation.[26] The dismissal of Touche Ross destroyed one of the checks and balances which had been incorporated into the system. It seems unlikely that they were dismissed for expressing reservations about Taurus. Such dissent was precisely what the chief executive wanted to hear. It is much more probable that the decision was indeed motivated by a desire to cut costs. It was imperative that the Stock Exchange reduced its overheads. The project monitors were apparently adding little value to Taurus. However, their role was symbolically significant: 'I quite liked their presence. . . . To have a resident whistle-blower was extremely important.' So, what was a sensible decision from one standpoint was 'disastrous' from another. It was the interplay between conflicting rationales that made the situation seem absurd.

The pursuit of multiple rationales is also evident in the organizational dichotomy between the technical team and the decision-makers in the Stock Exchange. Experimental scenarios assume that the business case and the professional case for continuance of a venture are identical. In the present example the professional case for continuance was arguably sound. Considerable technical ingenuity had been invested in the project. Moreover, respondents consistently maintained that the technicalities were 'doable, ultimately'. Whether the project justified such efforts was another issue.

Experimental scenarios further assume that in decision-making there is one right answer. In reality, professionals often differ in diagnosis and prescription. In the present case, for example, some players disagreed with the decision to buy a software package in principle, whereas others thought it was sensible, in principle. There were risks in utilizing a package but there were also risks in trying to build from scratch.

The notion of utility maximalization assumes that all options and their consequences are known. Since this is seldom the case, some decision theorists argue that, in practice, information serves to legitimize decision-making. In this case, evaluation procedures clothe decision-making with a rhetoric which gives it the appearance of scientific objectivity.[27] Ultimately choice depends upon the balance of power between the respective parties, that is, who ever is successful in establishing the dominant view: 'It's my decision.'

The divergences of opinion and conflicting priorities which emerged during the building of Taurus could only be addressed by a deep and sustained interchange between the decision-makers and the technical team. No mechanism existed to facilitate such an exchange. For example, there were no consultative committees, nor were the trade unions active in the organization. If anything the organizational arrangements worked to minimize the likelihood of informed debate.

Experimental evidence suggests that professionals are less likely to make escalatory judgements than inexpert decision-makers.[28] Again, the present case exemplifies the difference between experimental paper-and-pencil exercises and field conditions. Experiments test responses to the technical parameters of decisions such as whether to continue drilling in the face of so many abortive wells. Such scenarios tacitly assume a single decision-maker with full knowledge and authority to act. In the present study the Tayloristic separation of planning from execution and task division meant that few members of the technical team knew enough about the project to make an authoritative judgement.[29] Staff were briefed on a 'need-to-know basis'. For example, only a few members of the project team saw the contract with the Vista company. Experiments which utilize professionals as respondents may be testing the extent to which individuals subscribe to received practice. The proportion of respondents who opt to drill more wells or authorize further loans may not necessarily be making an irrational choice but may simply be using unconventional decision criteria. That does not necessarily mean that they are wrong.

The paucity of upwards communication mechanisms is traceable to the history and culture of the Stock Exchange. Organization culture is defined as 'the way we do things round here'.[30] The Stock Exchange, like many organizations in the City of London, was fairly authoritarian. It was perfectly legitimate for a manager to say, 'it's my decision,' and for that decision to be final. Moreover, the easy communication between staff and management found in some organizations was absent. Neither the chief executive, the chairman, or the Council (latterly the board) were much given to the practice of 'management by walking around'. Consequently they were largely unaware of staff concerns about the timetable commitments being entered into. Likewise when it was said that 'requirements are virtually finished,' there was little opportunity for junior staff to contradict this claim. By the time senior management realized that there were four groups in the Stock Exchange each giving different instructions to Vista, much damage had been done.

Despite all the resources that were lavished upon Taurus, gaps existed in the project infrastructure. For example, after the DTI declared that Taurus membership must be voluntary, John Watson was forced to concentrate on public relations at the expense of leading and managing the technical staff.

The present study suggests that what may appear as delusion or self-deception on the part of decision-makers may just reflect their obliviousness to the true state of affairs. In the present case structural weaknesses impeded the flow of information. Corporate optimism was partly the bliss of ignorance.

SYNTHESIS

Figure 10.1 attempts to synthesize the foregoing analysis into a coherent framework. At the macro-level escalation reflects an institutionalized acceptance of the perceived will of 'the great and the good'. Likewise, within the Stock Exchange, Taurus is still perceived as strategically important. Viewed from this perspective, persistence is explained by a political 'non-decision'[31] which allows expectations to be revised without the basic worth of the project being questioned.

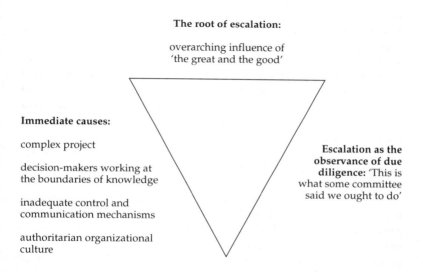

The root of escalation:

overarching influence of
'the great and the good'

Immediate causes:

complex project

decision-makers working at
the boundaries of knowledge

inadequate control and
communication mechanisms

authoritarian organizational
culture

**Escalation as the
observance of due
diligence:** 'This is
what some committee
said we ought to do'

FIG. 10.1 Escalation in decision-making

At the meso-level escalation emerges as the observance of due diligence. Due diligence reflects institutionalized acceptance of role prescriptions by the decision-makers. Everyone does what they are supposed to do, no more and no less. The institution of management, with its emphasis on accomplishment, authority, and scientific objectivity, contributes to escalation by using its skills to make Taurus work. The decision process resembles a sausage machine. Information is assembled and processed in accordance with received practice. Decision-makers ask predictable questions and receive predictable answers. The process is clothed in a rhetoric of scientific objectivity. Rhetoric imparts a sense of certainty to what is basically guesswork and opinion.

The observance of due diligence is escalatory because it becomes a substitute for taking effective action. Effective action, however, requires people to break out of their role prescriptions— for example, it requires a board member declaring, 'I want to talk to staff and see the situation for myself.' Since such behaviour would be regarded by others as unthinkable, it rarely occurs. Instead decision-makers know something is 'not quite right' and may even be heading for disaster, but feel powerless to stop it. Thus does 'escalation in decision-making' become 'decision-making in escalation.' Escalation is caused not so much by a breakdown in rationality as by rationality itself.

At the micro-level escalation is caused by weaknesses in the organizational control mechanisms which stifle debate and prevent important information from reaching the decision-makers. In the present case the situation was exacerbated by an authoritarian management culture. The effect was to lull decision-makers into a false sense of security. They knew things were not going well, but could not have realized just how bad they had become.

Each escalation paradigm is partial. As the three sides of the triangle are linked, however, it is possible to obtain a more holistic perspective.[32] To illustrate the point, let me take just one strand of the story. Viewed from a 'wide-angle' lens, Taurus survives because of a political 'non-decision'. The 'non-decision' is primarily the result of the overarching but largely invisible influence of the Group of Thirty but is also facilitated by the value premises of the institution of management. The chief executive, for example, still thinks the whole project is misconceived but his efforts are now directed at trying to make it work and discharging other organizational priorities. Besides, he has little idea of just how bad things are because no mechanism exists to alert him to the difficulties, and the culture of the Stock Exchange works against problem sharing and open debate. The organization's culture is a microcosm of management practice within the City itself: 'When they get in their dining rooms and decide that something will happen . . .'

CONCLUSIONS

It was expected that persistence would result either from information equivocality or from psychological and social pressures. There is little evidence to support either proposition. The present case belies the idea of decision-makers investing more resources in a desperate attempt to conceal failure or in order to cover embarrassment. Moreover, by 1991 it was clear that expectations had not been met by a substantial margin, and it was highly doubtful that reinvestment would result in Taurus being implemented by April 1993.

A striking feature of the data is that decision-makers' expectations prove to be highly flexible. When the timetable slips, expectations are revised without recomputing the cost–benefit equation. Moreover the board approves substantial reinvestment knowing that the new deadline is highly contingent. There was indeed nothing in the history of the project to justify optimism. Continuance occurs because of a political 'non-decision' which included the myth that settlement services were still strategically important to the Stock Exchange. In 1991 the dominant viewpoint had weakened, but it held.

The dominant viewpoint held principally because decision-makers were unable to surmount institutionalized norms about how they should behave. Escalation is characterized not by irrational persistence as depicted in the literature, but by the image of due diligence. It is the cumulative effect of so many parties discharging their duty in support of the dominant viewpoint and in the face of a stream of negative information which makes escalation appear bizarre.

In a nutshell, the project survived the crises of 1991 because building Taurus 'was what some committee said we ought to do'.

NOTES

1. Bowen (1987) suggests that it may be necessary to invoke social-psychological explanations if decision-makers proceed beyond a point where it is clear that expectations will not be met.

2. Ross and Staw (1986), Staw and Ross (1987*a*). The authors have subsequently modified this idea, pointing to the significance of political factors in escalation (Ross and Staw 1993). Drummond (1994*a*) concludes that escalation in complex organizations is basically political.

3. Conlon and Garland (1993: 412).

4. Bowen (1987).

5. Kahneman and Tversky (1979, 1982, 1984).

6. Drummond (1995) suggests that the factors thought likely to produce escalation might also be conducive to withdrawal and possibly irrational withdrawal. For example, when a decision turns sour decision-makers may actively look for trouble.

7. Northcraft and Wolfe (1984).

8. See, for example, Gist and Mitchell, (1992), Griffiths, (1990), Langer, (1975, 1983), and McCarthy, *et al.* (1993).

9. For example, Staw and Ross (1978), Conlon and Wolf (1980), Caldwell and O'Reilly (1982), O'Reilly (1980), and Borrgida and Nisbett (1977), Nisbett and Ross (1980).

10. The multi-paradigm approach to analysis draws on Burrell and Morgan (1979), Gioía and Pitre (1990), Gioía *et al.* (1989), Morgan (1980, 1986), Morgan and Smircich (1980).

11. See also, for example, Morgan (1986), Young (1989).

12. Allison (1971).

13. Institutionalization is defined after Bacharach and Baratz (1970), Berger and Luckmann (1966), Meyer and Rowan (1978), and Zucker (1977).

14. See, for example, Hales (1986), Mintzberg (1973), Stewart (1989).

15. Oliver and Marshall (1994).

16. Watzlawick *et al.* (1974).

17. Janis (1989) has suggested that NASA's 'gung-ho' culture was instrumental in causing the spaceship *Challenger* disaster.

18. Formal power here is defined as structurally sanctioned. For the purposes of the present study the definition embraces the concept of authority, that is, a manager's acknowledged right to command and an employee's obligation to obey (Gerth and Mills 1991).

19. For example, Devons (1961), Drummond (1991*a*), Feldman and March (1981), Gowler and Legge (1983), Meyer and Rowan (1978), Morgan (1986).

20. Aram (1989).

21. Intuition is defined here as a chain of reasoning which cannot be accounted for (e.g. Hayes and Allison 1994, Simon 1987). The idea of management as an institutionalized activity is emphasized by, for example, Alvesson and Willmott (1992), Frost (1980), Steffy and Grimes (1986). The institutionalised approach to information is drawn from Mintzberg (1994) and Mumby and Putnam (1992).

22. Schwenk (1986).
23. Bowen (1987).
24. See, for example, Drummond (1991*b*), Pfeffer (1981).
25. Staw and Ross (1987*a*, *b*).
26. For discussions of organizations as pluralities see, for example, Mintzberg (1985), Morgan (1986), Pettigrew (1973), Young (1989).
27. Devons (1961), Drummond (1991*a*), Meyer and Rowan (1978), Morgan (1986), Quaid (1993).
28. Brody and Lowe (1995), Garland *et al* (1990), Jeffrey (1992).
29. Braverman (1974).
30. See, for example, Ray (1986).
31. Bacharach and Baratz (1963, 1970).
32. Based upon Allison (1971), Gioía and Pitre (1990), and Morgan (1990). See Chap. 2 for a more detailed explanation.

11

The Final Months

'Are we any closer to the end?'
'We-ell, not really.'

(a member of the Taurus monitoring group)

1992 opened on a relatively optimistic note for Taurus. A new budget had been approved by the Stock Exchange board. The proposal for a thirteen-digit personal identification number had been dropped in favour of retaining some form of written contract note. The Government had abandoned its attempt to legislate for every aspect of Taurus. Instead, it was agreed that the Stock Exchange would produce its own code of practice. The project finances were set to improve as the chief executive had renegotiated some of the more expensive Taurus contracts:

One of the things I did to put salt on the tails of all these people who were working for the Exchange, . . . I decided, unilaterally, late in the day, to renegotiate some of those contracts, to improve the Exchange's position. . . . Some of those clauses [were] . . . a licence to print money. . . . it took as long as it took. I stopped that. I unilaterally modified the contract. People said to me, 'You can't do that.'

And I said, 'Watch me.'

And I just did. Somebody's got to stand and take some commercial views about some of these things.[1]

So, with a brake on costs and Taurus not expected to appear for at least another fifteen months, the way seemed clear for the project team to get on and finish the work.

By early summer, however, difficulties erupted once again. In May 1992, the specialist financial magazine *The Banker* published an article charting the outstanding work. The article was subtitled 'The Long, Long Road'. It seemed apt in the light of the stages and procedures still to be completed. Anyone reading it was bound to wonder how so much activity could possibly be crammed into the next eleven months.[2]

Besides, was the 'long, long, road' still worth travelling? Although the chairman of the Stock Exchange preferred to describe Taurus as 'much awaited' rather than 'long delayed'— 'Many superlatives spring to mind,' he told the press[3]—the market had long since sunk into depression. John Watson persistently reminded the City that Taurus was the largest single computer project in the UK and possibly Europe. That was precisely the problem. One asset manager recalls, 'He said it was on a scale most of us couldn't imagine, when we said, "All we want is a system that allows people to talk to one another." '[4]

In May 1992 Philip Hooker of Hoare Govett took the opportunity of a Coopers and Lybrand breakfast briefing to reiterate his views on Taurus. Taurus, he told the assembled representatives of the securities industry over their orange juice and croissants, was rapidly being overtaken by events. Operating costs would be much higher than originally estimated. Moreover, the anticipated upsurge in trading volumes which would have offset prices had failed to materialize. When Taurus was planned the Government had been keen to encourage wider share ownership. Now the policy had changed in favour of creating tax havens for private investors. Consequently, share ownership had deepened rather than widened. Conversely, Hooker warned that the need to streamline settlement was becoming ever more acute as the economic recession had cut profit margins in the securities industry. Hooker predicted that unless Taurus was simplified it would be bypassed in favour of cheaper and readily available solutions. Taurus, he argued, was conceived when investment in information technology was seen as the key to competitiveness. According to Hooker, received wisdom had changed:

Nowadays, people are not spending several years building an ideal system, they are instead determining their strategic direction and making a series of small, pertinent, low budget moves in that direction. . . . The trouble with TAURUS is that it is a Seventies idea, with an Eighties budget, which has become dislocated from the tough, competitive trading conditions of the Nineties.[5]

In July 1992 the consultancy firm Touche Ross published the results of an attitude survey entitled 'Taurus: Is the Market Ready?' The report claimed that the market was 'plagued by doubts' because of all the delays and changes to the design.[6]

According to Touche Ross, the market blamed the Stock Exchange for the problems and called for the Exchange to be more honest over timetables. The document also suggested that the market was entertaining second thoughts about the whole project. The following quotations purporting to be from leaders of the securities industry encapsulate the spirit of Touche's findings:

The full implications were not appropriately understood at the outset. (asset manager, p. 4)

Perhaps immobilisation would have been a faster and cheaper way to achieve the G30 recommendations. (custodian, p. 4)

The goal posts have been moved on several occasions, and now somebody had absconded with them. (asset manager, p. 1)

Although the Stock Exchange appeared impervious to criticism ('They lunched their way out of it,' said Brian Ludlow[7]), the message was not lost. Later that year Peter Rawlins visited a number of firms to see whether the Taurus design could be modified. The Taurus monitoring group also considered the possibilities. The problem was, as they both discovered, Taurus was inflexible. It was all or nothing.

'HOW THE HELL CAN I TELL?'

The date for implementation was now April 1993 provided there were no further delays. In June 1992 this assumption was destroyed when the prototype IBM communications server for the security interfaces failed to work. A member of the Taurus monitoring group recalls:

You realized that you were increasingly operating at the edge of available technology. We were constantly moving out to a point where not even the major suppliers could guarantee that what they were supplying would work.[8]

Although Peter Rawlins told reporters, 'It's going as well as a project of this size, scale and complexity can go,'[9] some City observers were now suggesting to the press that Taurus was destined never to appear.[10]

A month later another blow fell when the retail store chain known as Marks and Spencer declined to put dematerialization to a shareholder vote. Taurus, said a spokesperson for the company, was 'plagued by delays' and 'untested'.[11] Behind the scenes, there was another problem. John Watson accepted the post of project director on the understanding he had full authority over Taurus. Over the past two years, however, his ability to control Taurus had been undermined by the creation of a project executive with different staff responsible for the legal, marketing, and other aspects of Taurus. His ability to supervise the project had already been weakened by unlooked-for public relations burdens (see Chapter 9). The situation was now exacerbated by the need to liaise and negotiate with all the various Taurus functionaries.

By mid-1992 the project team had rewritten almost 50 per cent of the Vista software. The costs of tailoring Vista were approaching £14 million, many times more than had been estimated. As the summer wore on the technical team realized that Vista were proposing to proceed to testing on the basis of trial and error, that is, testing, fixing, and retesting. Whilst Vista's methodology was valid, the technical team considered it inappropriate for a system operating in the public domain. John Watson requested the secondment of another eighteen consultants from Coopers and Lybrand to cope with the situation. 'No,' said the chief executive; 'no more staff and no more money. This is what we are going with.'[12]

By November 1992 the project team were clearly under severe strain. Of necessity, heavy responsibilities had been thrust upon inexperienced juniors. Many staff had been working seventy to eighty hours a week for nearly three years, against a backcloth of a chief executive who seemed to take every opportunity to deride the project. At dinner parties, for example, he habitually referred to Taurus as 'his albatross', a 'bottomless pit', and 'a brick round his neck'.[13] The team were tired; morale was low. John Watson's momentary lapse at a press conference in November said it all. When reporters pressed him to name a new start date he shouted, 'How the hell can I tell? (Don't print that.)'.[14]

It was time to take stock. Watson decided to call a meeting to assess progress and to rekindle the team's enthusiasm and confidence. The meeting was attended by Peter Rawlins's *de facto* deputy Jane Barker. She was said to have been shocked by what she discovered.[15]

'IT WAS ALL STARTING TO BLOW UP.'

Meanwhile the Taurus monitoring group were growing deeply frustrated and concerned as they saw the project slipping month after month. Nothing seemed to change: 'There was always an answer. There was always another piece of work. There was always another dimension that was going to be investigated,' said one exasperated member of the group.[16]

The monitoring group knew that the critical path had been severely disrupted. Some members of the group, however, felt that they were beginning to lose sight of the path altogether. Although the Taurus monitoring group understood the difficulties involved in building Taurus, they were beginning to be overtaken by a sense of futility:

Whenever there was a delay we would say, 'In that case, would you do this, or would you do that?'
And they'd say, 'yes', and by and large it would get done. And then you'd say, 'Are we any further forward?'
And the answer is, 'Yes, you are further forward but you are no nearer the end, because the end keeps moving.'
It is only when the issues accumulate that you finally say, 'When is this going to end?'[17]

That was a question which the technical team were too busy to ask:

We were aware of the slowness of delivery. . . . We were concerned about how well the system that Vista were building would actually match with the one we were building . . . and thinking this is going to be a tricky task to bring to bed.[18]

A major source of tension was the contradiction between official reports and rumours emanating from the lower echelons of the technical team. Some members of the group were hearing informally that it was highly unlikely that future milestones would be achieved anywhere near to time.[19]

Then there was the emerging knowledge that significant portions of completed work were probably useless, as so much had changed in the intervening time. For instance, the coding had been built up over the years, changed, and changed again. Even when Taurus was finally implemented it was inconceivable that the system would plug in and work without some re-engineering.

How much re-engineering though? Would it be possible to patch flaws in the software and re-engineer them later, or, would testing reveal more fundamental problems? There was no way of knowing until testing commenced. Meanwhile uncertainty continued to fuel doubts. It was rumoured that hundreds of programming amendments would be required. It was even being whispered that Taurus might never work in the end. Against this backcloth, the technical team's habitual optimism was beginning to ring hollow. Another member of the monitoring group said:

I don't think anybody was withholding information. I think they were just optimistic and couldn't believe that it wouldn't work. They believed they knew how to make it work but it would just take longer and would cost a bit more. And you would have to put in phenomenal effort to prove that wasn't true.'[20]

Although much had changed in the City since 'Big Bang' it remained a relatively small, cohesive community. Many of the people connected with Taurus had known one another for a long time, perhaps having once worked for the same company, or having served on committees together. Moreover, for all its modern-day sophisticated electronic networks, personal contact has always been the City's most important mode of communication. In 1992 as the autumn leaves began falling, Taurus was increasingly a topic of conversation in firms' private dining rooms and in the City's pubs and wine bars. For example, one member of the monitoring group took supper with a partner of Coopers and Lybrand. The partner suggested that John Watson was being forced to present a brave public face. Why should he not have access to the board of the Stock Exchange?[21] Clandestine visits were made to Government officials and politicians close to the prime minister.[22] Some constituencies in the securities industry began to be briefed almost daily as a sense of impeding crisis enveloped the market: 'People were becoming conscious that certain features of this project were not as good as they [the technical team] were leading themselves to believe,' said a senior investment banker.[23] 'It was all starting to blow up,' said a retail broker.[24]

The question was, what should be done? A member of the Taurus monitoring group explained his dilemma:

All the time one had to be very careful that you weren't going behind people's backs. I was very conscious that if you serve on a group you don't go running round telling tales. . . . It had to be plainer than the nose on your face.[25]

In February 1993 Anthony Hilton, managing director of the *Evening Standard* received a visit from a senior figure in the securities industry allegedly 'desperate' to extricate his firm from Taurus. He supplied Hilton with secretly obtained intelligence indicating why 'the plug should be pulled' on Taurus.[26] Still nothing happened.

Meanwhile three or four dejected members of the Taurus monitoring group discussed with one another whether they should resign. They decided against the idea, fearful that such a drastic statement of 'no confidence' would destroy Taurus completely. Instead, the monitoring group decided that they must now draw the chief executive's attention forcibly to their concerns: 'Otherwise Rawlins will go away thinking he has got us tucked up again for a couple of months,' said one member.[27]

The meeting took place in early 1993. It began gently with members saying, 'We are a little bit concerned about this. . . . This doesn't feel right.'[28] The temperature began to rise as the discussion proceeded round the table and members perceived they were making little impression on the chief executive. The last person to speak pulled fewest punches: 'Baloney . . .,' he told Peter Rawlins. 'The cost equation as to whether it [Taurus] is worth doing doesn't stack up any more.'[29] The chief executive then reported that Stuart Senior, a most senior partner of Coopers and Lybrand, was about to review the project. 'We will prove you wrong,' Rawlins apparently replied.[30] The meeting ended with the customary thanks from Rawlins and an assurance that everything was under control. After he had left the room one member of the group shook his head and said, 'He doesn't know what's going on.'[31]

'I AM COMING UP TO SEE YOU TONIGHT.'

Shortly afterwards the testing schedules were postponed again. This was the last straw for the monitoring group:

Twelve meetings. A year has gone by and you said at the end of these twelve months, 'We haven't really made a hell of a lot of progress.' And at the end of eighteen months, 'We haven't made any progress at all.' And that is when we decided to do something.[32]

On Monday 8 March 1993, the group's chairman, Ian Cormak, sent a fax to Peter Rawlins: 'I said, "We have met and we think that this project is in a crisis." '[33] Rawlins telephoned Cormak immediately. Rawlins said, 'I am coming up to see you [at Citibank] tonight.'[34]

The monitoring group were not advocating closure. Ian Cormak was preparing to demand a change of personnel and a review of the project. Citibank is located on the fringes of the City, near the south bank of the River Thames. Peter Rawlins crossed the generous palm-court floor with its pine and chintz settees at six-thirty. His first words to the astonished chairman of the monitoring group were, 'I have scrapped it.'[35]

NOTES

1. Interview, Peter Rawlins, Oct. 1993.
2. 'Battling on All Fronts', (1992) *The Banker* (May1992), 46.
3. Hugh-Smith, A. H., 'The Time has Come for Investors to Take Taurus by the Horns', *The Times* (2 Sept. 1992), 19.
4. Interview, member of Taurus monitoring group, July 1994.
5. Hooker (unpub. mimeo, 1992).
6. Touche Ross (1992: 4).
7. Telephone interview, Brian Ludlow, Sept. 1994.
8. Interview, member of Taurus monitoring group, June 1994.
9. J. Ashworth, 'Taurus Costs Soaring', *The Times* (16 June 1992), 19.
10. S. Laurie, 'He Who Rides a Tiger', *The Banker* (Feb. 1992), 36–8.
11. P. Hosking, 'Cautious M & S Refuses to Put Taurus to the Vote', *The Independent* (18 July 1992), 17.
12. Interview, member of the Stock Exchange technical team, December 1994.
13. Interview, partner, Coopers and Lybrand Deloitte, December 1994.
14. 'Taurus Keeps City Guessing', *The Independent* (6 Nov. 1992), 29.
15. Telephone interview, partner, member of Stock Exchange technical team, June 1993.
16. Interview, member of Taurus monitoring group, June 1994.
17. Interview, member of Taurus monitoring group, July 1994.

18. Interview, member of Stock Exchange technical team, May 1994.
19. Interviews, member of Taurus monitoring group, Nov. 1993, June 1994, July 1994, Sept. 1994; Interview, Bank of England employee, May 1994.
20. Interview, member of Taurus monitoring group, July 1994.
21. Interview, member of Taurus monitoring group, Nov. 1993.
22. Ibid.
23. Interview, investment banker, May 1994.
24. Interview, retail banker, Nov. 1993.
25. Interview, member of Taurus monitoring group, Oct. 1993.
26. Telephone interview, Anthony Hilton, July 1994.
27. Interview, member of Taurus monitoring group, Sept. 1994.
28. Interview, member of Taurus monitoring group, July 1994.
29. Interview, member of Taurus monitoring group, Sept. 1994.
30. Ibid.
31. Interview, member of Taurus monitoring group, June 1994.
32. Ibid.
33. Interview, Ian Cormak, June 1994.
34. Ibid.
35. Ibid.

12

Revelation

> Every week someone was coming to me with this little prob-
> lem, saying, 'Don't worry, Peter, it will be alright.' But you
> know, we had another week here, and half a week there, and
> another quarter of a million there. . . . There were some peo-
> ple on my board who were embarrassed about it. I was furi-
> ous about it.
>
> (Peter Rawlins)

By mid-1992 the chief executive's mission to streamline the Stock
Exchange had been virtually accomplished. The old Council of
dinosaurs and its innumerable committees had been swept away.
Almost two-thirds of the professional staff had been made redundant.

Change had been accomplished at a price and there were signs of
resentment towards the chief executive. He had let it be known that
he had a poor opinion of many of the senior professional staff. The
human resources department was now nicknamed 'human
remains'. Hostility was fuelled when the chief executive announced
that some of his earlier reforms were in fact only temporary measures and the organization was restructured for a second time.[1]

More importantly, Peter Rawlins had ruffled the City establishment. He had made his deep dislike for the club culture felt. The
press summarized the situation:

Market makers are unhappy about the prospect of introducing order-dri-
ven systems. . . . Registrars are miserable about the delays to Taurus that
are costing them money. Private client firms are worried about being put
out of business by rolling settlement. Big firms are impatient about seg-
menting the market.[2]

Significantly, in July 1992 the Stock Exchange board passed a special vote of confidence in the chief executive. *The Independent*
newspaper conceded that some unpopularity was inevitable
given the magnitude of the changes spearheaded by Rawlins.

Nevertheless, the newspaper continued, 'It would be worrying if he has so damaged his relationships with colleagues, member firms, and investors that he can no longer work with them.'[3]

'I HAD HAD ENOUGH.'

Although Taurus was a 'pain in the neck' to Peter Rawlins, by July 1992 his thoughts were turning towards a possible use for the system.[4] One of his plans encouraging share ownership was to offer private investors automated trading facilities similar to the 'hole in the wall' machines operated by banks. Such a development was impossible in a paper-based environment, however. Taurus held the key to progress. Where was Taurus?

Where indeed? The *Financial Times* noted:

A strong sense of *déjà vu* at the Stock Exchange. Chief executive Peter Rawlins spoke yesterday of the 'very considerable progress' made in the past 12 months in building Taurus.

This time last year he said much the same. Indeed it seemed then that Taurus would have been launched by now . . . To the outside world, not much has changed.

Will Rawlins still be there making optimistic projections next year?[5]

The chief executive's public equanimity concealed his private anger. The latest delays emanating from the failed IBM security package (see Chapter 11) had provoked another hostile response from the Stock Exchange board: 'How much longer and how much more money?' they again demanded.[6] The chief executive's patience failed:

I had had enough two years on of people telling me, 'Don't worry, Peter. It will be with us soon.' All of my antennae telling me that my original instincts that this thing stank were right.[7]

Another cause of ill feeling in the City towards the chief executive was the appointment of Andersen Consultants (Rawlins's former employers) to review the Stock Exchange's trading and settlement computer systems. Competing firms were resentful because the appointment was made without competitive tender. Moreover, part of those services were subsequently contracted out to Andersen.[8]

Andersen commenced work at the Stock Exchange in early 1992. According to the press Taurus was outside their brief.[9] In October 1992, however, Rawlins commissioned them to examine Taurus:

I kept banging on because it didn't ring true to me. Everybody else was prepared to just tuck it under the carpet and keep on asking the easy question, 'How much longer?' . . . Almost superficial due diligence.[10]

The two vital questions he asked Andersen were:

1. 'Is the [Taurus] operating environment . . . wholly compatible with the technical architecture we have built into our trading front? '
2. 'Are you confident you can operate Taurus when it is handed over?'[11]

Andersen reported on 22 December 1992. The report was only eight pages long but it told the chief executive all he needed to know:

1. 'There is no operating system. There is no centre. It is not designed, let alone built.'
2. 'Are we going to be able to operate it? Well, here is a list of fifteen things we have reservations about.'[12]

The chief executive was deeply shocked. Not even his worst moments of doubt had prepared him for such a stark response. Although the technical team had quite openly and deliberately started building the outwards part of the system first, the significance of that decision only became clear to the chief executive as he read Andersen's report. Taurus was a distributed system of 500 computers communicating with one another. In order to do that the system required a unified architecture. Rawlins had not understood that in the rush to keep the market moving forward with what was increasingly seen as a cost burden, technical specifications had been issued before the design was finished. The chief executive was horrified to discover that as late as December 1992, three years after building had commenced, the design was still incomplete. Although requirements were said to have been 'virtually finished' in 1991 (see Chapter 10), the chief executive learned that the technical team were still issuing specifications even though they had begun testing parts of the system. Meanwhile, because of the continuous pressure and unforeseen problems, the technical team had neglected to do anything in the middle. For example, core elements of Taurus such as overnight reconciliation of share transactions and other internal control procedures had been classified as peripheral requirements and were therefore not due to be built until late 1993. It was like trying to construct a house by erecting the walls and roof first and digging the foundations last. As he read the report Peter Rawlins realized the project had reached nemesis:

I was now completely satisfied . . . that there was not an ice-cream's chance of it [Taurus] being built in less than another three years. It was then I decided to stop it, come what may, and to take the rap for it.[13]

'The rap', as Peter Rawlins realized, meant resignation. He spent an unhappy Christmas.[14]

'ONLY THEN IT CAME SCREAMING HOME TO ME . . .'

Stopping Taurus was no light undertaking. First, the chief executive needed more information. Andersen had been instructed to minimize disrupting the work of Coopers' staff.[15] They had therefore been unable to obtain certain definitive detail which the chief executive now needed. Besides, the chief executive knew he could hardly recommend closure on the basis of Andersen's report alone:

I needed them [Coopers and Lybrand] to agree because I knew my board would turn round and say, 'Coopers have been running this thing. This is Rawlins throwing a wobbly. He's lost his bottle.'[16]

Coopers and Lybrand, moreover, were unlikely to declare, 'That's what Andersen say. We agree.'

In January 1993, a senior partner of Coopers and Lybrand, known as Stuart Senior, arrived at the Stock Exchange to examine the project. Some people in the securities market were vaguely curious that 'Coopers had put one of their top men in.'[17] The technical team, however, attached little significance to this development as they were used to outside consultants poring over Taurus. Peter Rawlins recalls, 'To his [Stuart Senior's] credit, he didn't believe it was as bad as I was telling him when he arrived. Within a month he accepted that it was.'[18]

How bad was bad? As the detail emerged Rawlins realized that the whole approach was a nonsense: 'It was only then it came screaming home to me that nobody had really thought about it. Nobody had planned the thing. Nobody had analysed it.'[19] Time had taken its toll too:

There were God knows how many fatal flaws about the whole Taurus technical design, but one of them, one of many of them, was that they decided it was easier to build it around Talisman. . . . So the core of Taurus would have been Talisman. Talisman has been in place since 1979. Disaster! It was the right decision at the time. It was taken because they thought they would try to get the whole thing done in seven months and they thought, 'Let's not bother to change Talisman. We'll get round to changing it in due course.'[20]

Meanwhile the project team had been using a central simulation harness to test the system. Whereas people in the market may have thought they were linking with a real working computer, there was actually nothing in the middle. 'Very sexy,' remarked Rawlins. 'I had rocket scientists working for me.'[21]

The rationale for some decisions was a mystery to the chief executive. Recalling his earlier efforts on behalf of the project with the DTI and the Stock Exchange's suppliers, he said:

I felt that having moved heaven and earth to dig the guys out of their hole, let's get the bloody thing done and behind us. . . . I just never believed they could have done such crass things.[22]

For example:

Let's do it quick and cheerful . . . so, on-line system. On line? The boys had been spending two years buggering about with it to make it a batch system so that it was compatible with 1970s technology. It's brilliant! And daft![23]

It took Stuart Senior until early February to complete his investigation. Meanwhile there was other work to be done. Taurus involved a myriad of contractual relations, actual and potential. What was the legal position with Coopers and Lybrand and with Vista, for example? What about all the firms who had invested millions of pounds in preparing for Taurus? Would they be able to sue the Stock Exchange for damages? The human resources department were secretly instructed to plan for sudden large-scale redundancies and to draw up contingency plans to ensure that the Stock Exchange's other computer systems would continue to work when Taurus was disengaged. (Talisman, for example, is a live operating system settling thousands of share bargains worth millions of pounds every day.) The risk of sabotage by displaced staff was another worry.[24]

The chief executive was also instrumental in paving the way for a successor to Taurus. The successor would eventually be known as Crest. The sponsor was the Bank of England. Rawlins said:

I had my people looking at what the position would be if we stopped it dead, because if we stop it, we stop it. . . . I didn't want anyone panicking. I wanted it all trussed, tied up, and done.[25]

'OF COURSE WE CAN CARRY ON.'

For a brief period after Stuart Senior had completed his investigation the chief executive's hopes rose, as it seemed as if the project might be retrievable after all. He also wanted to see the results of the testing programme before finally making up his mind. Testing would expose just how ill prepared the market was: 'The drains would be up,' he said grimly.[26]

The chief executive's priority now was to identify a firm date for completion. Stuart Senior suggested fifteen months. Andersen's said two years. Both agreed that at least a year's testing would be required on top of that. It was then that the chief executive realized that his original prognostication was correct and that the Stock Exchange could not responsibly carry on:

Remember, this period I'm talking about is to be absolutely rock-solid certain that we would definitively finish everything we had to do. Which would itself then be followed by a period of testing which everybody agreed was no less than a year. So that was it. Depending on who you believed, minimum two, probably three years to get it done. All this to a world thinking Taurus is just round the corner.[27]

Taurus was only ever a means to an end. In the chief executive's opinion, it was viable only as a short-term project. It could be made to work but it could never do so in a cost-effective manner. 'Crazy,' Rawlins concluded.[28]

Now there was no alternative but to set the stage for abandonment. The chief executive had already been secretly preparing key players including the chairman of the Stock Exchange, trusted members of the board, leaders of the securities industry, and the Bank of England for this possibility.[29] The chief executive recalls the reaction:

I had to go through an awful lot of, 'gosh', you know, sinking jaws . . . City's prestige and all that sort of thing. They all had the same problem with the 'egg on face' bit. . . . I thought by saying to them, and I made it very clear to them, I said, 'Don't worry, I'll take the rap for this,' I thought that it might help them. It's funny, I know the establishment quite well. These were big men . . . [yet] the plain fact of the matter is that they were terrified. 'What do you mean we might have to stop this? How can you say that now? Whose fault?' [*sic*] They didn't believe it. . . . They wanted to believe I was wrong. They were fighting to find some reason to carry on.[30]

Peter Rawlins hammered out the message:

Of course we can carry on if you are prepared to vote the money, but I am telling you the issue is not the money. It is the time. . . . The only way to go forward now is . . . we say, 'Stop! Spend not one further penny. The Stock Exchange is going to finish building the central infrastructure which we should have done at the beginning. *Mea culpa*, we didn't. We are doing it now. We have no reason to doubt our ability to do it . . . and it is going to be fifteen months. We will then tell you that we are ready to start testing. . . . In the mean time, all you guys out there stand down your entire teams with no certain knowledge as to what you have still got to do. Any of you are going to vote for that? Bollocks! Are you going to vote for that? I remind you, this achieves nothing save a means to an end.[31]

There was also a significant risk that once the architecture had been constructed, part of the work already completed by the market would be redundant. Rawlins again:

One basic law of physics we couldn't change was that there are only twenty-four hours in a day. There were in excess of 2,000 batch programs that had to be run iteratively. As designed . . . it would have been behind from day one. . . . Of course it could have been fixed . . . . 'Forget the money,' I said, It is the time. And no guarantees that in fifteen months' time everything would just plug in.[32]

Besides, by now Rawlins had realized that time had overtaken Taurus. The likelihood of another bull market similar to that of the early 1980s seemed remote in the early 1990s. More importantly, part of the original problem had self-corrected. Brokers' back offices were now better organized than they had been in 1987 and were therefore better equipped to cope with an upsurge in trading volumes should it occur: 'There should have been a re-evaluation of whether [Taurus] . . . still made sense,' said the chief executive.[33]

As regards implementing the Group of Thirty's recommendations, rolling settlement was achievable regardless of Taurus provided the banking community were prepared to organize a quicker cash settlement system. Delivery versus payment was always possible within Talisman. The chief executive banged the table: 'I know it [Talisman] is archaic,' he said, 'but it is cheap, cheerful, and it bloody well works. Don't tell me you want Taurus.'[34]

Once the initial horror subsided, the chief executive discovered that the market's enthusiasm for Taurus had waned. The registrars were worried because of the emergent cost implications. The custodians said they could undertake the work themselves. The institutions might yet opt for an alternative system known as Euroclear. The banks were thought to be examining the possibility of a central register for shares, initially to act as 'company account controller' but which might eventually compete with Taurus. Rawlins again:

I thought, what is very odd in all of this, is now that I've actually grabbed people and thrust their noses in the muck, at last they agreed it smelt but I had to hold their heads down to do it. (Excuse my crude language but it was like that; they didn't want to believe what they were hearing.) Now, I have yet to find a single person who is saying that Taurus as it stands is what we should be doing. Nobody was fighting for it. Everybody had a problem with it. I understood the problems. I had problems with most of it. I wasn't saying that critically but having found nobody backing it, I thought, why carry on? . . . There wasn't a single faction that wanted it if you really pinned them down. So, without a single sponsor, with the absolute certainty you had got another two years, and in my belief three-plus years before you were there, it was a terribly easy decision to take . . . unassailable logic.[35]

The decision might be easy but what of the consequences? The chief executive told the board, 'Chaps, there is going to be a great row whatever we do.'[36] Perhaps, he suggested to the board, the Stock Exchange might be admired for taking such a courageous decision. Whatever happened, he was confident that his recommendation was correct: 'The decision is the right decision,' he told the board. 'We [the board], and I, can be criticized for many, many things but we will never be criticized for the decision.'[37]

'WHY DIDN'T YOU STEP IN?'

In late February the chief executive also learned that Ernst and Young, the consultants acting for the Government, were also unhappy about Taurus.

Ernst and Young were concerned about the correspondence between the system and the regulatory framework: 'I relied upon the team to go through those regulations with a fine-tooth comb and assure me they could deliver on them,' said Peter Rawlins bitterly. The project team had honoured their commitment to the chief executive. They thought they understood the complex legislation. Ultimately, however, the legal intricacies (see Chapter 8) had eluded them.[38]

Ernst and Young were not the only ones with serious concerns. Around that time the chief executive received a visitor. The visitor was Anthony Hilton, managing director of the *Evening Standard.* Hilton showed him information about the project which he had received from a confidential source. He was about to utilize the material in an article calling for Taurus to be scrapped (see Chapter 11).

'I implore you not to publish this,' said Rawlins.

'Why?' said Hilton.

'Because it's true,' Rawlins apparently replied. 'But if you print this people will think that the Stock Exchange is bowing to media pressure.'

'I'll give you a fortnight,' said Hilton.[39]

The board meeting was scheduled for March 11. A week and a half before then, board members received a confidential three-page memorandum recommending abandonment. When John Watson learned of the existence of the document he promptly faxed the chief executive and three members of the board imploring them to re-conside: ' "had to go forward, critical for London, all major problems overcome. . . . ." ' recounted Rawlins.[40] According to Anthony Hilton, Rawlins telephoned him shortly before the board meeting: 'Remember that story?' he said. 'It doesn't matter any more.'

'Why?' said Hilton. 'Have you been sacked?'

The chief executive laughed. 'Yes,' he replied.[41]

Hilton moved swiftly. On Wednesday 10 March the lunch-time edition of the *Evening Standard* carried a revised version of the report, whose title had changed from 'Taurus Should Be Scrapped' to 'Taurus Will Be Scrapped.'[42]

Although a few members of the securities industry knew or guessed what was about to happen, most were utterly astonished by the news. Richard Grayson, company secretary of BP and former member of Siscot and latterly the Taurus monitoring group, saw the article on the train going home. He was horrified, as BP's annual report containing details of the voting procedure on Taurus had just gone to press.[43] The technical team first received the news when someone returned from their lunch break with a copy of the newspaper. They reacted sceptically to the report. One said:

We were all lulled into this false sense of security by the fact that this may be a bit of a dog's breakfast coming up, but they've spent so much money on it, it really would be ludicrous to jack it in now.[44]

Not everyone in the Stock Exchange was utterly disbelieving. One technical manager had been puzzled by a remark made by Stuart Senior two weeks earlier during a chat about his career. Stuart Senior advised him to think of moving on. 'The Exchange is dead,' he said.[45] The technical manager was reminded of the conversation when, on the night of Tuesday 9 March, he was asked to compile lists of essential and non-essential computer personnel. It seemed an odd instruction. Even when it was followed by the article in the *Evening Standard*, it seemed incredible that the board would accept the chief executive's recommendation.[46]

Peter Rawlins had been planning to leave the Exchange at Christmas 1993, having originally contracted to serve three to five years. I asked him why he did not let Taurus run on for a few months and avoid the ignominy of resignation. 'I could have done all sorts of things,' he agreed. 'I could have ducked and dived and said "We are still working on this, that and the other." '[47] Indeed, in his darker moments subsequently, he said he wished he had but, he added, 'I couldn't have lived with myself

. . . I was brought in as a heavy hitter . . . when they hired me they hired a professional.'[48]

During January and February the chief executive had spoken with some of the junior staff working on Taurus. Accustomed to sophistication in the use of language, the chief executive was moved by their frankness about the project: 'I got straight answers. . . . I couldn't have lived with myself or asked them to work for me if I ignored that.'[49]

I asked Rawlins if he had to resign. He said he had considered the possibility of trying to stay on but decided against the idea:

I also came to the view [that] I'm not sure I want to hang around after this. I thought it would be a great liberating thing to have Taurus done. With Taurus behind us, the head count in the Exchange was down to under 800 . . . I thought, there's going to be nothing left to do now. I've slain the albatross, got it off everyone else's neck. Now its a care and maintenance job and I would have been very rapidly bored. . . . [Besides,] life might have become uncomfortable, . . . people would have wanted to have a go. So I thought the best thing to do was go. Indeed, it was instrumental in my strategy of getting the board to stop it.[50]

Would Taurus have worked in the end? Rawlins thought so but added:

For all I know the testing that had just started would have revealed the whole shambles sooner or later, but then the stink would have been directed partly externally because they weren't ready out there.[51]

The board meeting was apparently a bitter session.[52] Why, members demanded, had the chief executive not intervened sooner? Rawlins's reply was robust: 'Don't turn round and say "Why didn't I [sic] take it?" Why the hell didn't all of you? . . . You are the ones who have been pushing for it. Why didn't you step in?'[53]

NOTES

1. Interview, member of Stock Exchange technical team, July 1994.
2. Dobie, C., 'Rawlins Ruffles some Feathers', *The Independent* (24 July 1992), 25.
3. C. Dobie 'Rawlins Ruffles some Feathers', *The Independent* (24 July 1992), 25.

4. Interview, Peter Rawlins, Oct. 1993.
5. 'Under Fire', *Financial Times* (16 June 1992), 21.
6. Interview, Peter Rawlins, Oct. 1993.
7. Ibid.
8. Interview, member of Taurus monitoring group, Nov. 1993.
9. 'Anderson to Operate Exchange Computers', *The Times* (14 Apr. 1992), 18.
10. Interview, Peter Rawlins, Oct. 1993.
11. Ibid.
12. Ibid.
13. Ibid.
14. Ibid.
15. Ibid.
16. Ibid.
17. Interview, senior official, UK clearing bank, Aug. 1994.
18. Interview, Peter Rawlins, Oct. 1993.
19. Ibid.
20. Ibid.
21. Ibid.
22. Ibid.
23. Ibid.
24. Ibid.
25. Ibid.
26. Ibid.
27. Ibid.
28. Ibid.
29. Telephone interview, member of Stock Exchange board, Sept. 1994.
30. Interview, Peter Rawlins, Oct. 1993.
31. Ibid.
32. Ibid.
33. Ibid.
34. Ibid.
35. Ibid.
36. Ibid.
37. Ibid.
38. Interview, member of Stock Exchange technical team, Dec. 1994.
39. Telephone interview, Anthony Hilton, July 1994.
40. Interview, Peter Rawlins, Oct. 1993.
41. Telephone interview, Antony Hilton, July 1994.
42. M. Neill, 'Axe Poised over Taurus System', *Evening Standard*) 10 Mar. 1993), 29.
43. Interview, Richard Grayson, July 1994.
44. Interview, member of Stock Exchange technical team, May 1994.

45. Interview, member of Stock Exchange technical team, Nov. 1994.
46. Ibid.
47. Interview, Peter Rawlins, Oct. 1993.
48. Ibid.
49. Ibid.
50. Ibid.
51. Ibid.
52. Interview, member of Stock Exchange board, Sept. 1994.
53. Interview, Peter Rawlins, Oct. 1993.

13

Withdrawal

All credibility is gone.
(A member of the Taurus monitoring group)

The Stock Exchange invested over five years and £80 million in Taurus. The market allegedly spent £400 million in preparation for dematerialization plus countless hours of executive time spent in meetings and reading copious documentation. On 12 March 1993 the Stock Exchange publicly admitted that it had all been for nothing.

This chapter analyses the decision to cancel Taurus. The resolution of the story is important because most of the escalation literature concentrates on persistence as distinct from withdrawal. Very little is known about how, when, and why decision-makers opt to give up, and in so doing incur the ignominy of failure. The literature suggests two alternative possibilities. Decision dilemma theorists basically predict that market forces eventually curb unwarranted persistence. Social-psychological perspectives on escalation basically assert that market forces are often slow to act, that decision-makers persist with failing projects long after the rational point for withdrawal has been reached. An assumption common to both schools of thought is that withdrawal occurs in the conditions opposite those thought to favour persistence. According to decision dilemma theorists, withdrawal is principally a function of information. Feedback becomes more readily available and less ambiguous as time goes on. Accumulating negative feedback destroys commitment.[1] According to the social-psychological school of escalation, withdrawal is most probable if social, psychological, and organizational pressures surrounding a venture weaken, or if such pressures become sharply overridden by the costs of persistence.[2]

The focal decision for analysis is the board's decision to accept the chief executive's recommendation to cancel Taurus. Again, in order to understand escalation and withdrawal it is necessary to examine a series of decisions leading up to that point. The 'decision-maker' is defined as the board of the Stock Exchange, advised by the chief executive. Likewise it is necessary to consider the actions of other players, including the market and the Taurus monitoring group.

Ostensibly it is possible to make short work of the task of analysis. During 1992 it became abundantly clear to the market, the Taurus monitoring group, and the chief executive that Taurus was failing to meet its objectives to such an extent that commitment was destroyed: 'It was all starting to blow up.' If we were to leave it there the present study would conclude that accumulating negative feedback does indeed destroy commitment and render irrelevant such social-psychological pressures for persistence as may exist.

The problem with that conclusion is that it leaves much unanswered. Both decision dilemma theorists and social- psychological theorists assume that withdrawal is teleological, that is, given x, then y. Yet commitment to Taurus did not collapse of its own accord. Further, what constitutes clear and extreme negative feedback? Was Taurus an abject failure? The technicalities were said to be 'doable—ultimately'. Was it true that the commercial imperative had died? Back offices had improved but there was still risk and massive inefficiency in the system. What of the Stock Exchange's publicly avowed commitment to implement the Group of Thirty's recommendations?[3] Taurus represented a huge investment of time and money. Besides, given the still recent experience of Taurus 1 and Siscot, who would want to start all over again?

In order to answer such questions it is necessary to ask a different question. Escalation represents the breakdown of rationality. Instead of enquiring into what causes withdrawal, it seems more pertinent to ask how rationality is reasserted.

THAT DECISION MAKES ITSELF?

Decision dilemma theory forms the starting point for a new perspective on withdrawal. On 22 December 1992, the chief executive decided to close Taurus 'come what may'. He would have preferred to have closed it in early 1990. In 1990 nothing had been built whereas by 1993 a huge commitment had developed around the project. Why was he able to accomplish in 1993 what he had failed to achieve in 1990, when, in theory, objective conditions were much more favourable?

The intervening three years had certainly shown that the chief executive's initial reservations about Taurus were well founded. The Stock Exchange's repeated failures to meet time-scales and all the other difficulties with the project may be said to have destroyed the chief executive's remaining commitment to the project.[4] Moreover, the commercial imperative for Taurus had waned. It was becoming increasingly clear that Taurus would not meet the market's requirements in a timely and apposite fashion. Such emerging knowledge may be said to have destroyed the market's commitment to the venture.

Research never destroys a theory. It either suggests a more useful one or identifies how a theory can be modified to improve its explanatory power. The departure point of decision dilemma theory is that the decision to cancel Taurus did not make itself. The outcome was not obvious by any means. The dominant view was discredited not by unequivocal negative feedback *per se*, but by the application of a battery of power ploys of which information was but one part. The chief executive not only invested the phenomenal effort to disprove that all Taurus required was only a bit more money and a bit more time; he also had to fight his way through opposition: ' "Gosh", sinking jaws . . . City's prestige . . . "egg on face".'

The data suggest that withdrawal is best understood as a process, a power struggle whereby one myth competes with another for dominance.[5]

Power is defined here as the ability to produce 'intended effects'.[6] Capacity is partly a function of resources.[7] A significant move towards withdrawal occurred when the chief executive refused to allow the provision of additional staff and funding for the project at a critical time: 'No more staff and no more money. This is what we are going with.' According to decision dilemma theorists, such behaviour exemplifies decision-makers proceeding cautiously in the face of negative feedback, that is, minimizing additional investments whilst seeking a way out. The present study offers a complementary interpretation. Curtailing investment in Taurus exacerbated the difficulties, thus adding to the impression of a project in crisis. This may not have been the chief executive's intention, but it was instrumental nevertheless in constructing a new reality around the venture.[8] Such a move was impossible earlier because the chief executive was not in command of the project. It was only after a series of organizational restructures between 1990 and 1992 that he managed to achieve some control over Taurus.

The decisive act in the present case was the chief executive's decision to commission Andersen to review the project. In 1989 Peter Rawlins was unable to procure such 'heavy-hitting capability', nor were such resources available within the Stock Exchange. Indeed, he was forbidden to interfere with the project. It was only after he had consolidated his own power base that was able to intervene .[9]

Andersen's review wrested control of information from the project team.[10] An assumption common to both social-psychological and decision dilemma theories of de-escalation is that withdrawal is most probable given unambiguous negative feedback which shows that future expectations will not be met. If withdrawal were simply a function of information, surely Andersen's report would have enabled the chief executive to call an emergency board meeting and recommend closure. Instead he has to find a way of convincing the board that withdrawal is essential.

The Construction of a New Reality

In the present case withdrawal is characterized by force. Force succeeds by eliminating the other party's options.[11] The manner in which the board's options are eliminated is instructive. Decision dilemma theorists predict that withdrawal occurs when it becomes abundantly clear that future expectations will not be met. The theory assumes that expectations are fixed and immutable. It was suggested in Chapter 9 that this is by no means invariably the case. In 1991 the decision-makers revised their expectations several times when it became clear that the original time-scales would not be met. In early 1993 a subtle shift occurs in the opposite direction. Andersen's report detailed what they would need to operate the system. Similarly Ernst and Young were thought to be concerned about whether Taurus conformed to the complex regulations. In other words, part of the rationale for cancellation was Andersen's and Ernst and Young's criteria and not the Stock Exchange's.

In the present case there is no evidence that the criteria were racked up deliberately, cynically, or unreasonably. The point is important though as situations could arise where the decision-makers do just that in order to justify withdrawing their commitment. For example, in a marital relationship, one spouse may assert that the other promised not to work weekends when the actual commitment was to try to avoid working weekends. Such behaviour could be interpreted as a reversal of the unconscious information processing biases thought to produce escalatory decisions.[12] From a social-constructionist perspective such a tactic helps create an impression of failure by widening the gap between expectations and reality.

The chief executive anticipated that Coopers and Lybrand might dispute Andersen's conclusions. He eliminates their options by inviting them to see the project for themselves. This ploy also narrows the board's options. Its authority, however, rests less upon what is said (for apparently it tells the chief executive little that he does not already know), and more upon who is saying it, that is, 'one of Cooper's top men'.[13]

Yet even that is thought insufficient to overcome resistance. The chief executive next invokes his powers of access to leaders of the securities industry in order to prepare them for the possibility of abandonment. The present study suggests that withdrawal depends not just on information but the decision-maker's ability to force others to recognize the situation for what it has become. There was apparently resistance: 'They didn't believe it. . . . They wanted to believe I was wrong. They were fighting to find some reason to carry on.' Force is matched with force: 'I am telling you.'

Studied Ambiguity

According to decision dilemma theorists, commitment is most likely to be destroyed by unequivocal negative feedback. The present study highlights an intriguing counterpoint. What destroys Taurus is not certainty but ambiguity. Experimental scenarios present respondents with firm data as to future costs and time-scales to completion. No such certainty exists in the case of Taurus, however. Stuart Senior's assessment concluded that fifteen months would be required to finish the project. Andersen suggested two years. Added to that was at least one year's testing. The reaction of a member of the Taurus monitoring group was: 'I think anybody listening to that would have to double it because you would just say "Woah! All credibility is gone." '

In the present case equivocation served as a weapon. For example, the chief emphasizes that once the core is built, no guarantees exist that completed work will be usable. No such uncertainty attends closure. On the contrary, closing costs and all the other operational issues concerning disengagement were carefully researched and planned for. 'The decision is the right decision. . . . ,' he tells the board; 'we can never be criticized for the decision.'

In defining the case for closure the chief executive demolished one view of reality and substituted another. A striking feature of the data is that both realities are illusions. The case for closure was not quite as clear and definite as it may have seemed. For example, counsel's advice regarding the Stock Exchange's legal liability was not that claims were sure to be defeated, only that they were unlikely to succeed. There is, as Allison reminds us, an 'awesome crack between *unlikelihood* and *impossibility*'.[14] In the present case the 'crack' was to the tune of a possible liability of £400 million.

Degradation of the old order is thought to be an important prerequisite to ushering in the new.[15] The chief executive concentrates his attack upon the opportunity costs of continuance.[16] He points out that 'delivery versus payment' and rolling settlement could be achieved independent of Taurus. 'Don't tell me you need Taurus', he insists. That argument too was partial. One of the first decisions of the Crest task force was that dematerialization independent of Talisman was an essential prerequisite to achieving the highest levels of settlement efficiency.[17]

The effect of the chief executive's advocacy is to polarize the issue between certainty and uncertainty. The literature suggests that dramatic and stirring presentations may induce decision-makers to commit resources unwisely because such appeals detract from factual analysis.[18] The data suggest that the same tactic could be used to effect withdrawal. Hyperbole and denigration, ('Bollocks! Are you going to vote for that?') capture attention and add impetus to the sense of impending crisis. It is rather like watching the performance of a stage actor. Viewed close up a gesture seems overdone. Seen from the audience, however, it looks perfectly natural. To usher in a new reality the chief executive had to reach a distant and potentially unreceptive audience. The language and the gestures not only served to construct a new reality, they forced others to acknowledge it. In summary, the board is presented with two carefully contrasted options. One, closure, is apparently 'trussed, tied up, done'. The second, continuance, is apparently surrounded by massive uncertainty.

THROWING THE MARKET A LADDER

Much has been said in previous chapters about the overarching influence of the securities industry establishment, notably the Group of Thirty. An important feature of the process of withdrawal was to extricate the market from its obligations. The chief executive achieves this by offering the securities industry a diplomatic exit.

Ostensibly the data are consistent with previous experimental research which suggests that the level of project completion is more important than sunk costs: 'It is not the money, it is the time,' the chief executive repeatedly emphasizes.[19] Likewise a member of the Taurus monitoring group commented:

The City could have swallowed the money bit. They would have said, 'OK, there is an overspend of £100 million—let's fight about who is going to fund that, because we see the benefits coming through.' It was the time that killed them all.[20]

Yet was time really so critical? If it was, then surely the market would have demanded more information on alternative options for de-materialization before seeing Taurus scrapped. Moreover, when it later emerged that the earliest date for implementing Crest was not until 1996, why was Taurus not revived? Time became an issue because it was politically expedient to make it one in order to release the securities industry from its commitment.[21] The market's enthusiasm for Taurus had palpably weakened: 'Everybody had problems with it.' Emphasizing the time enabled the market to pay lip-service to the objective of improving settlement efficiency. It made them appear committed to the overarching myth when the reality lay elsewhere.

THE CHANGING FORTUNES OF TIME

A small minority of players disagreed with the decision to cancel Taurus. It is thought that John Watson was motivated by three factors.[22] These were, first, a sense of vocation, that is, to provide London with a new settlement system, which it badly needed. Second, the knowledge that he was close to achieving that goal. Third, the belief that the delays and cost overruns were worth while in view of the long-term benefits. Once implemented Taurus would serve for twenty years or more. Clearly such reasoning could be regarded as biased information processing motivated by the extreme pressures of a livelihood and reputation at stake.[23]

Yet that does not necessarily mean that Watson and other dissenters were wrong. Taurus failed because support for the project was withdrawn.[24] That does not mean that cancellation was the only option—far from it. 'Of course we can carry on,' Peter Rawlins tells the board. A fundamental assumption of escalation theory is that a rational point for withdrawal exists. The chief executive considers he has reached it: 'the decision is right,' he emphasized.

Yet history is a matter of received opinion at a particular point in time.[25] Until recently, for example, King John of England was cast as murderous, greedy, lecherous, and incompetent. Modern writers have attempted to modify this image by drawing attention to the monarch's strengths as an administrator and military strategist.[26] Likewise, the Tudor regime is thought to have tampered with portraits of King Richard III to emphasize the image of an ugly and sinister hunchback as part of a campaign to darken his reputation.[27]

According to the literature the logical course of action in decision-making is the option promising greatest return on investment.[28] Yet who is to know? In the nineteenth century two railway gauges existed in the UK, one narrow, the other broad. The broad gauge was technically far superior yet the narrow gauge was adopted because much of the network had already adopted the narrow gauge. Was that a case of irrational persistence? The Channel Tunnel was only ever a means to an end. Was it worth building, given the massive debts now surrounding the project?

By 1993 it had become clear that the cost–benefit equation was no longer valid. The equation did not stack up any more. The price of Taurus was one thing. What about its value? What constitutes worth? How significant are the quadrillions of pounds traded across the world which disappear into 'black holes' during the settlement process? How can time and opportunity costs be computed? John Watson apparently claimed that all the major technical problems had been overcome. Considering those that had already been solved, perhaps those that lay ahead were relatively simple: 'Of course it could have been fixed,' acknowledges the chief executive.

Similarly some members of the technical team disagreed with the suggestion of dropping everything in order to construct the central architecture: 'It would have taken for ever to do it that way,' said a member of the technical team.[29] That does not make either party right or wrong. Just as doctors have different views on the most effective forms of treatment for particular diseases, in many organizational situations there is no one correct answer, one indisputably rational course of action.

When Taurus was cancelled there was little dissent from the newly established dominant viewpoint. Almost everyone I interviewed between October 1993 and September 1994 agreed with the decision. Yet by November 1994, the signs were that some people were entertaining second thoughts. 'Taurus would have been in by now,' people began to say. 'Crest is not going to give us some of the services that Taurus offered . . . Taurus had some good features,' and so on.[30] That does not make the revisionists right either. After all, a major reason Taurus failed was that it was too ambitious. What the present case shows is that decisions which are perceived as right (or wrong) at time 1 may be viewed in a different light at time 2 and in another light at time 3.

RESPONSIBILITY AND THE LIMITS TO ESCALATION

The chief executive's behaviour seems to stand responsibility theory on its head. Responsibility for a decision is believed to be highly conducive to persistence, especially if the decision-maker's job is at stake.[31] In theory the chief executive was the person most likely to persist at all costs.

It could be argued that his freedom of action derived from the fact that he was not responsible for the initial decision. This might imply that withdrawal was ego-defensive. This seems a tenuous point as the chief executive knew that cancellation meant resignation and disgrace. It was suggested in Chapter 7 that low perceived responsibility is conducive to escalation. The data suggest that the reverse is also true. It was precisely because the chief executive was responsible for Taurus that he could not allow matters to continue as they were.

Confronting options is thought to be conducive to withdrawal.[32] Funding for Taurus expired in March 1993. The chief executive could not make a credible recommendation one way or the other without first establishing the state of the project. Once Andersen had reported, he could not responsibly conceal or ignore such information. Further, as the full picture emerged, imagine what the chief executive was confronted with:

Nobody had really thought about it. Nobody had planned the thing. . . . [Now,] minimum two, probably three years to get it done. . . . And no guarantees that everything would just plug in. All that to a world thinking Taurus was just round the corner.

This brings us back to the point made in Chapter 10 that emotion may precipitate action but it does not dictate what that action shall be.

Another important factor in the decision to withdraw was control. Peter Rawlins tells the board, 'There will be a great row whatever we do.' According to prospect theory, when a decision is framed as a choice between losses, decision-makers are risk-seeking and therefore likely to escalate.[33] Not so in the present case. Clearly there are indeed limits to escalation.[34] The limit may be reached where it becomes apparent that the costs of continuance outweigh the costs of withdrawal. What do we mean by costs, however? The present case suggests that the critical juncture may be reached when decision-makers perceive they are about to lose control of a situation. The market was about to withdraw: 'It was all starting to blow up.' Strategically that would probably have been an even worse loss than abandoning Taurus. It would have handed the market a fine opportunity to denigrate the Stock Exchange, hence the request to Anthony Hilton to delay publication of his article: 'I implore you not to publish this. . . . Because it is true.' Meanwhile the chief executive has to run the risk of losing control of the situation by giving the impression that he is still committed to the project: 'We will prove you wrong.' He succeeds so well that he creates a sense of desperation in the market: 'He doesn't know what's going on.' What appears as blindness to reality is a necessary risk in order to preserve secrecy.

Some respondents suggested that the board saw abandonment as an opportunity to be relieved of an unpopular chief executive. This seems unlikely, as there was no need to cancel Taurus to remove the chief executive if that was what the board wanted. The operation of informal power would suffice: 'We understand each other. You're going. You're on a short time-scale . . . couple of months, get someone in to replace you and you're off. Understood, gentlemen?'

Escalation theory might suggest that the ready availability of a scapegoat facilitated closure. Scapegoats act as lightning conductors. They release others from responsibility and provide them with freedom of action.[35] The present case qualifies this proposition. The chief executive's offer was initially brushed aside: 'I thought by saying to them, and I made it very clear to them, I said, "Don't worry, I'll take the rap for this," I thought that it might help them.' Perhaps scapegoats are only relevant after withdrawal has become inevitable.

THE RELATIONSHIP BETWEEN POWER AND MYTH-BREAKING TACTICS

Withdrawal emerges as a function of power. The data permit analysis to go a stage further and to suggest that a pattern exists between the decision-maker's power and the selection of myth-breaking tactics. According to the literature, myths may be destroyed in two ways. A myth may be undermined when a weakening of an old myth triggers a search for a new myth. A myth may be conquered when a new myth develops independently of an old myth.[36] The present study builds upon these ideas.

So far analysis has focused mainly on the actions of the chief executive. It is useful to consider the role of the Taurus monitoring group and the market, as they too were caught in an escalatory predicament by seeking to destroy the dominant viewpoint. The chief executive succeeded. The other two parties came close to succeeding. What differentiates their respective approaches?

It may be helpful at this juncture to imagine a myth as a castle. A castle may be brought to surrender by direct attack, or by being first undermined and then invaded, or by mounting a siege. The choice of tactic depends partly upon the attackers' resources. The chief executive possessed the strongest force. He commanded the most authoritative and comprehensive information. He had access to the board and leaders of the securities industry. Power is not only a matter of resources, however; it is also a function of dependency.[37] Since the chief executive knows resignation is inevitable and since he is not burdened with ever having previously been publicly identified with the project, of all the parties in the analytical frame he is the least dependent. High resources and low dependency enable him to adopt the most drastic course of action. He storms the ramparts: 'Don't tell me you need Taurus.'

Social-psychological theorists suggest that groups tend to act less responsibly and incur bigger risks than individuals.[38] The present study qualifies this idea. The actions of the Taurus monitoring group in response to the growing crisis are characterized by caution. The Taurus monitoring group had fewer resources than the chief executive. They were not party to Andersen's report or Stuart Senior's findings, for example. However, they did receive relatively detailed plans and accounts of progress. Such information was not as comprehensive as they might have wished, but it was sufficient for them to know for certain that the project had made little progress in eighteen months despite the enormous investments of time and money. Moreover, the group had access to the chief executive and to the board via the Stock Exchange's committee system. The group was also buttressed by their moral authority as responsible representatives of the external market. Such authority was also a restraining factor, however, in that they could not act in a manner which might be interpreted as a selfish and irresponsible attempt to 'scupper' Taurus. Conversely they could not be seen to preside over a fiasco. Finding themselves walking a tightrope, the monitoring group opted for the less risky tactic of undermining the ramparts by declaring a crisis. Such a move enabled them to be seen to be acting responsibly but not destructively.

The data concerning the market are scant but there are sufficient indicators to suggest insight. The market possessed the least concrete information about the project and lacked cohesion. Although the Stock Exchange was dependent upon the market to carry out preparatory work for Taurus, the possibility of open rebellion was negated by a commitment to improving settlement efficiency, by the market's previous behaviour over the central register (Taurus 1), and by its insistence on the time-scales and design complexity now beleaguering the project. As the weakest party, the market opted for the least risky and least expensive tactic by laying siege to Taurus. They achieved this mainly by quietly diverting resources from Taurus onto other projects. There was also a semi-orchestrated attempt to create a conscious reality of a project in crisis. Reports are circulated which articulate doubt.[39] Politicians and other potentially influential figures are secretly lobbied. Fact, rumour, and hyperbole are mingled and promulgated to concoct a vision of impending catastrophe, hence 'It was all starting to blow up.' The tactic succeeds when the retail chain store Marks and Spencer declines to put the issue of joining Taurus to a shareholder vote. It might have worked again with the publication of revelations in the *Evening Standard*.

Figure 13.1 summarizes the theoretical possibilities suggested by the data. The most drastic tactics are likely to be employed

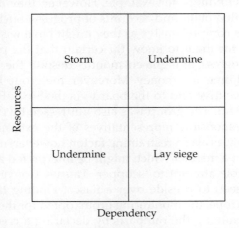

FIG. 13.1 Hypothesized relationships between power, dependency, and myth-breaking tactics

where resources are high and dependency is low. High resources coupled with medium dependency, or medium dependency coupled with high resources, are likely to result in a less bold approach. The most cautious response is expected where resources are low and dependency is high. Arguably such a model brings us back to decision dilemma theory by substituting 'commitment' for 'dependency' and 'information' for 'resources'. Yet if that were so, the project would have surely collapsed when it failed to materialize in 1991. In 1991 it became clear that expectations would not be met. Continuance beyond this point is explained by the time required for parties to position and otherwise empower themselves for withdrawal. A parallel can be drawn at the individual level where a spouse's behaviour destroys their partner's commitment. The partner cannot terminate the relationship immediately because he/she is emotionally and/or financially dependent upon the other person. The partner must first acquire the resources to enable them to reduce their dependency. In some instances resources will be the corollary of dependency, but not always, as was the case here, for example.

It could of course be said that decision-making is reducible to commitment; that is, that once the partner obtains the requisite resources they are able to withdraw the last vestiges of commitment. Yet if we are to understand persistence beyond a seemingly rational point, it is necessary to know what is sustaining commitment. Decision dilemma theorists suggest that information explains continuance and withdrawal. The present case suggests that power is the key.

Another factor in determining the choice of tactic used to destroy the dominant viewpoint will be the state of 'the castle's defence'. To extrapolate beyond the data a little, conceivably the strongest defences exist where the commitment to a venture is a moral one—the defence of a strategically worthless but emotionally significant city or fortress, for example. A purely financial commitment may prove more vulnerable if it amounts to a distinction between wanting to remain and needing to remain.[40]

BRAKES AND SWITCHES AS METAPHORS FOR
UNDERSTANDING WITHDRAWAL

In their introduction to their study of the closure of the Shoreham nuclear power plant Ross and Staw note that much is known about getting organizations moving but comparatively little about stopping them once they are bound in a particular direction.[41] The data suggest some additional metaphors which might provide a basis for future theorizing and research. One such is that of a switch. The analogy is borrowed from mechanical engineering. Since it is dangerous suddenly to halt a heavy machine with moving parts a switch mechanism is employed. A switch works by using a relatively small force to trigger a larger one, which in turn triggers a still larger one so that the machine is brought gradually to a standstill.

In the case of Taurus the first step was to instruct Andersen to review the project. This was a relatively small force. The second, more momentous move was to commission Stuart Senior's review. The third, still more momentous move was to 'soften up' important players for the possibility of abandonment. The final force was the memorandum to the board. To see the value of the metaphor, imagine the result if the chief executive had made such a recommendation cold, that is, without going through the preceding steps.

Another possible metaphor also suggested by engineering is that of applying a brake. A brake works by absorbing energy. In the present case the chief executive applies a brake when he refuses the request for additional staff. Likewise the secret planning and research activities and the 'softening-up' tactics absorb momentum. Ultimately nobody was fighting for Taurus because their energy had been absorbed by the chief executive.

Metaphors by definition are partial.[42] They illuminate one aspect of a phenomenon. The value of generating metaphors is that it helps illuminate multi-faceted situations capable of multiple meanings. A feature shared by the metaphors delineated in this chapter (the castle; the switch; brakes) is that they are rooted in the notion of power.

SYNTHESIS

Figure 13.2 attempts to synthesize the foregoing analysis. At the micro-level, the data bear out many of the factors thought to facilitate withdrawal. Organizational arrangements force the decision-makers to confront their options. The project has been overtaken by events. Closing costs are low. Alternatives are available. Pressure from vested interests has palpably receded. At the meso-level, withdrawal is an exercise in impression management whereby one myth is destroyed and another takes its place. Viewing withdrawal as the reassertion of rationality highlights the critical role of power in constructing a new reality. At the macro-level both escalation and withdrawal are evident. Taurus has crumbled but the overarching dominant viewpoint concerning the need to reform settlement is reasserted by the formation of the Bank of England's Crest task force.

Each paradigm provides a partial perspective. For example, low closing costs and alternative investment opportunities do not cause withdrawal. The alternatives always existed. Such factors

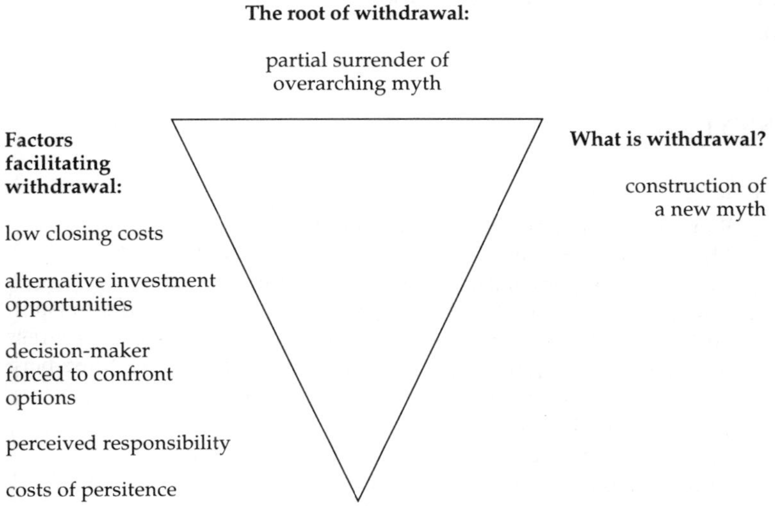

The root of withdrawal:

partial surrender of
overarching myth

Factors
facilitating
withdrawal:

What is withdrawal?

construction of
a new myth

low closing costs

alternative investment
opportunities

decision-maker
forced to confront
options

perceived responsibility

costs of persitence

Fig. 13.2 A synthesis of withdrawal

become weapons in the hands of the decision-makers. They help the chief executive to discredit the Taurus myth whilst still subscribing to the overarching viewpoint that settlement procedures must be reformed.

CONCLUSIONS

It was expected that withdrawal would occur either when it became abundantly clear that expectations would not be met or when the costs of persistence overrode psychological and social pressures for persistence.

The data are consistent with both propositions in so far as information played an important part in withdrawal, and the decision was influenced by the risk that the Stock Exchange might lose control of the situation if it did not take the initiative and cancel the project.

What emerges here, however, is that information is a necessary but insufficient condition for withdrawal. The notion of a clear-cut case for withdrawal or persistence is an illusion. Withdrawal amounts to the destruction of one myth and the creation of another. Power is the key to understanding how this process is accomplished.

NOTES

1. Bowen (1987).
2. Simonson and Staw (1992), Staw and Ross (1987*a*).
3. I have in mind Salancik's (1977) definition of commitment.
4. M. G. Bowen (personal communication, 1994).
5. The idea is articulated in Bowen (1987), citing Hedberg and Jonsonn (1977). It is also implicit in Kuhn's (1970) seminal thesis on progress in scientific research. Bacharach and Lawler (1980) and Mintzberg (1983) use different language to describe similar phenomena.
6. Derived from Wrong (1979).
7. See, for example, Clegg (1989), Etzioni (1975), Mechanic (1962).
8. This point is derived from Berger (1972), Berger and Luckman (1966), Burrell and Morgan (1979), Drummond (1991*b*), Dyer (1995), Gowler and Legge (1983), Morgan and Smircich (1980), and Quaid (1993).

9. In theory, organizations allot decision-makers the power they need to discharge their role obligations. In practice the balance between power and responsibility may be asymmetrical: see, for example, Drummond (1991b), Lukes (1974), Martin (1977), Mintzberg (1983), and Pfeffer (1992).

10. Possession of information needed for decision-making is synonymous with power: see, for example, Drummond (1991b), Mechanic (1962), Pettigrew (1973), Pfeffer (1981), Sterba (1978).

11. Wrong (1979).

12. See also Drummond (1995).

13. Zander (1982) argues that more attention is paid to high-status individuals than low-status individuals.

14. Allison (1971: vii).

15. Beyer and Trice (1987), Gephart (1978).

16. Northcraft and Neale (1986) suggest that making opportunity costs salient is conducive to withdrawal.

17. Bank of England (1993).

18. Schwenk (1986) suggests vivid presentations increase the risk of escalation. Singer *et al.* (1991) suggest the same tactic can facilitate de-escalation.

19. Conlon and Garland (1993). Interestingly, Heath (1995) suggests that people are more willing to invest money than time to salvage a sunk cost of time, even when time and money investments are of equal value. Special circumstances apply in the case of Taurus as the costs of the project were written off year by year.

20. Interview, member of Taurus monitoring group, Nov. 1993.

21. Allowing another party to reverse its position with dignity is thought to be an important negotiating tactic: see, for example, Fisher and Ury (1983).

22. Anonymous source close to John Watson.

23. For example, Bazerman (1994), Staw and Ross (1987a).

24. Saur (1993) defines failure in an IT context as withdrawal of support for a project.

25. See, for example, Berger (1972), Berger and Luckman (1966), Drummond (1991b), Dyer (1995).

26. R. V. Turner (1994).

27. For example, Drewett and Redhead (1990), Weir (1993).

28. Northcraft and Wolfe (1984). The idea is also implicit in Schwenk and Tang (1989).

29. Concurrent working is potentially much faster than sequential working (Drummond, 1992B). However, defining the system architecture is a fundamental prerequisite to the successful construction of computer systems (Daniels 1993).

30. Interview, member of Stock Exchange technical team, Nov. 1994.
31. See especially Brockner (1992) and Tetlock (1991).
32. Brockner and Rubin (1985), McCain (1986).
33. Kahneman and Tversky (1979, 1982, 1984), Tversky and Kahneman (1981). Whyte (1986) suggests that such framing effects can lead to escalation.
34. Goltz (1992), McCain (1986), Singer and Singer (1986a).
35. Simonson and Staw (1992).
36. Hedberg and Jonsonn (1977).
37. Emerson (1962).
38. Janis (1972, 1989), Whyte (1993).
39. I refer specifically to Hooker (unpub. mimeo, 1992) and Touche Ross (1992). There may have been other documents in circulation.
40. Etzioni (1975) suggests that we reconsider the idea that the relationship between power and involvement is systematic—a suggestion that has some empirical support (see Drummond 1993b). The impact of different forms of organizational commitment has been explored by Allen and Mayer (1990) and Becker (1992).
41. Ross and Staw (1993).
42. Morgan (1980, 1983, 1986).

14

Conclusions

It's brilliant! And daft!

(Peter Rawlins)

The focus of this study has been the phenomenon of escalation in decision-making. The central concern was to understand how and why organizations become involved in decision fiascos and why they persist once matters turn out badly. A basic theoretical question addressed by the present study is whether such persistence is erroneous, or whether it is basically an economically prudent response to difficult circumstances.

The research was pursued by means of a case-study. The case concerned a decision by the London Stock Exchange to build a multi-million-pound IT project known as Taurus, and the Stock Exchange's subsequent decision to cancel the project three years later whilst it was still under construction. Taurus is clearly a case of escalation. The project encountered a stream of negative feedback. The decision-makers were presented with at least two opportunities to withdraw but opted to persist. Moreover, the project's subsequent collapse was not what the decision-makers envisaged.

Some features of the case are unique, notably the Stock Exchange's dual role in the City of London as market regulator and as trading organization in its own right. However, Taurus contains much that is of general relevance to decision-making in organizations. Taurus was a large-scale infrastructure project which required the support of external constituencies. It was an IT venture which involved working at the boundaries of knowledge. The project was controversial and had far-reaching implications for an entire industry.

Two specific questions were raised by the present case. One was whether, and to what extent, persistence is dictated by social and psychological pressures. The second was whether, and to what extent, persistence is accounted for by paucity of information. The issue was addressed by asking the same question of the data at various critical junctures, that is, why persist?

The data were examined utilizing three conceptual lenses which examined persistence at the macro-, meso-, and micro-level. At the macro-level persistence was assumed to reflect deep-seated and potentially contradictory societal forces bound up with material gain. The basic question for analysis at this level was 'what is the root of escalation?' At the meso-level persistence was assumed to be an exercise in social construction. The basic question for analysis at this level was 'what is escalation?' At the micro-level persistence was assumed to be the product of specific causes. The question for analysis was at this level was 'what factors contribute to escalation?'

The aim was to triangulate analytical paradigms in order to obtain a holistic understanding of the phenomenon of escalation. This was attempted by taking a wide-ranging approach to analysis which involved tracing a chain of events starting with the origins of the project in the late 1960s, and considering the actions of players other than the immediate decision-maker.

The purpose in conducting research was to reconstruct events from the standpoint of key participants in the decision-making process. These were the board of the Stock Exchange advised by the chief executive; the Siscot committee, which designed Taurus; the monitoring groups, which subsequently oversaw progress; and the general market. Reconstruction was attempted by triangulating three principal data sources. The principal data sources were interviews with participants, documentary analyses, and a study of the media accounts.

THE DESCENT INTO THE BIZARRE

What emerges here is that escalation theory itself is predicated upon a myth. A myth was defined as something which cannot be tested objectively.[1] Escalation theory is bounded by the assumption that decisions are objectively verifiable. What the present study shows is that conceiving escalation as persistence beyond an economically defensible level misses the point. Decision rationales are something which people create for themselves.[2]

A striking feature of the present case is that it is impossible to say whether persistence with Taurus was rational or not. The rationale for the venture derived from the Stock Exchange's determination to reassert its authority and competitive position within the City. Social-psychological theorists might interpret persistence as socially determined, a matter of saving face.[3] Yet organizational survival is not merely a matter of technical rationality. The organization's perceived legitimacy within society may be a more important factor in determining its fate[4]—hence the importance attached to public relations and business ethics. Before 'Big Bang' the City's tradition of relationship-driven business was a source of considerable competitive advantage, epitomized in the slogan, 'My word is my bond.'[5]

Escalation theory says more about our own values than it does about how people behave in organizations. In particular it shows how our vision is constrained by narrow short-term economic criteria. The cost of Taurus was one thing. What of its value? Who can place a value on the risk attached to the quadrillions of pounds which disappear into 'black holes' during the settlement process? It has been argued that decision débâcles frequently cited as examples of irrational persistence were basically decision-makers' responding cautiously to difficult circumstances.[6] The present study suggests that it may be inappropriate to regard ventures such as Expo 86 and Shoreham as failures because they failed to turn out as expected.[7] Likewise it may be misleading to regard the pursuit of seemingly irrational business aims as foolish just because we fail to perceive the rationale or because the rationale does not meet an imposed set of criteria. It was suggested in Chapter 1, for example, that Forte's long quest to acquire control of the Savoy group is possibly an example of foolhardy persistence. Yet such a move could hold the potential to elevate the entire organization in the eyes of society and hence confer a long-term competitive advantage.

Decision dilemma theorists argue that persistence can only be regarded as irrational if decision-makers ignore information which clearly suggests that investment will not result in expectations being met. This proposition assumes that information is a neutral entity, and that it is used to inform decision-making. The case of Taurus lends credence to the idea that information is more important for what it symbolizes in decision-making than for its analytical potential.[8] In the present case the principal role of information is to lend the venture legitimacy by appealing to deeply stereotyped notions of what is appropriate.

The Stock Exchange went to considerable trouble to produce a series of costs–benefit analyses in order to demonstrate to the City that it was acting responsibly. Yet the exercise was hardly one of self-deception as social-psychological theory implies. The suggested benefits were potentially feasible. The costs–benefits equation was undermined because critical assumptions were subsequently negated, complete de-materialization, for example. The demonstration buttressed the legitimacy of the venture by suggesting that the benefits of Taurus would not just fall to the Stock Exchange and institutional investors. Basically the cost–benefit analyses and other trappings of decision-making functioned as devices to impose a rationale where none existed, hence 'It all looked marvellous in the prospectus.'

A MULTI-PARADIGM APPROACH TO RESEARCH

A feature of the present study has been the utilization of multiple conceptual lenses to examine decision-making. The use of a multi-paradigm approach is controversial because each conceptual lens makes fundamentally different assumptions about the nature of knowledge.[9] It does, however, highlight previously underemphasized aspects of escalation. In particular, the questions posed by the different paradigms enable us to see how escalation results not so much from people behaving irrationally, but more from people behaving logically.

Escalation theory tacitly assumes the existence of a single decision-maker faced with a single problem. Taking a multi-paradigm approach exposes a plethora of decision problems and a plethora of decision-makers, all influencing the decision that is the primary focus of analysis. What makes escalation predicaments seem bizarre is the cumulative impact of multiple and sometimes conflicting rationales.

Escalation at the Macro-Level

The case of Taurus shows the value of considering decisions in their wider context, of opening analysis to the possibility that domination is tied to the deep structure of power.[10] Part of the sheer power of 'the Establishment' is that it is seldom exposed or challenged. Taurus was driven by two agendas. One was the determination of the securities industry establishment, which is dominated by institutional investors, to reduce risk primarily for its own benefit and at the potential expense of other constituencies of the securities industry. The second agenda centred upon the Stock Exchange's competitive strategy.

Many decision débâcles may be ultimately traceable to macro-level forces. For instance, it has been suggested that the arrest of a serial murderer in the UK known as the 'Yorkshire Ripper' was delayed, and lives lost as a result, because of police antipathy towards prostitutes.[11] Likewise, why do roll-on roll-off ferries continue to operate when the dangers have been clearly demonstrated in two major accidents? It is surely not because marine architects are oblivious to reality or some board of directors is afraid of losing face?

Studying persistence at the macro-level enables us to see how organizations become involved in decision fiascos in the first place. It is concluded that the decisive juncture arrives when a venture becomes institutionalized, that is, is 'taken for granted' because of its rule-like status.[12] The present study conceptualizes decision-making as the establishment of a myth. A myth was defined as reflecting the dominant viewpoint about what should be done about a particular issue at a particular point in time. Escalation starts with the establishment of received opinion. In the present case, received opinion became the need to eliminate paper in order to streamline settlement and reduce risk.

Received opinion is what gives a decision its power. Two other potentially relevant features of the decision-making process were the settlements crisis, which provided the impetus to Taurus by legitimizing received objectives, and the fusion between ends and means. Fusion was what locked the decision-makers into Taurus. Taurus was an infrastructure project which by itself achieved nothing. It merely facilitated the reduction of risk by paving the way for rolling settlement and 'delivery versus payment'. By creating and promulgating a project rhetoric, however, the venture became an end in itself: 'Taurus is vital to London.' Such is the power of received opinion that the venture stood sacrosanct even though it drifted further and further away from the original objectives.

Some observers thought Taurus was a nonsense from the start. Few players were willing to issue a public challenge, however, for fear of being seen as attempting to 'scupper' a project which purported to serve the common good. Such reluctance to defy the dominant viewpoint was a restraining factor throughout the project's history. From a macro-perspective the roots of escalation lie in a series of political 'non-decisions':[13] 'No one stepped forward and said, "I don't really understand this." '

The Stock Exchange's determination to build Taurus was partly a response to a power struggle within the City. The project was seen as a potential route to organizational survival. The community responded by turning Taurus into a trial of the Stock Exchange's efficacy: 'There was a general belief it had all gone on too long, all that arguing, and what was the Exchange there to do?' Viewed from a wide-angle lens, escalation emerges as a political balancing act, a choice between the lesser of two evils. Taurus may have been a technically inferior solution but it was at least apparently feasible, 'complex but do-able'.

When all those forces are considered it becomes evident that the decision-makers persisted because there was no choice other than to 'Do the bloody thing.'

Escalation at the Meso-Level

At the meso-level escalation emerges as an irony, the enactment of the political will. The metaphor of the tragedy of the commons was evoked to encapsulate this process.[14] The 'long long march' towards cancellation reflects the unfolding of the destructive logic of the situation. Just as the commons were ruined by every peasant grazing one more beast, Taurus is destroyed by everyone pursuing their respective and sometimes conflicting interests.

Initially layer after layer of complexity is added to the design as members of Siscot attempt to chisel advantage for their respective constituencies. Thereafter persistence is characterized less by decision-makers attempting to conceal mounting failure, or fear of embarrassment, and more by the observance of due diligence.

Due diligence is produced and reproduced by decision-makers' institutionalized acceptance of their roles. The board asks correct and peremptory questions but stops short of demanding to see the situation for themselves or considering the broader and possibly more relevant issue: 'Is this the right project?' The chief executive and the Taurus monitoring group fulfil the role of managers as fixers, problem solvers, and negotiators[15] in trying to make Taurus work: 'Let's get the bloody thing done and behind us.' Likewise the technical team concentrate on the intricacies of coding and recoding, diligently bashing one peg down, seeing another fly up, bashing that one down too. Yet they never challenge the project despite the emerging knowledge that the culmination of their ingenuity and commitment is a 'dog's breakfast'.

Institutionalization also dictates the decision-maker's treatment of their information. The process functions like a sausage machine. Information is prepared and evaluated in accordance with received practice. Intuition, rumour, and informal evidence are inadmissible as evidence—however well founded they may be.[16] Consequently information which might lead decision-makers to the truth is disregarded whilst data which lead them away from reality is received.

Due diligence is characterized by first-order thinking.[17] When, for example, progress fails to match the charts and 'nice timetables' the decision-makers respond by demanding 'more of the same'. Such actions solve nothing because the real problem lies elsewhere. They do, however, enable the decision-makers to be seen to be managing the situation even though ultimately due diligence becomes 'almost superficial'.[18]

Due diligence is the means whereby decision-makers protect themselves against the possibility of failure. Like the doctor whose patient dies, it is better to have prescribed the textbook treatment, even if it was ineffective, than to have ventured into the realms of 'unsound' clinical practice, even though such action might have saved the patient's life.

In the present case absurdity piles on absurdity as the logic of the situation unfolds. The technical team commence building and purchasing software before the design is even complete. They leave the completion of the system architecture to the end. Although the decisions seem bizarre, tracing the sequence of events reveals that each move was entirely logical, the product of a previous decision.

The collision between multiple and sometimes conflicting rationales intensifies the impression of collective folly. The chief executive's mission is to cut costs. Accordingly he dismisses the project monitors, 'disastrous for a start'. Likewise, the chief executive is responsible for the project yet has no control over it: 'Keep out of this please.' By seeking to rebalance the equation by creating a project executive, the chief executive actually ends up undermining the project.

At the meso-level, escalation is basically an irony. The situation which had been reached in 1991 consisted of the Government demanding unprecedented security precautions and changing fundamental aspects of the project. The writing of software was taking much longer and proving more difficult than anyone had imagined. As the project timetable slipped further and further, the decision-makers redoubled their efforts and strained their ingenuity to make the project work, tackling one problem after another because 'This is what some committee said we ought to do.'

Escalation at the Micro-Level

At the micro-level persistence emerges as the product of organizational and project forces which restrict the decision-maker's options, impede the flow of information, and generally compound the situation. The sheer size and complexity of Project Taurus afforded little room for experimentation or redesign.[19] Working at the boundaries of knowledge meant that timetables were very difficult to predict: 'You realized that you were increasingly operating at the edge of available technology. . . . not even the major suppliers could guarantee that what they were supplying would work.'

These factors, plus constant changes to the design, plus inadequate organizational control and communication mechanisms prevented the decision-makers from fully appreciating exactly what they were committing themselves to when they authorized the project. Latterly, such weaknesses obscured the extent of the difficulties, facilitated questionable working practices, stifled debate, and hid serious resource shortages.

Such factors help to explain why the relationship between information and commitment may be imperfect. Commitment to a venture may be enhanced if the decision-makers fail to appreciate the ramifications of their actions or if negative feedback is slow in reaching them.

It is concluded that social-psychological theory may be confusing the causes of escalation with the symptoms. The data suggest that what may appear as unwarranted optimism or blindness to reality is actually traceable to other factors. For example, the overall state of Taurus only became clear in November 1992. Hitherto when the technical team offered assurances such as, 'Yes, yes, we have that under control', what they were saying was correct, but, such assurances applied only to specific aspects of the project. Social psychological theory suggests decision-makers deceive themselves. The present study shows how the situation can deceive decision-makers. Decisions are prismatic entities and it can be very difficult to maintain an holistic picture.

Decision dilemma theorists focus upon the relationship between information and commitment. The case of Taurus suggests that we can usefully build upon the model by exploring the factors which may impede the emergence of information. Organizational weaknesses are significant but so too are politics, the organizational ethos and more deeply rooted forces, notably the institution of management.

Likewise, face-saving and other socially conditioned behaviours presumed to cause escalation may actually be symptomatic of a loss of control. For example, John Watson's statement made in late 1991 that systems were 95 per cent complete was unconvincing. The extremity of the claim was a sign that the project was in crisis. Moreover, hitherto such behaviours have been interpreted in the literature as aimed at maintaining appearances in the face of failure. The present study suggests that maintaining appearances may mean attempting to conserve support for a venture. Such action is not necessarily irrational especially where a decision is highly contestable, as was the case here. There were some sectors of the securities industry who might have been undismayed to see Taurus collapse because of the long-term threat to business interest.

TRIANGULATION OF ANALYTICAL PARADIGMS

The value of a multi-paradigm approach is revealed when the three lenses are triangulated. A functionalist perspective would emphasize weaknesses in the organizational systems of control which enable deviations from technical rationality. A structuralist perspective would focus upon the tensions created by conflicting projected objectives and the inherent contradictions of management and control. A social-constructionist perspective would focus upon the ambiguity of human agency and the extent to which success and failure are things we create for ourselves. Counter-posing paradigms allows us to see how various levels of interpretation are linked and how escalation is a function of all three factors and the interplay between them.

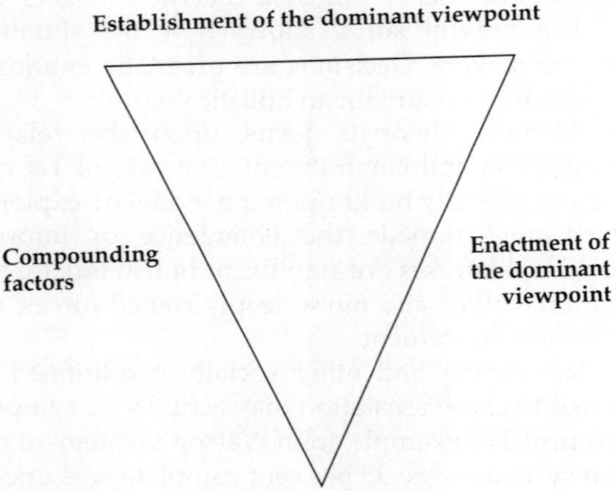

Establishment of the dominant viewpoint

Compounding factors

Enactment of the dominant viewpoint

FIG. 14.1 A synthesis of escalation

Figure 14.1 summarizes the analysis. Escalation begins with establishment of a myth. Persistence represents the enactment of the political will. Ironically, the playing out of the destructive logic of the situation is characterized by the observance of the due diligence, everyone, 'eyes down thinking this is going to be a tricky task to bring to bed.' Moreover, project and organizational factors combine to obscure reality. Persistence basically reflects a 'non-decision.' Although the venture becomes increasingly questionable those involved carry on because, 'this is what some committee said we ought to do.'

WITHDRAWAL AND THE DYNAMICS OF POWER

The present study has examined two competing views of withdrawal. Social-psychological theorists predict that withdrawal becomes more difficult as time goes on because of all the accumulated investments in a project. From a social-psychological standpoint withdrawal occurs either when social and psychological pressures weaken or when they are sharply overridden by the costs of persistence. Decision dilemma theorists suggest that withdrawal becomes easier with time as harsh reality destroys the decision-maker's commitment to a venture. An assumption common to both standpoints is that withdrawal is teleological.

The present study suggests that we need to move away from teleological assumptions and frameworks and instead focus upon the process whereby 'rationality' is reasserted. A striking feature of the present case concerns the impact of power in escalation and withdrawal.

Contrary to the idea that few commitments exist in the embryonic stages of a venture, the early phases may be the time when commitment is at its zenith. The chief executive was unable to stop the project even though nothing had been built because his arrival coincided with the institutionalization of the Taurus myth. The pressure to proceed with the project was immense: 'When are we going to build Taurus? Why can't it be quicker?' The chief executive's arrival also coincided with the emergence of a solution after a protracted debate. The situation had transformed itself into the paradox, 'where there is a way, there is a will.'[20] No one was interested in thinking again: 'We've had all those arguments. . . . forget it.' Further, although it was clear that the project was highly complex there was no evidence to suggest that it was unbuildable.

Thereafter, the myth begins to unravel. Ostensibly the data are consistent with decision dilemma theory. In 1991 it became clear that the ramifications of de-materialization were much more complex than had been realized. Accordingly the decision-makers took stock of the situation and decided, not unreasonably, to give the project another chance. However, when it became clear in 1993 that Taurus was going to need another two to three years-plus and another £50 million, they decided, again not unreasonably, to cancel the project.

ESCALATION AND WITHDRAWAL AS A POWER STRUGGLE

If we probe beneath the surface, however, the data suggest that a critical factor in explaining escalation and withdrawal is not information, but power. Indeed, the whole saga can be viewed as a power struggle.

The impetus to Taurus was the pursuit of vested interest. Taurus collapsed because the design became overly complex. Design complexity is traceable to the series of compromises rendered necessary because no one party was sufficiently powerful either to withdraw from participation or to get its own way over the design. The chief executive and the retail broking constituency were dismayed by the final decision but were powerless to stop the project: 'I did try to stop it and could not stop it,' says the chief executive. Subsequently, the Stock Exchange was insufficiently powerful to reject the Government's demands for investor protection, which gravely undermined the project.

Power is a dynamic phenomenon. However asymmetrical the relationship may be, the weaker party invariably has some power.[21] The dynamics of power are visible in the gradual undermining of the Taurus myth. The chief executive increases his control over the project by dint of reorganization and control of resources. The retail-broking constituency inflict severe damage via their unobtrusive campaign ('What if Mrs Snooks' shares get ripped off?'). Power increases exponentially as latterly a groundswell of negative opinion develops and is given conscious reality; hence, 'It was all starting to blow up.'

Withdrawal emerges as the creation of a new myth whereby one reality gives way to another. Withdrawal basically amounts to a struggle with all the forces for persistence: ' "gosh", . . . sinking jaws . . . City's prestige and all that sort of thing.' Information is a necessary but insufficient condition for this process to occur. The chief executive knew that the last thing he must do is take

Andersen's authoritative report straight to the board: 'This is Rawlins throwing a wobbly. He's lost his bottle.' Even when the chief executive manages to convince important players that there was not 'an ice-cream's chance' of Taurus being built in under two years, he still has to force them to concede abandonment: 'They wanted to believe I was wrong. They were fighting to find some reason to carry on.'

The present case lends empirical credence to the notion that information is potentially putty in the hands of decision-makers.[22] In the present case information serves as the basis for the construction of a competing rationale. However, it is not the information *per se* that is decisive but how it is interpreted and used. For example, cancellation is surrounded with an aura of certainty 'trussed, tied up, and done' whilst continuance is shot with doubt—'no guarantees'.

The chief executive uses a battery of weapons besides information to destroy commitment. He restricts the flow of resources to the project. He emphasizes the availability of alternatives: 'Don't tell me you need Taurus.' It is an example of domination through language.[23] Secrecy plays a vital part in withdrawal. Proponents of the old myth hardly have a chance to muster its defence.

Meanwhile the chief executive's behaviour in public seems bizarre. For instance, at the last meeting of the Taurus monitoring group members shake their heads and say, 'He doesn't know what's going on.' Latterly, persistence is explained by the time it takes to muster sufficient power to discredit the dominant viewpoint. In the present case it takes six months to close the project—almost 20 per cent of the total time-scale.

The present study highlights how escalation situations are capable of multiple meanings. The period from 1990 to 1993 is simultaneously a case of escalation, that is, commitment of resources, and a case of withdrawal.

WHAT IS A BAD DECISION?

Let me now ask a different question of the data. Instead of asking why the decision-makers persisted for so long, it could be asked, why they were able to withdraw at all and as soon as they were.

Reversing the analytical perspective in this way yields an insight which may provide an alternative to the perspective of economic rationality in explaining success and failure. At the risk of appearing contradictory, what made Taurus a 'bad' decision was that the project was never entirely institutionalized. The venture was never an entirely 'taken-for-granted' non-decision. In other words the difference between 'good' and 'bad' decisions resides in the level of sponsorship. A venture is judged legitimate and therefore rational if it is capable of commanding support.

IMPLICATIONS FOR SOCIAL-PSYCHOLOGICAL THEORIES OF ESCALATION

Although there are indications of social-psychological pressures in the data, these are not as pronounced as expected. This is arguably a reflection of the methodology. Weick argues that organizations obscure the behaviour of individuals. He suggests that if we want to understand organizations, we must stop studying them.[24]

The data in the present study suggest an alternative possibility. Organizations may limit the impact of individual behaviours. Although weaknesses existed in the Stock Exchange's system of checks and balances, it was not a total failure by any means and may have curbed escalatory tendencies. For example, the project team may have believed that they could make Taurus work given more time and more money. Persistence was curbed because the decision-makers eventually said, 'No more staff and no more money.'

It has been suggested that experimental scenarios underestimate escalatory tendencies. The present study is consistent with the corpus of literature which suggests that they exaggerate it.[25] Decisions in complex organizations are rarely made by one person operating in a vacuum. Budget reviews and other such devices may constrain a questionable course of action, as they did here.

Self-Justification Theory

The most significant theoretical insight from a social-psychological perspective concerns the impact of personal responsibility on decision-makers' behaviour. A major plank of social-psychological theory rests upon the presumed link between responsibility for a decision and escalation. It is thought that those responsible for a decision are more likely to persist when things turn out badly than are those who were not responsible for it.[26] In the present study the exact opposite happens. The chief executive as the person responsible for Taurus stops the project, knowing that the decision will cost him his job.

The issue is important because it has been argued that the acceptance of responsibility holds the key to preventing the tragedy of the commons.[27] Intervention in a 'commons' scenario requires power; that is, the ability to force individuals to abandon the pursuit of private interest where it conflicts with the common good. Significantly, the Stock Exchange was able to command such power over Talisman because it was a more homogeneous organization before 'Big Bang' revolutionized the balance of power in the City: 'Look, that may be your interest, but I ask you in the interest of the total institution, and of the totality of the savings world, not to press that point.'

The present case suggests a link between power and responsibility in predicting escalation. The hypothesized relationships are depicted in Figure 14.2. Basically, the greater the power to influence a decision and the less responsibility for its outcome, the

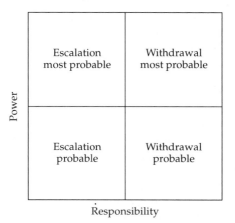

FIG. 14.2 Hypothesized relationships between power, responsibility, and escalation.

more likely it is that a decision will be corrupted. In the present case those least responsible for Taurus, that is, the securities market, had the power to inflict the greatest damage on the project. This power was evidenced mainly in the convoluted design followed by constant demands for change such that the requirements never stood still. The chief executive was always responsible for Taurus. Initially, however, his ability to influence the project was severely curtailed by organizational arrangements. In 1991 the chief executive had more power but his ability to take effective action was constrained by other priorities. Withdrawal was a probability but in the end came to nothing. Eventually, towards the end of 1992, the chief executive's sense of responsibility prompts him to develop his power. Withdrawal becomes highly probable under conditions of high power and high responsibility.

Extrapolating a little beyond the data, conceivably escalation is also probable under conditions of moderate power and moderate responsibility. These are the conditions most likely to result in escalation through strategic drift. Since the decision-makers are neither burdened with a sense of responsibility, nor likely to be fired by a sense of potency, they may decide to let things be.

Self-justification theory assumes that decision-makers accept responsibility for their actions. The present case suggests that, in practice, they may try to avoid blame by distancing themselves from the venture. A feature of the Taurus saga is the number of voices which were silent when the project collapsed. Conversely, people in organizations may claim responsibility when a decision turns out better than expected.

NEW DIRECTIONS FOR RESEARCH

The most exciting developments in research typically derive from discarding the bounding assumptions of theory or approaching the phenomenon from a different angle. If we abandon the assumption that decisions are capable of objective verification, what new possibilities does that open up for research?

Instead of focusing upon the notion of irrational persistence, it might be more fruitful to investigate how decision-makers allocate scarce resources. What rationale do they adopt, and in what circumstances?

The case of Taurus enables us to see not just escalation in decision-making, but decision-making in an escalatory predicament. The image portrayed by the data is one of a series of gambles. The literature largely assumes that gambling in the face of poor odds arises from overstimulation or overconfidence.[28] The present study suggests that the time is ripe to redress the balance. Instead of assuming such behaviour is *de facto* irrational, we need to understand how decision-makers weigh risk and potential reward, and how scarcity may force them into sub-optimal decisions.

Likewise, instead of assuming decision-makers interpret their information in a biased manner when things are turning out badly, it might be fruitful to consider more precisely how decision-makers evaluate feedback. For example, I suggested in Chapter 10 that in autumn 1991, the level of project completion was nil. The decision-makers, however, apparently believed the project was '50 per cent of the way there, 60 per cent of the way'. This suggests that decision-makers equate elapsed time with partial project completion. This is not necessarily irrational but probably reflects a complex calculation based on a combination of 'hard' information and crude projection. The present study suggests that there may be much to be gained from building upon studies which have examined the impact of time, uncertainty, and a venture's perceived importance upon decisions to persist with a course of action.[29]

Much has been said about the impact of received practice. An interesting avenue for research would be to investigate the circumstances in which decision-makers disregard professional norms and practices. For example, a decision to refuse credit facilities to a 'triple A' rated institution[30] might be highly unusual but not necessarily an example of irrational withdrawal.

PARADIGM DEVELOPMENT

Hitherto, escalation studies have been almost entirely rooted in the functionalist tradition. Studying escalation from a social-constructionist perspective has enabled a less frequently asked question to be posed, that is, what is escalation? Examining the logic of the situation and the structure of power relations enables us to understand why decision-makers may persist in the face of highly negative information and yet such persistence is not necessarily irrational.

Adopting an unconventional conceptual lens has yielded new metaphors which may not only help us grasp the nature of escalation, but also suggest new plausible hypotheses for research. In particular, the image of attacking a castle was invoked to suggest that the tactics used to destroy a myth may relate systematically to the decision-makers' perceived power.

Perhaps the most exciting way forward lies in identifying a battery of metaphors to understand and explore escalation. Hitherto research has focused on isolating possible causes and synthesizing these into macro-variables. Such an approach assumes that escalation is caused by one major force at any point in time. The present study suggests that we need to move away from simple cause-and-effect explanations and instead develop more complex equations.

A useful metaphor might be that of the 'deadly cocktails', that is, particular combinations of factors where interaction increases potency beyond the sum of its parts, just as the combination of alcohol and narcotics is highly dangerous even in low doses. In the present case one such 'cocktail' consisted of the perceived importance of Taurus combined with inadequate knowledge and an illusory sense of control. The perceived importance of Taurus provided the impetus to persist with the project whilst the other ingredients obscured the risks involved.

Another potentially exciting avenue for research is to conduct multiple-case comparisons. Escalation theory is riveted by the notion of fiasco. Some misguided-decision fiascos, perhaps the majority, simply peter out—the Stock Exchange's multi-million pound electronic trading floor that lasted six weeks (see Chapter Four), for example. The operation of power and political behaviours can produce good decisions as well as bad ones. Moreover, they can be deployed to close potentially successful ventures. There is probably much to be learned from studying 'good' decisions and examples of 'irrational' withdrawal as distinct from the seemingly more obvious débâcles like Taurus. The key may be to stand back from the notion of irrational persistence and instead base research upon tracing the establishment and development of decisions as myths.

A highly fruitful site for research may be to trace the seemingly mundane and bizarre practices we see in organizations. I am reminded here of an episode in my own career where I encountered three clerks inputting nutritional values of school meals into a computer. 'We used to have to do it by law,' explained the manager. 'It's not so important now but we still do it.' Mundanity is an illusion. If we were to investigate this tiny episode of persistence it would probably reveal much about the link between the establishment and partial destruction of a myth and resource-allocation decisions.[31]

Ultimately it would probably show that 'irrational persistence' is capable of being understood but is not necessarily attributable to specific causes. A striking feature of the present case is that whilst project and organizational factors compounded the loss, they did not cause escalation. It is perhaps impossible to say what causes escalation. It is something that we create largely for ourselves.

SOME PRACTICAL AND POLICY IMPLICATIONS

Taurus was a highly public failure. Decision débâcles occur day-in, day-out in organizations. The waste is incalculable. What can Taurus teach us that may be useful for the future?

Managers and policy-makers need to recognize a decision for what it is, that is, the establishment of the dominant viewpoint. Ventures become sacerdotal because people make them so. No project, however vital it may seem, is beyond challenge. A critical point in Taurus was the fusion between ends and means. The question which leaders need to impress upon management teams is 'what are you trying to achieve?' In the present case every layer of complexity that was added to the design led decision-makers further away from their objectives.

In the present case the greatest damage is inflicted by people behaving correctly. History is full of examples of people who were rewarded for subscribing to received opinion—for example, the generals who sent thousands of troops 'over the top'. Conversely, the convoy system was facilitated by smuggling a junior officer into Downing Street. Breaking out of institutionalization requires decision-makers to behave like the celebrated jury who, knowing the local situation, delivered the verdict, 'not guilty provided he returns the sheep,' and when challenged by the judge, duly reconsidered and concluded, 'not guilty and he can keep the sheep.'[32]

Taurus also lends credence to the idea espoused in the 'total quality management' literature of integrating specialisms from the start. IT professionals cannot divorce themselves from the business ramifications of decisions or confine their role to 'doing the bloody thing'. Likewise, nor can general managers perform properly with scant knowledge of the technical implications of their decisions. Communication rather than technical literacy is the key.

Taurus also teaches us that it is not the decision-makers' information that is important so much as knowing the limits of their data.

Finally, Taurus is one more reminder that the odds are stacked against large and complicated IT projects.[33] As risk is difficult to quantify and control, why create it?

BRILLIANT AND DAFT

After Taurus collapsed a small team of staff were retained to archive the project. It was a soul-destroying task, working in empty rooms, moving through rows of deserted work stations, lifting pens and papers lying just as colleagues had left them when the fateful announcement was broadcast. Inevitably the question arises: was cancellation 'the right decision' after all?

It could be argued that the Stock Exchange abandoned a successful line of action in 1981 when Council decided against investing more money in 'Mr Gascoigne's schemes'. Then again, 'Big Bang' was already in the air. The Stock Exchange must put its own house in order, said the partners of the big firms.

What if the Stock Exchange had gone ahead? Would Taurus have 'been in by now' as some observers have suggested, or would it have collapsed anyway as the testing programme revealed the whole shambles? In that case, might Taurus have brought the Stock Exchange down with it? Assuming it had been implemented, would it have been regarded as a good system or a 'dog's breakfast'? Talisman, it was said, was not a particularly good system. It just had the merit of working. It also came to generate almost 50 per cent of the Stock Exchange's income. Did the Bank of England really start with a 'clean sheet' in designing Crest, the successor to Taurus? Or is Crest an example of first-order thinking, the securities industry basically trying 'more of the same', a familiar tune transposed to a different key? Does it mean that the vested interests that underscored Taurus have succeeded in reasserting themselves?

I am not suggesting that persistence and withdrawal were either right or wrong. I conclude that each was a plausible response to circumstances. Ultimately it is all a matter of opinion. More importantly, what emerges here is that the idea of a 'clear-cut case' for persistence or for withdrawal based on 'unassailable logic' is an illusion. There are no absolutes. The decisive factor is received opinion at a particular point in time. We could conclude that Taurus was daft. We could perhaps argue that it was brilliant. What the present case shows is that in decision-making, it is whose opinion that is received that is decisive.

NOTES

1. Hedberg and Jonsonn (1977), Meyer and Rowan (1978).
2. The point is articulated in Funder (1987). See also Devons (1961), Meyer and Rowan (1978), Morgan (1986), Quaid (1993).
3. For example, Brockner *et al.* (1981), Brockner *et al.* (1984), Teger (1980).
4. Brunnson (1989), Kamens (1977), Meyer and Rowan (1978).
5. Kay (1993), London Business School (1995).
6. Bowen (1987).
7. As is suggested by, respectively, Ross and Staw (1986) and Ross and Staw (1993).
8. Devons (1961), Feldman and March (1981), Gowler and Legge (1983), Quaid (1993).
9. Principally derived from Allison (1991), Burrell and Morgan (1979), Gioía and Pitre (1990), and Morgan (1990).
10. Clegg (1981), Giddens (1979), Luke (1974).
11. Yallop (1993).
12. Bacharach and Baratz (1970), Berger and Luckman (1966), Meyer and Rowan (1978), Zucker (1977).
13. Bacharach and Baratz (1963).

14. Hardin (1968). See also Aram (1989).
15. See, for example, Downs (1967), Hales (1986), Mintzberg (1973), Stewart (1989), Thompson (1967), and Wilmott (1987).
16. Mintzberg (1994) and Mumby and Putnam (1992).
17. Watzlawick *et al.* (1974).
18. Meyer and Rowan (1978).
19. Collingridge (1992), Etzioni (1989), Perrow (1984), Willcocks and Griffiths (unpub. mimeo, n.d.).
20. Cohen *et al.* (1972).
21. Principally Lukes (1974), Martin (1977), Pfeffer (1992), Simmel (1950).
22. See, for example, Drummond (1991*b*), Pettigrew (1973), Pfeffer (1981), Toffler (1992).
23. O'Barr (1984).
24. Weick (1974).
25. For example, Drummond (1994*a*, 1995), Goltz (1992), Hantuala and Crowell (1994*a*, *b*), McCain (1986), Singer and Singer (1986*a*).
26. See, or example, Brockner (1992), Staw (1976, 1980, 1981), Tetlock (1991).
27. Hardin (1968).
28. For example, Langer (1975, 1983), Griffiths (1990), Schwenck (1986).
29. Brockner and Rubin (1985) and Rubin and Brockner (1975).
30. 'Triple A' denotes high creditworthiness.
31. Weick (1974).
32. Gilbert (1986).
33. For example, Willcocks and Griffiths (no date).

POSTSCRIPT

It is now almost three years since Taurus was cancelled. Much has happened since then. NatWest have disposed of their registration business. Barclay's too is said to be for sale. The global custodian industry is apparently undergoing a massive restructuring. Famous City firms—Barings, Kleinwort-Benson, and Warburg's—are about to lose their independence in what appears to be a second 'Big Bang', the death throes of the old club culture. The irony is that the City of London retains its supremacy as a world financial centre though control of its institutions is increasingly passing to foreign firms.

An organization known as Tradepoint has opened up as a possible rival to the Stock Exchange. For its part, the Stock Exchange is considering the creation of its own interdealer broker service, an intermediary for share transactions between market professionals in direct competition with its own member firms. Five-day rolling settlement has been achieved within a paper-based environment though at some cost, especially to the more poorly organized brokers. Crest is nine months away from implementation. The consensus of opinion seems to be that unlike Taurus, it will be implemented because it is underwritten by the authority of the Bank of England.[1] Whether Crest will be a success is another question. It is a very simple system devoid of some of the better features of Taurus. Then again, the sheer complexity of Taurus was one reason why it collapsed. Moreover, some observers are suggesting that Crest has cost the City the opportunity to create an integrated settlement infrastructure embracing all trading activities in finance and commodities. Others disagree, arguing that Crest is paving the way for this very development.[2] One thing which has emerged is the commercial potential of providing settlement services. The back office is no longer 'the province of Gladys'. That, of course, was what some of the more sophisticated players in the Taurus saga saw all along.

Many of the people who suffered redundancy following the cancellation of Taurus have since found work, though sometimes only to lose it again. Some of the former Taurus technical staff see one another occasionally at seminars about Crest and at other events. The 'dinosaurs' still meet as a dining club, their numbers diminishing with the passing years.[3]

One of the last visits in connection with this research was to the Guildhall Library. It was a poignant experience watching scholars poring over old ledgers, patiently deciphering crackled pages of black lettering, carefully undoing the faded pink tape on a quire of papers. One day the Taurus archive may be deposited here, 'trussed, tied up, and done'. What will business historians have to say about it a century from now?

The library was an appropriate setting to reflect upon the possibility that time does indeed travel backwards as well as forwards. The Stock Exchange's apparently life-expired Talisman system will soon be scrapped: 'We will be back to settling in each other's offices,' said Patrick Mitford-Slade.[4] Well, perhaps some of the fun might come back into the City. People are already beginning to congregate in coffee houses to connect into the information highway. How long before auction notices, news sheets, and price-current lists including 'The Course of the Exchange and Other Things' are to be found there, and what surcharge will be levied in the twenty-first century for 'bread, cookin, and taters'?

Meanwhile, what of the people who disappeared into Taurus working groups to deal with corporate actions, rules, and so forth? In spirit they are still there. The issues may have changed but the questions are the same: 'Whether this way or that way . . . we-ell, the network's not there, anyway it doesn't work very well, and besides, . . . can all the firms cope?' Ultimately, 'all that arguing' and indeed the copious volumes of decision theory come down to one question: 'Is this really the right way to go?'

There never is an answer.

Liverpool
5 November, 1995.

NOTES

1. Patrick Mitford-Slade, (personal communication, Oct. 1995).
2. Partner, Coopers and Lybrand Deloitte, (personal communication, Sept. 1995).
3. Patrick Mitford-Slade, (personal communication, Sept. 1995).
4. Ibid.

NEWSPAPER AND MAGAZINE ARTICLES ON TAURUS, 1986–1993

(in chronological order)

Wolman, C., 'Stock Exchange to Computerise Transfers', *Financial Times* (22 May 1986), 48.

Shale, T., 'The Sharp End of Borrowing and Lending', *Euromoney* (Sept. 1987), 421.

Cane, A., 'From Here to Maturity', *Financial Times* (30 Oct. 1987), 33.

Brandenberg, M., 'Winners and Losers in the Wake of Big Bang', *Accountancy* (Oct. 1988), 67–9.

Lascelles, D., 'Share Transfer "Fraud Risk" ', *Financial Times* (17 Jan. 1989), 8.

Cane, A., 'SE Revises Plans for Technology', *Financial Times* (29 Jan. 1989), 8.

Wolman, C., 'Taurus is a Sign of Troubled Times to Come', *Financial Times* (6 Feb. 1989), 6.

'London Bids Farewell to a Transparent Stockmarket', *The Economist*, 25 Feb. 1989), 89–90.

Wolman, C., 'Share Settlement Plan Scaled Down', *Financial Times* (17 Mar. 1989), 1.

——, 'Questions Linger after Settlements Decision', *Financial Times* (17 Mar. 1989), 90.

'Taurus', *Financial Times* (20 Mar. 1989), 26.

Grayson, R. C., 'Telescope on Taurus', *Financial Times* (28 Mar. 1989), 23.

Wolman, C., 'Opposition to Sepon Share Registration Option Grows', *Financial Times* (3 Apr. 1989), 8.

——, 'Stock Exchange to Have Paperless Share Register', *Financial Times* (4 Apr. 1989), 10.

'Taurus', *Financial Times* (4 Apr. 1989), 24.

Day, C., 'A Modern Settlement', *Public Finance & Accountancy*, 28 Apr. 1989), 7.

Wolman, C., 'Rebellion Expected over SE Settlements', *Financial Times* (30 May 1989), 1.

Shale, T., 'Is ISE too Ambitious about its Technology?', *Euromoney* (May 1989), 117.

Waters, R., 'Paperless Trading to be Eased', *Financial Times* (15 June 1989), 10.

——, 'Compromise Imminent on Share Settlement Plans', *Financial Times* (21 June 1989), 10.

Murphy, P., 'The Long, Long March', *The Banker* (July 1989), 163.

Riley, B., 'Meeting Small Brokers' Objections', *Financial Times* (7 July 1989), 4.

Marsden, H., 'Taurus and the Private Client', *Financial Times* (15 July 1989), 7.

Murphy, P., 'One on the Nose for ISE', *The Banker* (Aug. 1989), 24.

Waters, R., 'Paperless Share Deals Scheme to be Delayed', *Financial Times* (17 Aug. 1989), 18.

——, 'Exchange Scheme for Paperless Trading Alarms Listed Companies', *Financial Times* (4 Sept. 1989), 6.

——, 'Rawlins May Head Stock Exchange', *Financial Times* (19 Sept. 1989), 1.

'New Boy at the Exchange', *The Economist* (7 Oct. 1989), 116.

Waters, R., 'Disagreement Threatens to Stall Work on City's Taurus Project', *Financial Times* (9 Oct. 1989), 22.

——, 'Taurus Plan Enters Critical Phase', *Financial Times* (9 Oct. 1989), 10.

Stevens, D. A., 'Share Dealing Costs', *Financial Times* (20 Nov. 1989), 25.

Waters, R., 'Further Changes Planned for SE's Taurus', *Financial Times* (30 Nov. 1989), 26.

Riley, B., 'SE Taurus Settlement System Criticised', *Financial Times* (6 Dec. 1989), 8.

Campbell, C., 'Dealing with Taurus', *Financial Times* (7 Dec. 1989), 23.

Waters, R., 'SE's Taurus Expected to be Given Go-ahead Today', *Financial Times* (13 Dec. 1989), 7.

——, 'Taurus System is Approved for SE Settlements', *Financial Times* (14 Dec. 1989), 8.

'Pumping Life into the London Exchange's Heart', *The Economist* (20 Jan. 1990), 103.

'Bruce Goes', (1990) *Financial Times* (26 Jan. 1990), 18.

'SE's Taurus System Comes Closer', *The Times* (24 Feb. 1990), 18.

Freeman, A., 'Rolling Settlement "Will Delay Taurus" ', *Financial Times* (9 Mar. 1990), 33.

Waller, D., 'Stock Exchange Prepares Traders for Paperless Settlement', *Financial Times* (10 Mar. 1990), 4.

Freeman, A., 'Taurus System Expected to Save £255m', *Financial Times* (10 Mar. 1990), 24.

'Taurus', *Financial Times* (10 Mar. 1990), 24.

'Abolition will Coincide with Introduction of Taurus System', *Financial Times* (21 Mar. 1990), 18.

Waters, R., 'Share-Dealing to Cost 25% Less', *Financial Times* (24 Mar. 1990), 5.

Goldstein-Jackson, K., 'Taurus—and the Bear Market', *Financial Times* (28 Apr. 1990), 6.

Wilson, N., 'The Emperor's New Clothes', *The Banker* (May 1990), 16.

Watson, J., 'Stock Exchange Takes Bull by the Horns with Taurus', *The Times* (28 May 1990), 31.

Freeman, A., 'SE Says Taurus May Cost 3,000 jobs', *Financial Times* (31 May 1990), 24.

Tate, M., 'Taurus "Likely to Cost up to 3,000 Jobs" ', *The Times* (31 May 1990), 21.

Freeman, A., 'Taurus Loan Arranged', *Financial Times* (1 June 1990), 31.

Waller, D., 'DTI Seeks Comment on Taurus', *Financial Times* (12 July 1990), 6.

Financial Staff, 'Warning on Cost of Taurus to Companies', *Financial Times* (3 Sept. 1990), 8.

Cane, A., 'Taurus Users will Pay only for Services Needed', *Financial Times* (27 Sept. 1990), 8.

'Taurus Snag', *The Times* (28 Sept. 1990), 23.

Chalton, S., 'Dematerialisation of Financial Instruments', *Computer Law & Practice* (Sept./Oct. 1990), 30–4.

Waters, R., 'Frequent Share Checks will Cost More under Taurus', *Financial Times* (2 Oct. 1990), 10.

'Order, Order', *The Economist* (6 Oct. 1990), 128.

Seargeant, G., 'Lending of Shares Set to Grow', *The Times* (24 Oct. 1990), 26.

Mallet, P. L. V., 'Taurus is Bad News for Technology-Shy Investors', *Financial Times* (15 Dec. 1990), 7.

'Taking Taurus by the Horns', *Financial Times* (27 Dec. 1990), 12.

Sergeant, P. A., 'Does Taurus Mean the End of the Private Shareholder?', *Financial Times* (8 Jan. 1991), 15.

Dobie, C., 'Draft Rules for Taurus will Miss Target Date', *The Independent* (23 Jan. 1991), 23.

Barchard, D., 'Stock Exchange Delays Taurus Launch to Next Year', *Financial Times* (26 Jan. 1991), 5.

'Taurus', *Financial Times* (26 Jan. 1991), 22.

Dobie, C., 'Delay by DTI Reprieves Share Certificates', *The Independent* (26 Jan. 1991), 17.

Campbell, C., 'Taurus Delayed after Deadline Proves too Demanding', *The Times* (26 Jan. 1991), 29.

'Taurus Delay an International Blow', *The Independent* (29 Jan. 1991), 23.

Marland, D., 'Stock Exchange Must Realise Taurus Cannot be All Things to all Men', *Financial Times* (31 Jan. 1991), 19.

Waters, R., 'Hold-up for Taurus', *Financial Times* (2 Feb. 1991), 4.

Willett, J., 'Taurus Mystery', *Financial Times* (26 Feb. 1991), 17.

Summers, D., 'Pay Stall Brings Fear of Delay to Taurus', *Financial Times* (1 Mar. 1991), 11.

Bennett, N., 'Exchange to Boost Security', *The Times* (5 Mar. 1991), 21.

'Taurus Safeguards', *Financial Times* (8 Mar. 1991), 7.

'Getting Ready for Taurus', *The Independent* (16 Mar. 1991), 22.

Waters, R., 'Compensation for Share Fraud Losses to Rise', *Financial Times* (21 Mar. 1991), 8.

Prynn, J., 'Taurus Safety Set as Priority', *The Times* (21 Mar. 1991), 30.

——, 'ISE Fund Debate Continues', *The Times* (6 May 1991), 30.

Dobie, C., '£250,000 Taurus Compensation Scheme Planned by Exchange', *The Independent* (21 Mar. 1991), 30.

'Reshaping the Exchange', (1991) *Financial Times* (9 Apr. 1991), 24.

Waters, R., 'Dispute May Delay Taurus Project', *Financial Times* (29 Apr. 1991), 18.

'Taurus', *The Financial Times* (30 Apr. 1991), 22.

Waters, R., 'Share Trading Compensation Row', *Financial Times* (4 May 1991), 24.

'Heel-Dragging Threatens City', *The Independent* (8 May 1991), 25.

Dobie, C., '£100m Compensation Fund Set for Taurus', *The Independent* (11 May 1991), 17.

'Decision Due on Taurus', *The Times* (13 May 1991), 21.

Waters, R., 'City Regulators Angry over Taurus Decision', *Financial Times* (14 May 1991), 8.

McRae, H., 'Shared Blame for Taurus Delays', *The Independent* (16 May 1991), 29.

'Taurus', *Financial Times* (17 May 1991), 22.

'Taurus Date', *The Times* (17 May 1991), 27.

Seargeant, G., 'Protective Measures will Cover Taurus', *The Times* (17 May 1991), 27.

Waller, D., 'Minister Commends Taurus Rules', *Financial Times* (17 May 1991), 8.

'Plans for Taurus Charge Ahead', *Financial Times* (18 May 1991), 4.

Dunham, R., 'Countdown to Taurus', *Accountancy* (May 1991), 107.

Waters, R., 'Stock Exchange Reports £5.1m Deficit', *Financial Times* (14 June 1991), 7.

'Taurus Criteria', *Financial Times* (28 June 1991), 8.

Holmes, G., and Sugden, A., 'The Stock Exchange in the Ring', *Accountancy* (June 1991), 72–3.

Jones, D., 'Banks Step Up Taurus Preparations', *Banking World*, (June 1991), 42.

Rennison, A., 'The Bull Charges Forward', *Banking World* (July 1991), 16–78.

Mercer, C., 'Taurus and the London Stock Exchange Paperless Securities Transfers', *Computer Law & Practice* (July / Aug. 1991), 238–46.

Coggan, P., 'Taurus Info Campaign', *Financial Times* (3 Aug. 1991), 4.

Scott, M., 'Stock Exchange Aims for a Bull's Eye with Taurus', *The Independent* (3 Aug. 1991), 19.

'Taurus Safeguards to be Reviewed', (1991) *Financial Times* (7 Aug. 1991), 6.

Waters, R., 'SE Deals Computer Faces Threat of Renewed Delays', *Financial Times* (10 Aug. 1991), 5.

Dobie, C., 'Taurus Hit by Further Delays', *The Independent* (10 Aug. 1991), 15.

Prynn, J., 'Delays Threaten Taurus Launch', *The Times* (10 Aug. 1991), 24.

Waters, R., 'Stockbrokers Fear Rise in Costs after Changes to Trading System', *Financial Times* (12 Aug. 1991), 14.

'Home Thoughts from Abroad', (1991) *The Economist* (17 Aug. 1991), 74.

Goldstein-Jackson, K., 'The Hidden Costs of Taurus', *Financial Times* (31 Aug. 1991), 6.

'Bull in a China Shop', (1991) *The Banker* (Aug. 1991), 39–42.

Narbrough, C., 'Exchange Brings in Outside Directors', *The Times* (3 Sept. 1991), 19.

Dobie, C., 'Taurus is the Test for the Exchange', *The Independent* (3 Sept. 1991), 21.

Watson, J. S., 'Anxieties about Taurus are Natural but Unfounded', *Financial Times* (7 Sept. 1991), 7.

Waters, R., 'Taurus Settlement System "Likely to Miss Target Date"', *Financial Times* (16 Sept. 1991), 1.

——, 'Man with a Bull by the Horns', *Financial Times* (18 Sept. 1991), 11.

'Director of Taurus Under Fire', *The Independent* (19 Sept. 1991), 28.

Seargeant, G., 'Taurus Rethink Urged by Law Society', *The Times* (25 Sept. 1991), 21.

'New Wounds for Troubled Taurus : Footnote', *The Times* (25 Sept. 1991), 23.

Dunham, R., 'Taurus to Go Live Next Year', *Accountancy* (Sept. 1991), 84.

Carter-Ruck, P., 'Beware Computers', *The Times* (1 Oct. 1991), 26.

Hunter-Smart, A., 'Need for a Rethink on Taurus', *The Times* (1 Oct. 1991), 26.

Dobie, C., 'Taurus Costs Rise for Exchange', *The Independent* (3 Oct. 1991), 29.

——, 'Complaints force Taurus redraft' *The Independent* (15 Oct. 1991), 25.

Kinsella, R. P., 'Taurus Requires a More Credible Timetable', *The Times* (15 Oct. 1991), 27.

London, S., 'Timetable for Introduction of Taurus Revealed', *Financial Times* (18 Oct. 1991), 36.

Cole, R., 'Taurus to be Delayed for a Year', *The Independent* (18 Oct. 1991), 22.

Seargeant, G., 'Taurus Delayed until Spring 1993', *The Times* (18 Oct. 1991), 23.

'Rawlins Takes Bull by the Horns', *The Times* (18 Oct. 1991), 25.

London, S., 'Taurus Delay', *Financial Times* (19 Oct. 1991), 4.

Leonard, C., 'Ruthless Enemy of the Status Quo', *The Times* (19 Oct. 1991), 19.

'London Stock Exchange Unsettled Taurus', *The Economist* (26 Oct. 1991), 130.

'Gearing up for Taurus' (1991) *Banking World* (Oct. 1991), 29–30.

Waters, R., 'Taurus Poised to Clear Final Hurdles', *Financial Times* (20 Dec. 1991), 17.

'Taurus Code Leaves Gap', *The Independent* (8 Jan. 1992), 23.

'Computer Review Ordered at Exchange', *Financial Times* (18 Jan. 1992), 4.

'Consultants Code Change at Exchange for Taurus', *The Independent* (20 Jan. 1992), 20.

Owen, D., 'Mowlam Opens Attack on Regulation of Taurus', *Financial Times* (29 Jan. 1992), 10.

Dobie, C., 'Labour Sees New SIB Role', *The Independent* (29 Jan. 1992), 25.

Waters, R., 'Parliament Approves Taurus Change', *Financial Times* (12 Feb. 1992), 28.

——, 'Clearing Banks Delay Plans to Join Taurus', *Financial Times* (18 Feb. 1992), 30.

——, 'Banks Look at Central Register for Shares', *Financial Times* (21 Feb. 1992), 20.

Cohen, N., 'Stock Exchange Passes Taurus System Milestone', *Financial Times* (24 Feb. 1992), 6.

Laurie, S., 'He Who Rides a Tiger', *The Banker* (Feb. 1992), 36.

Temple, P., 'Taurus and its Traumas', *Accountancy* (Mar. 1992), 94.

'New Issues for Securities Traders', *Banking World* (Mar. 1992), 29.

Smith, A. H., 'Taurus Protects the Investor', *The Times* (3 Apr. 1992), 25.

'Exchange Contracts Out IT Operation', *Financial Times* (14 Apr.), 10.

'Anderson to Operate Exchange Computers', *The Times* (14 Apr. 1992), 18.

Watson, J. S., 'Taurus Role in Cutting Cost of Share Registration', *Financial Times* (30 Apr. 1992), 21.

Waters, R., 'SE Reviews Privileges of its Market Makers', *Financial Times* (19 May 1992), 7.

Prynn, J., 'SE to Review System of Market-Making', *The Times* (19 May 1992), 17.

'Battling on All Fronts', *The Banker* (May 1992), 46.

'Swift Busters Strike Out', *The Banker* (May 1992), 44.

Rennison, A., 'Taurus and Collateral—What the Future Holds', *Banking World* (May 1992), 13–19.

Corrigan, T., 'SE Issues Proposed Taurus Regulations', *Financial Times* (6 June 1992), 7.

'Under Fire', *Financial Times* (16 June 1992), 21.

'London Stock Exchange', *Financial Times* (16 June 1992), 22.

Ashworth, J., 'Taurus Costs Soaring', *The Times* (16 June 1992), 19.

Tyler, C., 'What if Taurus should get a Virus?' *The Times* (4 July 1992), 32.

Fagan, M., 'Brokers "Wasted £100m on Systems" ', *The Independent* (14 July 1992), 23.

Hosking, P., 'Cautious M&S Refuses to Put Taurus to the Vote', *The Independent* (18 July 1992), 17.

Watson, J., 'Taurus Offers Data Security', *The Times* (23 July 1992), 21.

Dobie, C., 'Rawlins Ruffles some Feathers', *The Independent* (24 July 1992), 25.

Bear, H., 'Taurus is a Triumph of Monopoly', *The Times* (29 July 1992), 21.

Franklin, A. H. B., 'Welcome for Taurus', *The Times* (1 Aug. 1992), 20.

Paxton, J., 'Not Bullish on Taurus', *The Times* (6 Aug. 1992), 19.

Ackers, G., 'Marks and Spencer Shareholders did not Vote Against Joining Taurus', *The Times* (13 Aug. 1992), 19.

Maddrell, G., 'Taurus May Prove too Complex for Private Investors', *The Times* (18 Aug. 1992), 19.

Gates, D. J., 'Reasons to Take Taurus by the Horns', *The Times* (20 Aug. 1992), 19.

Waters, R., 'Cloudy Future for Taurus', *Financial Times* (22 Aug. 1992), 5.

Montier, D., 'Taurus Hampers Private Investors', *The Times* (24 Aug. 1992), 17.

Paxton, J., 'Taurus Inhibits Wider Share Ownership', *The Times* (28 Aug. 1992), 21.

Bear, H. F., 'Stock Exchange should Talk, not Dictate, to Private Shareholders', *The Times* (28 Aug. 1992), 21.

Hugh-Smith, A. H., 'The Time has Come for Investors to Take Taurus by the Horns', *The Times* (2 Sept. 1992), 19.

Woodgate, T. D. W., 'Taurus and the Private Investor', *The Times* (3 Sept. 1992), 19.

'Unsettled Controversies', *The Economist* (5 Sept. 1992), 110.

Collie, G. F., 'Out of Touch with the Man in the Street over Taurus', *The Times* (8 Sept. 1992), 19.

Pope, J., 'Where a Computer is Found Wanting', *The Times* (8 Sept. 1992), 19.

Santilhano, F., 'How Quickly will I Know I have Sold?' *The Times* (8 Sept. 1992), 19.

Jackson, J. D., 'Taurus Worry', *The Times* (15 Sept. 1992), 21.

Bellwood, M., 'Quicker Taurus', *The Times* (16 Sept. 1992), 23.

Bateman, M., 'Be Magnanimous and Forget the Trials of Taurus', *The Times* (29 Sept. 1992), 23.

Dobie, C., 'City Still Unprepared', *The Independent* (21 Oct. 1992), 25.

Smith, A. H., 'Taurus Strengthens Shareholder Safeguards', *The Times* (22 Oct. 1992), 30.

Baggott, S. D., 'Gilts Excluded', *The Times* (2 Nov. 1992), 38.

Miller, G. B., 'Bucking at Implementation of the Taurus Share System', *The Times* (4 Nov. 1992), 25.

'Taurus Keeps City Guessing', *The Independent* (6 Nov. 1992), 29.

Corrigan, T., 'SE Chief Urges Greater Powers for Regulators', *Financial Times* (24 Nov. 1992), 20.

Hotten, R., 'Exchange's Taurus Set for Further Delay', *The Independent* (24 Nov. 1992), 27.

Seargeant, G., 'Bank Charges Taurus in Firing Line', *The Times* (11 Jan. 1993), 36.

Oldham, G. D. R., 'Taurus Need Not Bring an Increase in Charges', *The Times* (14 Jan. 1993), 27.

Waters, R., 'Taurus Delay Prolongs Stamp Duty on Shares', *Financial Times* (18 Jan. 1993), 13.

Shamash, D., 'US Has Shown How Taurus Could Be Run', *The Times* (22 Jan. 1993), 23.

Waters, R., 'Taurus the Octopus', *Financial Times* (22 Jan. 1993), 10.

Paterson, D., 'Software Houses Bear High Costs of SE's Taurus', *Financial Times* (29 Jan. 1993), 14.

Neill, M., 'Axe Poised over Taurus System', *Evening Standard* (10 Mar. 1993), 29.

Waters, R., 'City May Scrap Trading Scheme', *Financial Times* (11 Mar. 1993), 1.

'Horns of a Dilemma', *Financial Times* (11 Mar. 1993), 24.

Waters, R., 'Stock Exchange Takes a Matador to Taurus', *Financial Times* (11 Mar. 1993), 25.

Ashworth, J., 'Taurus Runs into Gresh Problems', *The Times* (11 Mar. 1993), 25.

'Angry City Takes Stock of Lost Money and Time', *The Financial Times* (12 Mar. 1993), 11.

Waters, R., 'Stock Market Chief Quits', *Financial Times* (12 Mar. 1993), 1.

——, 'Harsh Post-Mortem Reveals Flaws', *Financial Times* (12 Mar. 1993), 11.

Peston, R., 'Stock Exchange Chief Failed to Tame the Bull', *Financial Times* (12 Mar. 1993), 11.

Waters, R., 'The Plan that Fell to Earth', *Financial Times* (12 Mar. 1993), 19.

'Paper Trail', *Financial Times* (12 Mar. 1993), 19.

'Taurus Done to Death', *Financial Times* (12 Mar. 1993), 19.

Seargeant, G., 'Chief of Stock Exchange Quits in Computer Fiasco', *The Times* (12 Mar. 1993), 1.

'This Bull Called Taurus', *The Times* (12 Mar. 1993), 21.

Ashworth, J., 'Stopgap Plan Urged after Taurus Fiasco', *The Times* (12 Mar. 1993), 25.

Ashworth, J. and Seargeant, G., 'Taurus Finally Succumbs to Fatal Errors of Conception', *The Times* (12 Mar. 1993), 29.

'What is a Stock Exchange For?', *The Economist* (13 Mar. 1993), 119.

Waters, R., 'Task Force Studies Taurus Successor', *Financial Times* (13 Mar. 1993), 1.

——, 'Few Mourn the Death of Taurus', *Financial Times* (13 Mar. 1993), 3.

——, 'City Settles on the Way Ahead after Taurus', *Financial Times* (13 Mar. 1993), 5.

'Taurus the Victim of Unclear Objectives', *Financial Times* (13 Mar. 1993), 9.

Keegan, V., 'Short Circuit in the Square Mile', *Financial Times* (13 Mar. 1993), 24.

Cook, L., 'Taurus Relief', *The Times* (13 Mar. 1993), 25.

Ashworth, J., 'Bank Task Force Considers Future without Taurus', *The Times* (13 Mar. 1993), 23.

Hamilton, K., 'Taurus : Bank Takes Bull by the Horns', *Sunday Times* (14 Mar. 1993),2, p. 3.

'A Certificate in Hand Beats Taurus in Bush', *The Sunday Times* (14 Mar. 1993),4, p. 2.

'Exchanging Bosses', *Financial Times* (15 Mar. 1993), 13.

Dobie, C., and Willcock, J., 'Companies Alarmed at Taurus Option', *The Independent* (15 Mar. 1993), 22.

Moate, R., 'Collapse of Taurus', *The Times* (15 Mar. 1993), 15.

Stevenson, T., 'Hoskyns Warns of Cancelled Projects', *The Independent* (16 Mar. 1993), 23.

Waters, R., 'Group Debates Life After Taurus', *Financial Times* (17 Mar. 1993), 9.

Gard, D., 'Bear Necessity', *The Times* (18 Mar. 1993), 27.

Waters, R., and Cane, A., 'Sudden Death of a Runaway Bull', *Financial Times* (19 Mar. 1993), 11.

Abrams, C., 'Talisman the Ideal Basis for SE's Taurus Mark II', *Financial Times* (19 Mar. 1993), 14.

Waters, R., 'Failure of Taurus Blamed on Lack of City Leadership', *Financial Times* (19 Mar. 1993), 16.

Willcock, J., ' "Split market" advocated', *The Independent* (19 Mar. 1993), 25.

Seargeant, G., 'Bank Stopgap Urged in Wake of Taurus', *The Times* (19 Mar. 1993), 25.

Smith, E. F., 'Factors behind Stock Exchange Computer Failure', *The Times* (19 Mar. 1993), 19.

'When the Bull Turned', *The Economist* (20 Mar. 1993), 111.

Pearson, T., 'No Time to Waste in Filling Vacuum Left by Taurus', *The Times* (20 Mar. 1993), 22.

'After Taurus: City Lessons', *Financial Times* (23 Mar. 1993), 21.

Willcock, J., and Rogers, P., 'Two-Tier System Wins City Support', *The Independent* (23 Mar. 1993), 23.

'Bank's Settlement Plea', *The Times* (23 Mar. 1993), 26.

Pembroke, A. M. F., 'Beware the Bulldozer', *The Times* (24 Mar. 1993), 25.

Powell, W. H., 'Filled with Delight at the Demise of the Taurus System', *Financial Times* (25 Mar. 1993), 20.

Seel, G. H., 'Talisman No Successor to Taurus', *Financial Times* (26 Mar. 1993), 18.

Willcock, J., 'Tradepoint Learns from the Lessons of Taurus', *The Independent* (29 Mar. 1993), 25.

'Completing the Electronic Chain', *Banking World* (Mar. 1993), **11**, 32, & 34.

Gandy, T., 'Exchanges Take Stock', *The Banker* (June 1993), 59.

BIBLIOGRAPHY

ACKER, B. (1995), 'Another Fine Mess', *The Banker* (Apr.), 57–9.

ACKROYD, S., and CROWDY, P. A. (1990), 'Can Culture be Managed? Working with Raw Material: The Case of English Slaughtermen', *Personnel Review*, 19: 3–13.

ADDISON, W. (1953), *English Fairs and Markets*, London.

ADLER, P. A., and ADLER, P. (1988), 'Intense Loyalty in Organizations: A Case Study of College Athletics', *Administrative Science Quarterly*, 33: 401–17.

ALLEN, N. J., and MAYER, J. P. (1990), 'The Measurement and Antecedents of Affective, Continuance and Normative Commitment to the Organization', *Journal of Occupational Psychology*, 63: 1–18.

ALLISON, G. T. (1971), *Essence of Decision: Explaining the Cuban Missile Crisis*, Boston.

ALVESSON, M., and WILLMOTT, H. (1992), 'On the Idea of Emancipation in Management and Organization Studies', *Academy of Management Review*, 17: 432–64.

ANDERSON, P. A. (1983), 'Decision Making by Objection and the Cuban Missile Crisis', *Administrative Science Quarterly*, 28: 201–22.

ARAM, J. D. (1989), 'The Paradox of Interdependent Relations in the Field of Social Issues in Management', *Academy of Management Review*, 14: 266–83.

ARKES, H. R, and BLUMER, C. (1985), 'The Psychology of Sunk Costs', *Organisational Behavior and Human Performance*, 35: 124–40.

ARMSTRONG, J. S., COVIELLO, N., and SAFRANEK, B. (1993), 'Escalation Bias: Does it Extend to Marketing', *Journal of Academy of Marketing Science*, 21: 247–53.

ASSAD, T. (1987), 'On Ritual and Discipline in Medieval Christian Monasticism', *Economy and Society*, 16: 159–203.

ASTLEY, W. G., and VAN DE VEN, A. (1983), 'Central Perspectives and Debates in Organization Theory', *Administrative Science Quarterly*, 28: 245–73.

AUSTIN, G. (1991), *The Equity International Guide to Taurus*, Global Market Publications.

BACHARACH, P., and BARATZ, M. S. (1963), 'Decisions and Non-Decisions: An Analytical Framework', *American Political Science Review*, 57: 632–42.

—— —— (1970), *Power and Poverty: The Theory and Practice*, New York.

BACHARACH, S. B. (1989), 'Organizational Theories: Some Criteria for Evaluation', *Academy of Management Review*, 14: 496–515.

BACHARACH, S. B. and LAWLER, E. J. (1980), *Power and Politics in Organizations*, San Francisco.

BANK OF ENGLAND [Task Force on Securities Settlement] (1993), *Report to the Governor of the Bank of England*, London.

BARTON, S. L, DUCHON, D., and DUNEGAN, K. L. (1989), 'An Empirical Test of Staw and Ross's Prescriptions for the Management of Escalation of Commitment Behaviour in Organizations', *Decision Sciences*, 20: 532–44.

BARTY-KING, H. (1977), *The Baltic Exchange*, London.

BATEMAN, T. (1983), 'Resource Allocation after Success and Failure: The Role of Attributions of Powerful Others and Probabilities of Future Success', Working Paper Department of Management, Texas A. & M. University, College Station, Tex.

—— and ZEITHMAL, C. P. (1989), 'The Psychological Context of Strategic Decisions: A Model and Convergent Experimental Findings', *Strategic Management Journal*, 10: 59–74.

BAZERMAN, M. H. (1994), *Judgement in Managerial Decision Making*, New York.

—— BEEKUN, R. I., and SCHOORMAN, F. D. (1982), 'Performance Evaluation in a Dynamic Context: The Impact of a Prior Commitment to the Ratee', *Journal of Applied Psychology*, 67: 873–6.

—— GIULIANO, T., and APPLEMAN, A. (1984), 'Escalation in Individual and Group Decision Making', *Organizational Behavior and Human Performance*, 33: 141–52.

BECKER, H. S. (1958), 'Problems of Inference and Proof in Participant Observation', *American Sociological Review*, 23: 652–60.

—— (1960), 'Notes on the Concept of Commitment', *American Journal of Sociology*, 66: 32–40.

—— (1967), 'Whose Side Are We On?', *Social Problems*, 14: 239–47.

BECKER, T. E. (1992), 'Foci and Bases of Commitment: Are They Distinctions Worth Making?', *Academy of Management Journal*, 35: 232–44.

BECKETT, S. (1986), *The Complete Dramatic Works*, London.

BEDFORD, S. (1989), *The Best We Can Do*, Harmondsworth.

BELBIN, R. M. (1981), *Management Teams*, London.

BENYON, D. (1990), *Information and Data Modelling*, Oxford.

BERGER, J. (1972), *Ways of Seeing*, Harmondsworth.

BERGER, P., and LUCKMAN, T. (1966), *The Social Construction of Reality*, London.

BETTLEHEIM, B. (1943), 'Individual and Mass Behaviour in Extreme Situations', *Journal of Abnormal and Social Psychology*, 38: 417–52.

—— (1990), *Recollections and Reflections*, London.

BEYER, J., and TRICE, H. (1987), 'How an Organization's Rites Reveal its Culture', *Organizational Dynamics*, 15: 5–23.

BOBOCEL, D. R., and MEYER, J. P. (1994), 'Escalating Commitment to a Failing Course of Action—Separating the Roles of Choice and Justification', *Journal of Applied Psychology*, 79: 360–3.

BORRGIDA, E., and NISBETT, R. (1977), 'The Differential Impact of Abstract Versus Concrete Information on Decisions', *Journal of Applied Social Psychology*, 7: 258–71.

BOWEN, M. G. (1987), 'The Escalation Phenomenon Reconsidered: Decision Dilemmas or Decision Errors?', *Academy of Management Review*, 12: 52–66.

—— and POWER, F. C. (1993), 'The Moral Manager: Communicative Ethics and the Exxon Valdez Disaster', *Business Ethics Quarterly*, 3: 97–115.

BOWER, J. L. (1983), *The Two Faces of Management: An American Approach to Leadership*, Boston.

BOWER, T. (1991), *Maxwell: The Outsider*, London.

BRAVERMAN, H. (1974), *Labour Monopoly Capital*, New York.

BROAD, W., and WADE, N. (1982), *Betrayers of the Truth*, London.

BROCKNER, J. (1992), 'The Escalation of Commitment to a Failing Course of Action: Toward Theoretical Progress', *Academy of Management Review*, 17: 39–61.

—— and RUBIN, J. Z. (1985), *Entrapment in Escalating Conflicts: A Social Psychological Analysis*, New York.

—— SHAW, M. C., and RUBIN, J. Z. (1979), 'Factors Affecting Withdrawal from an Escalating Conflict: Quitting Before It's Too Late', *Journal of Experimental Social Psychology*, 15: 492–503.

—— RUBIN, J. Z., and LANG, E. (1981), 'Face-Saving and Entrapment', *Journal of Experimental Social Psychology*, 17: 68–79.

—— NATHASON, S., FRIEND, A., HARBECK, J., SAMUELSON, C., HOUSER, R., *et al.* (1984), 'The Role of Modelling Processes in the "Knee Deep in the Big Muddy" Phenomenon', *Organizational Behavior and Human Performance*, 33: 77–99.

—— HOUSER, R., BIRNBAUM, G., LLOYD, K., DEITCHER, J., NATHASON, S., *et al.* (1986), 'Escalation of Commitment to an Ineffective Course of Action: The Effect of Negative Feedback having Negative Implications for Self Identity', *Administrative Science Quarterly*, 31: 109–26.

BRODY, R. G., and LOWE, D. J. (1995), 'Escalation of Commitment in Professional Tax Payers', *Psychological Reports*, 76: 339–44.

BRUNNSON, N. (1989), *The Organization of Hypocrisy: Talk, Decisions, and Actions in Organizations*, Chichester.

BRYMAN, A. (1988), *Quantity and Quality in Social Research*, London.

—— (1993), *Charisma and Leadership in Organisations*, London.

BURK, K. *Morgan Grenfell 1838–1988*, Oxford.

BURNS, T. (1961), 'Micro-Politics: Mechanisms of Institutional Change', *Administrative Science Quarterly*, 6: 257–81.

BURRELL, G., and MORGAN, G. (1979), *Sociological Paradigms and Organizational Analysis*, Chicago.

BUTLER, R. A. (1971),. *The Art of the Possible*, London.

CALDWELL, D. F., and O'REILLY, C. A. (1982), 'Responses to Failures: The Effects of Choices and Responsibility on Impression Management', *Academy of Management Journal*, 25: 121–36.

CAMPBELL, D. T. (1969), 'Reforms as Experiments', *American Psychologist*, 24: 409–29.

CARTWRIGHT, J. (1978), 'A Laboratory Investigation of Group Think', *Communication Monographs*, 45: 229–46.

CASSIS, Y. (1988), 'Merchant Bankers and City Aristocracy', *British Journal of Sociology*, 39: 114–26.

CHALTON, S. (1990), 'Dematerialisation of Financial Instruments', *Computer Law and Practice*, 7: 30–4.

CHAPMAN, C. (1991), *How the Stock Markets Work*, London.

CHAPMAN, S. D. (1984), *The Rise of Merchant Banking*, London.

—— (1986), 'Aristocracy and Meritocracy in Merchant Banking', *British Journal of Sociology*, 38: 180–93.

CLARK, A. (1990), 'Taurus: New Developments and Implementation Plans', International Stock Exchange and Bank of England, London.

CLARKE, W. M. (1979), *Inside the City*, London.

CLEGG, S. R. (1981), 'Organizations and Control', *Administrative Science Quarterely*, 26: 545–62.

CLEGG, S. R. (1989), 'Radical Revisions: Power, Discipline and Organizations', *Organization Studies*, 10: 97–115.

COBBETT, D. (1986), *Tales of the Old Stock Exchange before Big Bang*, London.

COHEN, M., JAFFRAY, J., and SAID, T. (1987), 'Experimental Comparisons of Individual Behaviour under Uncertainty for Gains and for Losses', *Organizational Behavior and Human Decision Processes*, 39: 1–22.

COHEN, M. D., MARCH, J. G., and OLSEN, J. P. (1972), 'A Garbage Can Model of Organizational Choice', *Administrative Science Quarterly*, 17: 1–25.

COLLINGRIDGE, D. (1992), *The Management of Scale*, London.

CONLON, D. E. and GARLAND, H. (1993), 'The Role of Project Completion in Resource Allocation Decisions', *Academy of Management Journal*, 36: 402–13.

CONLON, E. J., and WOLF, G. (1980), 'The Moderating Effects of Strategy, Visibility and Involvement on Allocation Behavior: An Extension of Staw's Escalation Paradigm', *Organizational Behavior and Human Performance*, 26: 172–92.

—— and PARKS, J. M. (1987), 'Information Requests in the Context of Escalation', *Journal of Applied Psychology*, 72: 344–50.

COOPER, D. (1983), 'Tidiness, Muddle and Things: Commonalities and Divergences in Two Approaches to Management Accounting Research', *Accounting, Organizations and Society,* 8: 269–86.

COOPERS AND LYBRAND DELOITTE (1991), 'Taurus Briefing', issues 1–9, London.

—— (1992), 'Taurus Briefing', issues 10–15, London.

CRICK, B. (1976), *In Defence of Politics,* Harmondsworth.

CYRET, R., and MARCH, J. G. (1963), *A Behavioural Theory of the Firm,* Englewood Cliffs, NJ.

DANIELS, C. L. (1993), *Information Technology: The Management Challenge,* Reading, Mass.

DARLEY, J. M., and LATANE, B. (1968), 'Bystander Intervention in Emergencies: Diffusion of Responsibility', *Journal of Personality and Social Psychology,* 8: 377–83.

DATE, C. J. (1990), *An Introduction to Data Base Systems,* Reading, Mass.

DEVONS, E. (1961), *Statistics as a Basis for Policy,* London.

DIXON, N. (1976), *On the Psychology of Military Incompetence,* London.

DOWNS, A. (1967), *Inside Bureaucracy,* Boston.

DREWETT, R., and REDHEAD, M. (1990), *The Trial of Richard III,* Gloucester.

DRUMMOND, H. (1991a), *Effective Decision Making,* London.

—— (1991b), *Power: Creating it, Using it,* London.

—— (1992a), 'Another Fine Mess: Time for Quality in Decision Making', *Journal of General Management,* 18: 1–14.

——(1992b), *The Quality Movement,* London.

—— (1993a), 'Measuring Management Effectiveness', *Personnel Management* (Mar.), 38–41.

—— (1993b), *Power and Involvement in Organizations,* Aldershot.

DRUMMOND, H. (1994a), 'Escalation in Organizational Decision Making: A Case of Recruiting an Incompetent Employee.' *Journal of Behavioral Decision Making,* 7: 43–55.

—— (1994b), 'Les Liasons Dangereuses', *New Law Journal,* 144: 93–4.

—— (1994c), 'The Pig-Headed Way to Lose Your Money', *Financial Times* (2 Apr.), iv.

—— (1994d), 'Too Little Too Late: A Case Study of Escalation in Decision Making', *Organization Studies,* 15: 590–605.

—— (1995), 'De-escalation in Decision Making: A Case of a Disastrous Partnership', *Journal of Management Studies,* 32: 265–81.

—— and CHELL, E. (1992), 'Decisionless Decisions and Entrepreneurs', *New Law Journal,* 142: 1480–1.

—— —— (1994), 'Crisis Management in a Small Business: A Tale of Two Solicitors', *Management Decision,* 32: 37–40.

DTI (Department of Trade and Industry) (1991), 'The Uncertificated Securities Regulations: A Consultative Document', London.

DUHAIME, I., and SCHWENK, C. (1985), 'Cognitive Simplification Processes in Acquisition and Divestment Decision Making', *Academy of Management Review*, 10: 287–95.

DUNEGAN, K. J. (1993), 'Framing, Cognitive Modes, and Image Theory: Toward an Understanding of a Glass Half Full', *Journal of Applied Psychology*, 78: 419–503.

DURHAM, K. (1992), *The New City*, London.

DYER, G. (1995), *The Missing of the Somme*, Harmondsworth.

DYER, W. G., Jr., and WILKINS, A. L. (1991), 'Better Stories, not Better Constructs to Generate Better Theory: A Rejoinder to Eisenhardt', *Academy of Management Review*, 16: 613–19.

EISENHARDT, K. M. (1989), 'Building Theories from Case Study Research', *Academy of Management Review*, 14: 532–50.

EMERSON, R. H. (1962), 'Power-Dependence Relations', *American Sociological Review*, 27: 31–41.

ETZIONI, A. (1975), *A Comparative Analysis of Complex Organizations*, London.

—— (1989), 'Humble Decision Making', *Harvard Business Review*, (July / Aug.), 122–6.

FELDMAN, M. A., and MARCH, J. G. (1981), 'Information in Organizations as Signal and Symbol', *Administrative Science Quarterly*, 26: 171–86.

FESTINGER, L. (1957), *A Theory of Cognitive Dissonance*, Stanford, Calif.

FIEGENBAUM, A. and THOMAS, H. (1988), 'Attitudes toward Risk and Risk Return Paradox: Prospect Theory Explanations', *Academy of Management Journal*, 31: 86–106.

FISHER, R., and URY, W. (1983), *Getting to Yes*, London.

FISHER, S. (1993), 'The Pull of the Fruit Machine: A Sociological Typology of Young Players', *Sociological Review*, 41: 446–74.

FLOWERS, M. (1977), 'A Laboratory Test of some Implications of Janis' Group Think Hypothesis', *Journal of Personality and Social Psychology*, 1: 288–99.

FORTE, C. (1987), *Forte: The Autobiography of Charles Forte*, London.

FOX, F., and STAW, B. M. (1979), 'The Trapped Administrator: The Effects of Job Insecurity and Policy Resistance upon Commitment to a Course of Action', *Administrative Science Quarterly*, 24: 449–71.

FROST, P. (1980), 'Toward a Radical Framework for Practising Organizational Science', *Academy of Management Review*, 5: 501–7.

FT (*Financial Times*) (1986), 'The City Revolution', *Financial Times Survey*, (27 Oct.), sect. 2.

FUNDER, D. C. (1987), 'Errors and Mistakes: evaluating the accuracy of social judgement', Psychological Bulletin, 101: 75–90.

GALBRAITH, J. K. (1984), *The Anatomy of Power*, London.

GARLAND, H. (1990), 'Throwing Good Money after Bad: The Effect of Sunk Costs on the Decision to Escalate Commitment to an Ongoing Project', *Journal of Applied Psychology*, 75: 728–31.

—— and CONLON, D. E. (unpub. mimeo, n.d.) 'Too Close to Quit: The Role of Project Completion in Escalation of Commitment', University of Delaware, Newark, Del.

—— and NEWPORT, S. (1991), 'Effects of Absolute and Relative Sunk Costs on the Decision to Persist with a Course of Action, *Organizational Behavior and Human Decision Processes*, 48: 55–69.

—— SANDEFUR, C. A., and ROGERS, A. C. (1990), 'De-escalation of Commitment in Oil Exploration: When Sunk Costs and Negative Feedback Coincide', *Journal of Applied Psychology*, 75: 721–7.

GEPHART, R. (1978), 'Status Degradation and Organizational Succession: an Ethnomethodological Approach', *Administrative Science Quarterly*, 23: 553–81.

GERSICK, C. J. (1994), 'Pacing Strategic Change: The Case of a New Venture', *Academy of Management Journal*, 37: 9–45.

GERTH, H. H., and MILLS, C. W. (eds.) (1991), *From Max Webster: Essays in Sociology*, London.

GIDDENS, A. (1979), *Central Problems in Social Theory*, Berkeley.

GILBERT, M. (1986), *The Oxford Book of Legal Anecdotes*, Oxford.

GIOIA, D. A., and PITRE, E. (1990), 'Multi-Paradigm Perspectives on Theory Building', *Academy of Management Review*, 15: 584–602.

—— DONNELLON, H. P., and SIMS, J. R. (1989), 'Communication and Cognition in Appraisal: A Tale of Two Paradigms', *Organization Studies*, 10: 503–30.

GIOVANNITTI, L., and FREED, F. (1967), *The Decision to Drop the Bomb*, London.

GIST, M. E., and MITCHELL, T. R. (1992), 'Self-Efficacy: A Theoretical Analysis of its Determinants and Malleability', *Academy of Management Review*, 17: 183–211.

GLASER, B. G., and STRAUSS, A. L. (1967), *The Discovery of Grounded Theory: Strategies for Qualitative Research*, London.

GOLTZ, S. M. (1992), 'A Sequential Learning Analysis of Decisions in Organizations to Escalate Investments despite Continuing Costs or Losses, *Journal of Applied Behaviour Analysis*, 25: 561–74.

GOWLER, D. and LEGGE, K. (1983), 'The Meaning of Management and the Management of Meaning; A View from Social Anthropology', in M. Earl (ed.), *Perspectives on Management: A Multidisciplinary Analysis*, Oxford, 197–233.

GRIFFITHS, M. D. (1990), 'The Cognitive Psychology of Gambling', *Journal of Gambling Studies*, 6: 31–43.

GROSSMITH, G., and GROSSMITH, W. (1945 edn.), *Diary of a Nobody*, Harmondsworth. (1st pub. 1892).

HALES, C. P. (1986), 'What Do Managers Do? A Critical Review', *Journal of Management Studies*, 23: 88–115.

HALL, M. (1987), *The City Revolution*, London.

HAMILTON, D. J. (1968), *Stockbroking Today*, London.

HANTUALA, D. A. (1992), 'The Basic Importance of Escalation', *Journal of Applied Behaviour Analysis*, 25: 579–83.

—— and CROWELL, C. R. (1994a), 'Behavioral Contrast in a Two Option Analog Task of Financial Decision Making', *Journal of Applied Behavior Analysis*, 27: 607–17.

—— —— (1994b), 'Intermittent Reinforcement and Escalation Processes in Sequential Decision Making: A Replication and Theoretical Analysis', *Journal of Organizational Behavior Management*, 14: 7–36.

HARDIN, G. (1968), 'The Tragedy of the Commons', *Science*, 162: 1243–8.

HARRISON, P. D., and HARRELL, A. (1993), 'Impact of "Adverse Selection" on Managers' Project Evaluation Decisions', *Academy of Management Journal*, 36: 635–43.

HARWOOD, G. B., PATE, J. L., and SCHNEIDER, A. (1991), 'Budgeting Decisions as a Function of Framing: An Application of Prospect Theory's Reflection Effect', *Management Accounting Research*, 2: 161–70.

HASSARD, J. (1991), 'Multiple Paradigms and Organizational Analysis: A Case Study', *Organization Studies*, 12: 274–99.

HAWKING, S. W. (1988), *A Brief History of Time*, London.

HAYES, J., and ALLINSON, C. W. (1994), 'Cognitive Style and its Relevance for Management Practice', *British Journal of Management*, 5: 53–71.

HEATH, C. (1995), 'Escalation and De-escalation of Commitment in Response to Sunk Costs: The Role of Budgeting in Mental Accounting', *Organizational Behavior and Human Decision Processes*, 62: 38–54.

HEDBERG, B., and JONSONN, S. (1977), 'Strategy Formulation as a Discontinuous Process', *International Studies of Management and Organization*, 7: 88–109.

HEIDER, F. (1958), *The Psychology of Interpersonal Relations*, New York.

HELLER, H. (1989), *The Decision Makers*, London.

HENNESSY, P. (1992), *Never Again*, London.

HENNESTED, B. (1990), 'The Symbolic Impact of Double Bind Leadership: Double Bind in the Dynamics of Organizational Culture', *Journal of Management Studies*, 27: 265–81.

HIBBERT, C. (1992), *The Story of England*, London.

HICKSON, D. J., BUTLER, R. J., CRAY, D., MALLORY, G. R., and WILSON, D. C. (1986), *Top Decisions*, Oxford.

HILTON, A. (1987), *City within a State*, London.

HIRSCH, P. M. (1975), 'Organizational Effectiveness and the Institutional Environment', *Administrative Science Quarterly*, 20: 327–44.

HOBSON, D. (1991), *The Pride of Lucifer*, London.

HODGES, R. (1988), *Primitive and Peasant Markets*, Oxford.

HOGARTH, R. (1980), *Judgement and Choice: The Psychology of Decision*, Chichester.

HOLLOWAY, W. (1991), *Work Psychology and Organizational Behaviour*, London.

HOOKER, P. (unpub. mimeo, 1990), 'The Trouble with Taurus', Hoare Govett, London.

—— (unpub. mimeo, 1992), 'Taurus in Context', Hoare Govett, London.

INDUSTRIAL WELFARE SOCIETY (1990), *The City at Work*, London.

ISHIKAWA, K. (1985), *What is Total Quality Control? The Japanese Way*, Englewood Cliffs, NJ.

JANIS, I. (1972), *Victims of Groupthink*, Boston.

—— (1989), *Crucial Decisions: Leadership in Policy Making and Crisis Management*, New York.

JEFFREY, C. (1992), 'The Relation of Judgement, Personal Involvement and Experience in the Audit of Bank Loans', *Accounting Review*, 67: 802–19.

JENKINS, A. (1973), *The Stock Exchange Story* London.

JENKINS, H., and CLARK, A. (1990), 'The Planning for Taurus Conference: 15 November', London.

JONES, E. E., and DAVIS, K. E. (1965), 'From Acts to Dispositions: The Attribution Process in Person Perception', in L. Berkowitz (ed.), *Advances in Experimental Social Psychology*, New York, vol. 2.

JURKUS, A. F. (1990), 'Requiem for a Lightweight: The Northrop F–20 Strategic Initiative', *Strategic Management Journal*, 11: 59–68.

KAHN, R. L., WOLFE, D. M., QUINN, R. P., and SNOEK, J. D. (1964), *Organizational Stress: Studies in Role Conflict and Ambiguity*, New York.

KAHNEMAN, D., and TVERSKY, A. (1979), 'Prospect Theory: An Analysis of Decision under Risk', *Econometrica*, 47: 263–91.

—— —— (1982), 'The Psychology of Preferences', *Scientific American*, 246: 162–70.

—— —— (1984), 'Choices, Values and Frames', *American Psychologist*, 39: 341–50.

KAMENS, D. H. (1977), 'Legitimating Myths and Educational Organization: the relationship between organizational ideology and formal structure', *American Sociological Review*, 42: 208–19.

KAY, J. (1993), *Foundations of Corporate Success: How Business Strategies Add Value*, Oxford.

KERMAN, M. C., and LORD, R. G. (1989), 'The Effects of Explicit Goals and Specific Feedback on Escalation Processes', *Journal of Applied Social Psychology*, 19: 1125–43.

KETS DE VRIES, M. F. R., and MILLER, D. A. (1987), 'Interpreting Organizational Texts', *Journal of Management Studies*, 24: 233–48.

KIM, S. H., and SMITH, R. H. (1993), 'Revenge and Conflict Escalation', *Negotiation Journal*, 9: 37–43.

KNIGHTS, D., and ROBERTS, J. (1982), 'The Power of Organization and the Organization of Power', *Organization Studies*, 3: 47–63.

Kuhn, T. S. (1970), *The Structure of Scientific Revolutions*, 2nd edn., Chicago.

Kynaston, D. (1988), *The Financial Times: A Centenary History*, London.

—— (1991), *Cazenove and Co: A History*, London.

—— (1994), *The City of London. Vol. I: A World of its Own*, London.

—— (1995), *The City of London. Vol. II: Golden Years*, London.

Krantz, J., and Gilmore, T. N. (1990), 'The Splitting of Leadership and Management as a Social Defense', *Human Relations*, 43: 183–204.

Langer, E. J. (1975), 'The Illusion of Control', *Journal of Personality and Social Psychology*, 33: 311–28.

—— (1983), *The Psychology of Control*, Beverly Hills, Calif.

Lasswell, H. D. (1963), *Politics: Who Gets What, When, How*, New York.

Lawler, E. E. (1985), 'Challenging Traditional Research Assumptions', in E. E. Lawler, A. T. Mohrman, Jr., S. A. Mohrman, G. E. Ledford, Jr., T. G. Cummings, and Associates (eds.), *Doing Research that is Useful Both for Theory and Practice*, San Francisco.

Leana, C. (1985), 'A Partial Test of Janis' Group Think Model: Effects of Group Cohesiveness and Leader Behavior on Defective Decision Making', *Journal of Management*, 11: 5–17.

Leatherwood, M. L., and Conlon, E. J. (1987), 'Diffusibility of Blame: Effects on Persistence in a Project', *Academy of Management Journal*, 30: 836–48.

Lewis, M. (1990), *Liar's Poker*, London.

Light, D., Jr. (1979), 'Surface Data and Deep Structure: Observing the Organization of Professional Training', *Administrative Science Quarterly*, 24: 551–9.

Lindblom, C. E. (1959), 'The Science of Muddling Through', *Public Administration Review*, 19: 79–88.

—— (1979), 'Still Muddling, Not Yet Through', *Public Administration Review*, 39: 517–26.

London Business School (1992), 'The City Research Project: Interim Report, Executive Summary', The City Research Project, London.

—— (1993a), 'The Costs and Effectiveness of the UK Financial Regulatory System', The City Research Project, London.

—— (1993b), 'Equity Settlement in London: Its Importance to London as a Financial Centre', The City Research Project, London.

—— (1995), 'The Competitive Position of London's Financial Services: Final Report', The City Research Project, London.

London Stock Exchange (1970), *Report of the WorkingParty on Securities Handling* (The Heasman Report), London.

—— (1982), *Securities Industry Consultative Document: Report on Equity Settlement* (The Powell Report), London.

—— (1989A), *Report of the Securities Industry Steering Committee on Taurus* (SISCOT), London.

—— (1989b), 'Tauruscope: The Taurus Newsletter' (Dec.), London.

—— (1989c), 'The Way Forward for LSE Trading Services', London.

—— (1990a), 'Project Taurus: A Prospectus for Settlement in the 1990's', London.

—— (1990b), 'Project Taurus: Strategic Background and Cost Savings', London.

—— (1991a), 'Project Taurus: A Prospectus for Settlement in the 1990's, Prospectus 2', London.

—— (1991b), 'Taurus: Participation Criteria Progress Report', London.

—— (1991–2), 'Taurus Bulletin', London.

—— (1992a), 'Taurus Briefing', London.

—— (1992b), 'Taurus: Dress Rehearsal and Data Capture Guide', London.

—— (1992c), 'Taurus: The Input of Investor Details: Talisman and Taurus', London.

—— (1993), *Fact Book*, London.

—— (n.d.), 'Consultataive Document for the Listed Companies Access Service', draft, London.

LONG, J. (1978), *Inside the Stock Exchange*, London.

LORD, R. G., and MAHER, K. J. (1990), 'Alternative Information-Processing Models and their Implications for Theory, Research and Practice', *Academy of Management Review*, 15: 9–28.

LUKES, S. (1974), *Power: A Radical View*, London.

McCAIN, B. E. (1986), 'Continuing Investment under Conditions of Failure: A Laboratory Study of the Limits of Escalation', *Journal of Applied Psychology*, 71: 280–4.

McCARTHY, A. M., SCHOORMAN, F. D., and COOPER, A. C. (1993), 'Reinvestment Decisions by Entrepreneurs: Rational Decision-Making or Escalation of Commitment?' *Journal of Business Venturing*, 8: 9–24.

McGUIRE, T., KIESLER, S., and SIEGEL, J. (1987), 'Group and Computer Mediated Discussion Effects in Risk Decision Making', *Journal of Personality and Social Psychology*, 52: 917–30.

McNEIL, B., PAUKER, S., SOX, H., and TVERSKY, A. (1982), 'On the Elicitation of Preferences for Alternative Therapies', *New England Journal of Medicine*, 306: 1259–62.

MANTLE, J. (1992), *For Whom the Bell Tolls*, London.

MARCH, J. G. (1962), 'The Business Firm as a Political Coalition', *Journal of Politics*, 24: 662–3.

—— and OLSEN, J. P. (1976), *Ambiguity and Choice in Organizations*, Oslo.

—— and SIMON, H. A. (1958), *Organizations*, New York.

MARTIN, R. (1977), *The Sociology of Power*, London.

MECHANIC, D. (1962), 'Sources of Power of Lower Participants in Complex Organizations', *Administrative Science Quarterly*, 7: 349–64.

MERCER, C. (1991), 'Taurus and the London Stock Exchange Paperless Securities Transfers', *Computer Law and Practice* 7: 238–46.

MEYER, J. W., and ROWAN, B. (1978), 'Institutionalized Organizations: Formal Structure as Myth and Ceremony', *American Journal of Sociology*, 83: 340–63.

MILES, M. B. (1979), 'Qualitative Data as an Attractive Nuisance: The Problem of Analysis', *Administrative Science Quarterly*, 24: 590–600.

MILLER, J. D. B. (1962), *The Nature of Politics*, London.

MILLS, C. W. (1959), *The Sociological Imagination*, Oxford.

MINTZBERG, H. (1973), *The Nature of Managerial Work*, New York.

—— (1979), 'An Emerging Strategy of Direct Research', *Administrative Science Quarterly*, 24: 582–9.

—— (1983), *Power in and around Organizations*, Englewood Cliffs.

—— (1985), 'The Organization as Political Arena', *Journal of Management Studies*, 22: 133–54.

—— (1992), 'Crafting Strategy', in H. Mintzberg and B. Quinn (eds.),, *The Strategy Process: Concepts and Contexts*, Englewood Cliffs, NJ.

—— (1994), *The Rise and Fall of Strategic Planning*, London.

—— RAISINGHAM, D., and THOERET, A. (1976),. 'The Structure of Unstructured Decision Processes', *Administrative Science Quarterly*, 21: 146–75.

MITCHELL, J. C. (1983), 'Case and Situation Analysis', *Sociological Review*, 31: 187–211.

MORGAN, E. V. and THOMAS, W. A. (1962), *The Stock Exchange*, London.

MORGAN, G. (1980), 'Paradigms, Metaphors and Puzzle Solving in Organization Theory', *Administrative Science Quarterly*, 25: 605–22.

—— (1983), 'More on Metaphor: Why we Cannot Control Tropes in Administrative Science', *Administrative Science Quarterly*, 28: 601–7.

—— (1986), *Images of Organization*, London.

—— (1990), 'Paradigm Diversity in Organizational Research', in J. Hassard and W. Pym (eds.), *The Theory and Philosophy of Organizations*, London.

—— and SMIRCICH, L. (1980), 'The Case for Qualitative Research', *Academy of Management Review*, 5: 491–500.

MORTIMER, T. (1969 edn.), *Every Man His Own Broker*, Farnborough, 1st pub. 1765.

MUMBY, D. K., and PUTNAM, L. L. (1992), 'The Politics of Emotion: A Feminist Reading of Bounded Rationality', *Academy of Management Review*, 17: 465–86.

MURPHY, W. P. (1980), 'Secret Knowledge as Property and Power in Kpelle Society—Elders versus Youth', *Africa*, 50: 193–207.

MURRAY, C. (1992), *Black Mountain*, Edinburgh.

MURRAY, V. and GANDZ, J. (1980), 'Games Executives Play: Politics at Work', *Business Horizons* (Dec.), 11–23.

MUSCOVICI, S., and FAUCHEUX, C. (1972), 'Social Influence, Conformity Bias, and the Study of Active Minorities', in L. Berkowitz (ed.), *Advances in Experimental and Social Psychology*, New York, vol. 6.

—— and PERSONNAZ, B. (1980), 'Minority Influence and Conversion Behaviour in a Perceptual Task', *Journal of Experimental Social Psychology*, 16: 270–82.

MYERS, D. and LAMM, H. (1976), 'The Group Polarization Phenomenon', *Psychological Bulletin*, 83: 602–27.

MYNATT, C., and SHERMAN, S. J. (1975), 'Responsibility Attribution in Groups and Individuals: A Direct Test of the Diffusion of Responsibility Hypothesis', *Journal of Personality and Social Psychology*, 32: 1111–18.

NATHASON, S., BROCKNER, J., BRENNER, D., SAMUELSON, C., COUNTRYMAN, M., LLOYD, M., *et al.* (1982), 'Toward the Reduction of Entrapment', *Journal of Applied Social Psychology*, 12: 193–208.

NEUSTADT, R. E., and MAY, E. R. (1986), *Thinking in Time: The Uses of History for Decision Makers*, London.

NISBETT, R., and ROSS, L. (1980), *Human Inferences: Strategies and Shortcomings of Social Judgement*, Englewood Cliffs, NJ.

NORTHCRAFT, G. B., and NEALE, M. A. (1986), 'Opportunity Costs and the Framing of Resource Allocation Decisions', *Organizational Behaviour and Human Decision Processes*, 37: 348–56.

—— and WOLFE, M. A. (1984),. 'Dollars Sense and Sunk Costs: A Life Cycle Model of Resource Allocation Decisions', *Academy of Management Review*, 9: 225–34.

O'BARR, W. M. (1984), 'Asking the Right Questions about Language and Power', in *Language and Power*, C. Kramarat, M. Schultz, and W. M. O'Barr (eds.), Beverly Hills.

OLIVER, M. S., and MARSHALL, E. A. (1994), *Company Law*, London.

O'REILLY III, C. A. (1980), 'Individuals and Information Overload in Organizations: Is More Necessarily Better?', *Academy of Management Journal*, 23: 684–96.

PARKER, M., and McHUGH, G. (1991), 'Five Texts in Search of an Author: A Response to John Hassard's "Multiple Paradigms and Organizational Analysis" ', *Organization Studies*, 12: 451–6.

PARKER TRIBUNAL (1958), *Report of the Tribunal Appointed to Inquire into Allegations of Improper Disclosure of Information Relating to the Raising of the Bank Rate*, Cmnd. 350, London.

PERROW, C. (1984), *Normal Accidents*, New York.

PETERS, T., and WATERMAN, R. H. (1982), *In Search of Excellence: Lessons from America's Best-Run Companies*, New York.

PETTIGREW, A. (1973), *The Politics of Organizational Decision Making*, London.

PFEFFER, J. (1977), 'The Ambiguity of Leadership', *Academy of Management Review*, 2: 104–12.
—— (1981), 'Management as symbolic action', in L. Cummings and B. Staw (eds.), *Research in Organizational Behaviour*, Greenwich, Conn.
—— (1982), *Power in Organizations*, Boston.
—— (1992), *Managing With Power*, Boston.
—— and SALANCIK, G. R. (1978), *The External Control of Organizations: A Resource Dependence Perspective*, New York.
PLENDER, J. and WALLACE, P. (1985), *The Square Mile: A Guide to the City of London*, London.
PREBBLE, J. (1975), *The High Girders: The Story of the Tay Bridge Disaster*, Harmondsworth.
QUAID, M. (1993), 'Job Evaluation as Institutional Myth', *Journal of Management Studies*, 30: 239–60.
RANDALL, D. M. (1987), 'Commitment and Organization: The Organization Man Revisited', *Academy of Management Review*, 12: 460–71.
RAPHAEL, M. (1995), *Ultimate Risk*, London.
RAY, C. A. (1986), 'Corporate Culture: The Last Frontier of Control', *Journal of Management Studies*, 23: 287–99.
REES, G. L. (1972), *Britain's Commodity Markets*, London.
REICH, C. (1980), 'The Confessions of Siegmund Warburg', *Institutional Investor* (Mar.), 167–201.
REID, M. (1988), *All Change in the City*, Basingstoke.
ROBERT, R. J. (ed.) (1974), *Winston S. Churchill: His Complete Speeches 1897–1963*, 8 vols., London.
ROBERTS, R. (1973), *The Classic Slum*, Harmondsworth.
—— (1992), *Schroders: Merchants and Bankers*, London.
—— (1993), 'What's in a Name? Merchants, Merchant Bankers, Accepting Houses, Issuing Houses, Industrial Bankers and Investment Bankers', *Business History*, 35: 22–38.
ROLT, L. T. C. (1978), *Red For Danger*, London.
ROSEN, M. (1985), 'Breakfast at Spiro's: Dramaturgy and Dominance', *Journal of Management*, 11: 31–48.
ROSS, J., and STAW, B. M. (1986), 'Expo 86: An Escalation Prototype', *Administrative Science Quarterly*, 31: 379–91.
—— —— (1991), 'Managing Escalation Processes in Organizations', *Journal of Managerial Issues*, 3: 15–30.
—— —— (1993), 'Organizational Escalation and Exit: Lessons from the Shoreham Nuclear Power Plant', *Academy of Management Journal*, 36: 701–32.
RUBIN, J. Z., and BROCKNER, J. (1975), 'Factors Affecting Entrapment in Waiting Situations: The Rosencrantz and Guildenstern Effect', *Journal of Personality and Social Psychology*, 31: 1054–63.

—— —— SMALL-WEIL, S., and NATHASON, S. (1980), 'Factors Affecting Entry into Psychological Traps', *Journal of Conflict Resolution*, 24: 405–26.

RUSBULT, C. E. (1980*a*), 'Satisfaction and Commitment in Friendships', *Representative Research and Social Psychology*, 11: 78–95.

RUSBULT, C. E. (1980*b*), 'Commitment and Satisfaction in Romantic Associations: A Test of the Investment Model', *Experimental and Social Psychology*, 16: 172–86.

SALANCIK, G. R. (1977), 'Commitment and Control of Organizational Behaviour and Belief', in B. M. Staw and G. R. Salancik (eds.), *New Directions in Organizational Behaviour*, Malabar, Fla., 1–54.

SAMPSON, A. (1962), *Anatomy of Britain*, London.

SANDLANDS, L. E., BROCKNER, J., and GLYNN, M. A. (1988), 'If At First You Don't Succeed, Try, Try Again: Effects of Persistence-Performance Contingencies, Ego Involvement, and Self-Esteem on Task Persistence', *Journal of Applied Psychology*, 73: 208–16.

SAUR, C. (1993), *Why Information Systems Fail*, Henley-on-Thames.

SCHATTSNIEDER, E. E. (1960), *The Semi-Sovereign People: A Realist's View of Democracy in America*, New York.

SCHAUBROECK, J., and DAVIS, E. (1994), 'Prospect-Theory Predictions when Escalation is Not the Only Chance to Recover Sunk Costs', *Organizational Behaviour and Human Decision Processes*, 57: 59–82.

—— and WILLIAMS, S. (1993), 'Type A Behaviour Pattern and Escalating Commitment', *Journal of Applied Psychology*, 78: 862–7.

SCHLESINGER, Jr., A. M. (1965), *A Thousand Days: John F. Kennedy in the White House*, London.

SCHOORMAN, F. D. (1988), 'Escalation Bias in Performance Appraisals: An Unintended Consequence of Supervisor Participation in Hiring Decisions', *Journal of Applied Psychology*, 73: 58–62.

—— MAYER, R. C., and HETRICK, C. T. (1994), 'Escalation of Commitment and the Framing Effect', *Journal of Applied Social Psychology*, 24: 509–28.

SCHWARTZ, H., and JACOBS, J. (1979), *Qualitative Sociology: A Method to Madness*, New York.

SCHWENK, C. R. (1985), 'The Use of Participant Recollection in the Modelling of Organizational Decision Processes', *Academy of Management Review*, 10: 496–503.

—— (1986), 'Information, Cognitive Biases and Commitment to a Course of Action', *Academy of Management Review*, 11: 290–310.

—— (1988), 'Effect of Devil's Advocacy on Escalating Commitment', *Human Relations*, 41: 769–82.

SCHWENK, C. R. and MEINDL, J. (1984),. 'Corporate Attributions as Management Illusion of Control', *Administrative Science Quarterly*, 29: 238–54.

SCHWENK, H. E., and TANG, M-JE. (1989), 'Economic and Psychological Explanations for Strategic Persistence', *Omega International Journal of Management Science*, 17: 559–70.

SHAW, M. E. (1981), *Group Dynamics*, New York.

SHILTS, R. (1988), *And the Band Played On: Politics, People and the Aids Epidemic*, Harmondsworth.

SHIRVASTAVA, P. (1994), 'Technological and Organizational Roots of Industrial Crises: Lessons from Exxon-Valdez and Bhopal', *Technological Forecasting and Social Change*, 45: 237–53.

SILVERMAN, D. (1993), *Interpreting Qualitative Data*, London.

SIMMEL, G. (1950), *The Sociology of George Simmel*, tr. K. H. Wolff, Glencoe, Ill.

SIMON, H. (1957), *Models of Man*, New York.

—— (1960), *The New Science of Management Decision*, New York.

—— (1978), 'Rationality as a Process and Product of Thought', *American Economic Review*, 68: 1–16.

—— (1987), 'Making Management Decisions: The Role of Intuition and Emotion', *Academy of Management Executive* (Feb.), 57–64.

SIMONSON, I., and STAW, B. M. (1992), 'Decision Strategies: A Comparison of Techniques for Reducing Commitment to Losing Courses of Action', *Journal of Applied Psychology*, 77: 419–26.

SINGER, A. E., LYONSKI, S. L., SINGER, M., and HAYES, D. (1991), 'Ethical Myopia: The Case of Framing by Framing', *Journal of Business Ethics*, 10, 29–36.

SINGER, M. S. (1990), 'Individual differences in adaption, innovation and the escalation of commitment paradigm', *Journal of Social Psychology*, 130: 561–3.

—— and SINGER, A. E. (1986a), 'Individual Differences and the Escalation of Commitment Paradigm', *The Journal of Social Psychology*, 126: 197–204.

—— —— (1986b), 'Is There Always Escalation of Commitment?', *Psychological Reports*, 56: 197–204.

SKAPINKER, M. (1994), 'Knives Out at Heartbreak Hotel', *Financial Times* (30 July), 9.

SMITH, A. L. (1970), *Dictionary of City of London Street Names*, Newton Abbot.

SOUTH WEST THAMES REGIONAL HEALTH AUTHORITY (1993), *Report of the Inquiry into the London Ambulance Service*, London.

SPIEGELBERG, R. (1973), *The City: Power Without Accountability*, London.

STAW, B. M. (1976), 'Knee-Deep in the Big Muddy: A Study of Escalating Commitment to a Chosen Course of Action', *Organizational Behaviour and Human Performance*, 16: 27–44.

—— (1980), 'Rationality and Justification in Organizational Life', in B. M. Staw and L. Cummings (eds.), *Research in Organizational Behaviour*, Greenwich, Conn.

—— (1981), 'The Escalation of Commitment to a Course of Action', *Academy of Management Review*, 6: 577–87.

—— and Fox, F. V. (1977), 'Escalation: The Determinants of Commitment to a Chosen Course of Action', *Human Relations*, 30: 431–50.

—— and Hoang, H. (unpub. mimeo, 1994), 'Sunk Costs in the NBA: A Behavioral Determinant of Playing Time and Survival in Professional Basketball', University of California.

—— and Ross, J. (1978), 'Commitment to a Policy Decision: A Multi-Theoretical Perspective', *Administrative Science Quarterly*, 23: 40–64.

—— —— (1980), 'Commitment in an Experimenting Society: An Experiment on the Attribution of Leadership from Administrative Scenarios', *Journal of Applied Psychology*, 65: 249–60.

—— —— (1987a), 'Behaviour in Escalation Situations: Antecedents, Prototypes and Solutions', in L. L. Cummings and B. M. Staw, (eds.), *Research in Organization Behaviour*, London, vol. 9, pp. 39–78.

—— —— (1987b), 'Knowing When to Pull the Plug', *Harvard Business Review*, 65: 68–74.

—— —— (1989), 'Understanding Behaviour in Escalation Situations', *Science*, 246: 216–20.

—— McKechnie, P. I., and Puffer, S. M. (1983), 'The Justification of Organizational Performance', *Administrative Science Quarterly*, 28: 582–600.

Steffy, B. D., and Grimes, A. J. (1986), 'A Critical Theory of Organization Science', *Academy of Management Review*, 11: 322–36.

Sterba, R. L. A. (1978), 'Clandestine Management in the Imperial Chinese Bureaucracy', *Academy of Management Review*, 3: 67–78.

Stewart, R. (1989), 'Studies of Managerial Jobs and Behaviour: The Ways Forward', *Journal of Management Studies*, 26: 1–10.

Taguchi, G., and Wu, Y. (1985), *Introduction to Off-Line Quality Control*, Nagoya, Japan.

Taylor, A. J. P. (1969), *War by Timetable: How the First World War Began*, London.

Taylor, S., and Thompson, S. (1982), 'Stalking the Elusive "Vividness" Effect', *Psychological Review*, 89: 155–81.

Teger, A. I. (1980), *Too Much Invested to Quit*, New York.

Tetlock, P. E. (1991), 'An Alternative Metaphor in the Study of Judgement and Choice: People as Politicians', *Theory and Psychology* 1: 451–75.

Tey, J. (1988), *The Daughter of Time*, Harmondsworth.

Thatcher, M. (1993), *The Downing Street Years*, London.

Thomas, W. A. (1986), *The Big Bang*, London.

Thompson, J. D. (1967), *Organizations in Action*, New York.

Toffler, A. (1992), *Powershift*, London.

TOPPING, P. (1989), *Topping: The Autobiography of the Police Chief in the Moors Murder Case*, London.

TOUCHE ROSS [Management Consultants] (1989a), 'Taurus Business Case: Cost–Benefit Analysis' (Apr.), London.

—— (1989B), 'Taurus Business Case: Presentation of Initial Findings to the Committee' (Feb.), London.

—— (1989c), 'Taurus Business Case: Principal Report' (Mar.), London.

—— (1992), 'Taurus: Is the Market Ready?', London.

TREVOR-ROPER, H. (1972), *The Last Days of Hitler*, London.

TUCHMAN, B. W. (1984), *The March of Folly*, New York.

TURNER, B. (1983), 'The Use of Grounded Theory for the Qualitative Analysis of Organizational Behaviour', *Journal of Management Studies*, 20: 333–48.

—— (1994), 'Patterns of Crisis Behaviour', in A. Bryman and R. G. Burgess (eds.), *Analyzing Qualitative Data*, London.

TURNER, R. V. (1994), *King John*, Harlow.

TVERSKY, A., and KAHNEMAN, D. (1981), 'The Framing of Decisions and the Psychology of Choice', *Science*, 211: 453–63.

VAN MAANEN, J. (1979a), 'Observations on the Making of a Policeman', *Human Organization*, 32: 407–18.

—— (1979b), 'Reclaiming Qualitative Methods for Organizational Research: A Preface', *Administrative Science Quarterly*, 24: 520–6.

—— (1988), *Tales of the Field*, Chicago.

VAN VELSEN, J. (1967), 'The Extended-Case Method and Situational Analysis', in A. L. Epstein (ed.),, *The Craft of Social Anthropology*, London, 129–49.

WALSH, P., and HENDERSON, C. M. (1989), 'An Attributional Analysis of Decisions about Making Commitments', *Journal of Social Psychology*, 130: 533–49.

WATZLAWICK, P., WEAKLAND, J. H., and FRISH, R. (1974), *Change: Principles of Problem Formation and Resolution*, New York.

WEBB, C. H. (1987), *The Bigger Bang: Growth of a Financial Revolution*, London.

WEBB, E. J., CAMPBELL, D. T., SCHWARTZ, R. D., and SCHREST, L. (1966), *Unobtrusive Measures: Non-reactive Research in the Social Sciences*, Chicago.

WEICK, K. E. (1974), 'Amendments to Organizational Theorizing', *Academy of Management Journal*, 17: 487–502.

—— (1989), 'Theory Construction as Disciplined Imagination', *Academy of Management Review*, 14: 516–31.

WEIR, A. (1993), *The Princes in the Tower*, London.

WHITE, M., and GRIBBIN, J. (1992), *Stephen Hawking: A Life in Science*, Harmondsworth.

WHYTE, G. (1986), 'Escalating Commitment to a Course of Action: A Reinterpretation', *Academy of Management Review*, 11: 311–21.

—— (1989), 'Groupthink Reconsidered', *Academy of Management Review*, 14: 40–56.

—— (1991), 'Diffusion of Responsibility: Effects on the Escalation Tendency', *Journal of Applied Psychology*, 76: 408–15.

—— (1993), 'Escalating Commitment in Individual and Group Decision Making: A Prospect Theory Approach', *Organizational Behaviour and Human Decision Processes*, 54: 430–55.

WHYTE, W. F. (1984), *Learning from the Field*, London.

WILLCOCKS, L., and GRIFFITHS, C. (unpub. mimeo, n.d.), 'Management and Risk Issues in a Large-Scale IT Projects: A Comparative Analysis', Oxford, Oxford Institute of Information Management.

WILLMOTT, H. (1987), 'Studying Managerial Work: A Critique and a Proposal', *Journal of Management Studies*, 24: 249–70.

WILSON COMMITTEE (1980), (Committee to Review the Functioning of Financial Institutions), *Report and Appendices*, Cmnd. 7937, London.

WILSON, D. C., BUTLER, R. J., CRAY, D., HICKSON, D. J., and MALLORY, G. R. (1986), 'Breaking the Bounds of Organization in Strategic Decision Making', *Human Relations*, 39: 309–31.

WOODCOCK, A., and DAVIS, M. (1978), *Catastrophe Theory*, Harmondsworth.

WRONG, D. H. (1979), *Power, Its Forms, Bases and Uses*, Oxford.

YALLOP, D. (1993), *Deliver us from Evil*, London.

YIN, R. K. (1989), *Case Study Research*, Beverly Hills, Calif.

—— (1993), *Applications of Case Study Research*, Beverly Hills, Calif.

YOUNG, E. (1989), 'On the Naming of the Rose: Interests and Multiple Meanings as Elements of Organizational Culture', *Organization Studies*, 10: 187–206.

ZANDER, A. (1982), *Making Groups Effective*, San Francisco.

ZEIGLER, P. (1988), *The Sixth Great Power: Barings 1762–1929*, London.

ZUCKER, L. G. (1977), 'The Role of Institutionalization in Cultural Persistence', *American Sociological Review*, 42: 726–43.

INDEX

Note: The following are abbreviated in sub-entries:
Stock Exchange ('SE'), and Taurus ('T')